American Liberty & Justice

Gordon Morris Bakken
Series Editor

Also in the series

Broke, Not Broken: Homer Maxey's Texas Bank War
Broadus Spivey and Jesse Sublett

A Clamor for Equality: Emergence and Exile of an Early Californio Activist
Paul Bryan Gray

A Conservative and Compassionate Approach to Immigration Reform: Perspectives from a Former U.S. Attorney General
Alberto R. Gonzales and David N. Strange

Hers, His, and Theirs: Community Property Law in Spain and Early Texas
Jean A. Stuntz

Lone Star Law: A Legal History of Texas
Michael Ariens

Quite Contrary: The Litigious Life of Mary Bennett Love
David J. Langum, Sr.

The Reckoning: Law Comes to Texas's Edwards Plateau
Peter R. Rose

Sex, Murder, and the Unwritten Law: Courting Judicial Mayhem, Texas Style
Bill Neal

Treasure State Justice: Judge George M. Bourquin, Defender of the Rule of Law
Arnon Gutfeld

showdown in the BIG QUIET

showdown in the BIG QUIET

LAND, MYTH, AND GOVERNMENT IN THE AMERICAN WEST

John P. Bieter, Jr.

Foreword by Gordon Morris Bakken

Texas Tech University Press

This book is typeset in Monotype Amasis. The paper used in this book meets the minimum requirements of ANSI/NISO Z39.48-1992 (R1997). ♾

Designed by Kasey McBeath

Library of Congress Cataloging-in-Publication Data
Bieter, John P., Jr.

Showdown in the Big Quiet : land, myth, and government in the American West / John P. Bieter, Jr. ; foreword by Gordon Morris Bakken.

pages cm. — (American liberty & justice)

Summary: “"Examines the area known as the Big Quiet, the role of environment, the history of this area in the West, and the power of Western mythology”— Provided by publisher.

Includes bibliographical references and index.

ISBN 978-0-89672-902-5 (hardback : alkaline paper) — ISBN 978-0-89672-903-2 (paperback : alkaline paper) — ISBN 978-0-89672-904-9 (e-book) 1. Owyhee County (Idaho)—History. 2. Owyhee County (Idaho)—Environmental conditions. 3. Land use—Government policy—Idaho—Owyhee County—History. 4. Law—Social aspects—Idaho—Owyhee County—History. 5. Community life—Idaho—Owyhee County—History. 6. Social justice—Idaho—Owyhee County—History. 7. Owyhee County (Idaho)—Politics and government. 8. Frontier and pioneer life—West (U.S.)—Historiography. 9. West (U.S.)—In popular culture. 10. West (U.S.)—Mythology. I. Title.

F752.O97B43 2015
979.6'21—dc23

2014036327

15 16 17 18 19 20 21 22 23 / 9 8 7 6 5 4 3 2 1

Texas Tech University Press
Box 41037 | Lubbock, Texas 79409-1037 USA
800.832.4042 | ttup@ttu.edu | www.ttupress.org

FOR MY WIFE, ALEXANDRA J. LAURENZ

CONTENTS

Illustrations *xi*
Foreword *xiii*
Preface *xv*
Acknowledgments *xvii*

Introduction 3

Chapter One
The Owyhees 15

Chapter Two
The Eagle's Silver Heart 32

Chapter Three
The Battle of Shoshone Mike 56

Chapter Four
"An Asset and Not a Liability": *Omaechevarria v. State of Idaho* 88

Chapter Five
The Power of Myth, Marketing, and Government in the West 116

Chapter Six
Claude Dallas: The Myth Comes to Life 133

Chapter Seven
Saylor Creek Bombing Range: A Modern Range War 172

Chapter Eight
The Owyhee Canyonlands: Showdown to Collaboration 202

Conclusion
Lesions and Lessons from the West 231

Notes *237*
Bibliography *271*
Index *281*

Illustrations

The dramatic walls of the Owyhee Canyonlands. 11

The snow-capped Owyhee Mountains
beyond a homestead. 12

The arid high desert country with mesa in background. 13

Map of Native American tribes in Idaho. 17

Shoshone-Bannock Indians at the Fort Hall
Indian Reservation, 1885. 18

The Bannock tribe of the Northern Paiute. 20

Map of Owyhee County, Idaho. 21

Owyhee Dam near Nyssa, Oregon. 24

Historic mining community of Silver City, about 1867. 26

Murphy Outpost Days, 2013. 27

Poorman Mine on War Eagle Mountain, 1867–68. 33

Mill buildings at the Oro Fino Mine on War Eagle Mountain in 1866. 34

A band on the balcony of the Silver City Wells Fargo
& Company office in the late 1860s. 43

View of Silver City, circa 1885. 44

J. Marion More portrait. 53

Snake River Agency, Fort Hall Indian Reservation, Idaho, 1872. 61

Slain Basque sheepherders, Little High Rock Canyon,
Nevada, February 1911. 73

Captain J. P. Donnelly's posse that pursued Shoshone Mike, 1911. 75

Location of slaying, Little High Rock Canyon, Nevada. 83
Ranchers have worked the Owyhee range since the 1860s. 90
Basque sheepherder on horse. 93
Basque family in front of farmhouse. 95
Basque sheepherder with sheep dogs. 97
US Supreme Court Justice Louis Brandeis. 112
Poster of Buffalo Bill's Wild West and Congress of Rough Riders of the World. 120
Buffalo Bill and Sitting Bull. 121
Map of federal land as a percentage of total state land area. 123
Frederic Remington's sculpture ***Bronco Buster,*** created in 1909. 125
Movie poster for ***The Virginian,*** 1929. 126
Movie poster for ***The Vanishing American,*** 1925. 128
Idaho Fish and Game warden Bill Pogue. 141
Idaho Fish and Game warden Conley Elms. 143
Claude Dallas under arrest, March 12, 1987. 155
Cover of Jack Olsen's ***Give a Boy a Gun.*** 161
Cover of Jeff Long's ***Outlaw: The True Story of Claude Dallas.*** 161
Reward poster for Claude Dallas. 162
F-15Es on a low-level training mission out of Mountain Home Air Force Base. 175
Live munitions range clearance in Saylor Creek Bombing Range, 2012. 180
Idaho Governor Cecil Andrus working at his desk, 1975. 181
Saylor Creek Bombing Range warning sign. 199
Owyhee Canyonlands. 203
Simplot employees on a trail drive in southwestern Idaho, 2007. 205
Rafting down the Owyhee River. 209
Tim Lowry gets ready for spring branding. 215
Shoshone-Paiute Tribes chairman Terry Gibson, speaks during a 2004 meeting in Murphy, Idaho, regarding the Owyhee Initiative process. 221
The Owyhee Initiative, signed into law by President Barack Obama on March 29, 2009. 226
Bruneau Canyon. 229

Foreword

John Bieter, Jr.'s, study of the Big Quiet extends the tradition of Frederick Jackson Turner's call for "the study of the West as a developing region."[1] Or, as Bieter shows, a region in which the mythology that marketed the American West became as central a player as the evolving role of government and law. Contemporaneously, Josiah Royce called for a new sense of place or community, a sense of regional identity that reflected the interplay of geography, people, and socioeconomic factors.[2] So too, Walter Prescott Webb found on the Great Plains the essence of regionalism in identity emerging over time in a specific place because of the environment and culture.[3] Kansas historian James C. Malin rejected geographic determinism and credited the relationships of land, settlers, and regional culture for shaping identity.[4] Bridging the historiographical gap between Turner and the new western historians, Bieter demonstrates not only the vitality of regional studies but also the power of mythology, and his focus on the Big Quiet even more certainly fixes the forces of change in landscapes, environment, and local culture. In many ways, it resonates with Gretel Ehrlich's *The Solace of Open Spaces* (1985), set in Wyoming sheep country. Ehrlich made "year-by-year accommodation to the chilling winds, hot summers, and open skies of her adoptive state."[5] The wind blew hot and cold in the Big Quiet and landforms directed the flow. People adapted accordingly.

As immigrants moved west, they brought law with them. John Phillip Reid examined the writings and conduct of people on the Overland Trail and found "that for nineteenth-century Americans the definition of binding 'law,' vesting rights and imposing obligations, was not limited to a command or set of commands from some 'sovereign' backed by threats or by force."[6] Law was not some abstraction derived from nature. It was not a universal rule or rules. "Law was the taught, learned, accepted customs of a people."[7] Yet law was not the law of the folk, the clan, or a closely related community. "Rather it was the expression of an agrestic, community-centered world we have lost, a custom bottomed on the sovereign's law, learned by living in a coercive state, and instilled in the marrow of social behavior."[8] That was law as immigrants left the trail, became settlers, and made the Big Quiet their home.

Law evolved in time and place for special circumstances, new industries, and old conflicts in a new regional setting—and as Bieter reveals—not uninfluenced by Western mythology, even in the New West of the late twentieth century. As people such as placer miners faced new problems, territorial or state lawmakers passed legislation hoping to solve them.[9] So, too, the Big Quiet's people faced contentious issues. Bieter's work resonates also with Mark R. Ellis's *Law and Order in Buffalo Bill's Country: Legal Culture and Community on the Great Plains, 1867–1910* (2007). Ellis studied Lincoln County, Nebraska, and found it quiet compared to the mining towns of California, Nevada, or Montana. Even with the Union Pacific pushing through the country, Lincoln County residents carried a legal culture with them, and the lawyers of the area pushed for the trappings of due process of law.[10] Law and order at the operational level was as much a product of a "shared legal culture" as economic self-interest.[11] Demonstrating how mythology can resonate so deeply with cultural identity that it becomes truth, Bieter's work adds an important chapter to the legal history of the American West and the liberty and justice that Americans pursued making communities whether in Lincoln County or the Big Quiet.

Gordon Morris Bakken
California State University, Fullerton

Preface

The stories we tell reveal much of who we think we are. Both this book and the writing of it have stories. Although I was unaware of it at the time, this book really began when I was twelve and my parents took our family to the Basque region of Spain (a story I tell in chapter 5). That's the first time I began to question origins of American identity. Later, while conducting research for another book, I came across a US Supreme Court case (*Omaechevarria v. State of Idaho*) involving the arrest of a Basque herder for trespassing on private grazing land. This legal battle between sheep and cattle interests revealed a deeper debate over race, ethnicity, and accepted definitions of American identity. As I read for context about this conflict, other episodes of struggle over land use surfaced—both legal and violent. These conflicts exposed deeply held values regarding proper definitions of land use, the role of government, and what it means to be American.

As I researched, the episodes aligned themselves into two groups. One set, from the last third of the nineteenth century, included three "Old West" stories of battles in mines, with Native Americans, and over rangeland. The "New West" disputes from the 1980s to the present involved conflicts over trapping, bombing ranges, and environmental conservation. Each chapter displays conflict over proper land use, government, and identity; however, throughout each episode the mythologized American western character often impacted events.

And, so what? Many new western historians have dealt with similar themes: what's new about this work? Ultimately this book bridges the historiographical gap between Frederick Jackson Turner and the work of these new western historians. The core of Turner's thesis argued that the interaction on the frontier formed American characteristics of rugged individualism, democracy, aggression, and innovation. The new western historians of the late 1970s discredited this view. They showed the diversity of the West, reminded us of the role of the environment, and demonstrated that rather than settling "free land" as Turner suggested, settlers and later corporations—both with the assistance of government—conquered land wrested away from Native Americans. Both Turner and the new western historians were right. However, neither side fully realized the power of mythology. Although often historically inaccurate, Turner's interpretation, when mythologized, became "true"—like a B western brought to life. Despite the new western historians' attempts to shoot holes in Turner's thesis, the stories and myths simply resonated too deeply with the national and international sense of the American identity. *Showdown in the Big Quiet* demonstrates how the "Old West" speaks to the "New." The chronological gap between the collections of episodes demonstrates how the power of western mythology moved from background to central character.

Acknowledgments

Many books begin with acknowledgment of the major intellectual contributions to the subject. I too owe a tremendous amount to all those authors from whose work I draw. I deeply appreciate the countless hours that went into their scholarship. However, as I finished writing, I also realized the debt I owe to all those who helped prepare me to take on this work—the wonderful teachers I have had in my life. They inspired in me a love of ideas and the tools to pursue them. My elementary school teacher, Mrs. Bigler, made class so enjoyable I did not want to move on. In high school, Mr. Dave Skinner modeled a balanced life of academics and activities while we laughed every day in his class. Dr. Tom Mooney was the greatest teacher I have had, and he and Dave Skinner inspired me to become a teacher myself. Father Vincent Rush at the University of St. Thomas had a deep intellect and a wonderful sense of humor and prompted countless conversations in Ireland Hall. Todd Shallat at Boise State University mentored me into becoming a historian; I owe him more than he knows. While I was in graduate school at Boston College, David Quigley about worked us to death that first semester. I thank him for his exceptional efforts, professionalism, and kindness. Without my doctoral dissertation committee—Kevin Kenny, Lynn Johnson, and Jim O'Toole—this work simply would not have happened. I so appreciate the way they approach the study of history and am forever thankful that I was able to look over their shoulders and watch how it should be done. Special thanks to Lynn, for her extra efforts and time, and to Jim, the consummate professional—

outstanding in his field, an exceptional teacher, and so caring for his students—who became a friend.

I would like to thank the Basque Museum and Cultural Center in Boise, Idaho, for its support while I carried out this project. Christy Echevarria, Jeff Johns, Michael Vogt, and especially Patty Miller were extremely helpful and supportive. Thanks to Pam Marcum from the Committee for Idaho's High Desert and Roger Singer from the Sierra Club for the generous use of their records; to Chad Gibson and Craig Gehrke and all those who gave of their time for interviews; to Joe Demshar, Brittany Lindstrom, and all those who work so hard at the Owyhee Historical Society Museum and Library; to Eileen Herman for her tireless work in research; to Brenda Richards and to John Brown of the *Owyhee Avalanche* and to Jim Duran and Cheryl Oestreicher from Boise State University's Special Collections and Archives, who helped with photos; to John Herber for all of his computer assistance; to Mike Pape for flying us over Owyhee County and providing that unique perspective; to Jim and Nicole Pape for their editing skills and countless meals; to Tom Miller and Chris Bieter for their legal advice; to the Hoeppners for being the Hoeppners; and special thanks to Mark Bieter and Meggan Laxalt Mackey for being willing to read and edit this work. Finally, I want to acknowledge my deceased parents, Pat and Eloise Bieter. They afforded me the wealth of experiences, and the model of lifetime learning, that provided much of the inspiration behind this work.

showdown in the BIG QUIET

Introduction

Not many stayed around for the last talk. On an especially warm July 12th evening in 1893, on the second day of the World's Congress of Historians and Historical Students, put on in conjunction with the Columbian Exposition in Chicago, thirty-two-year-old Frederick Jackson Turner, a historian from the University of Wisconsin who had earned his doctorate just two years earlier, gave the last of five presentations that day. He had finished preparing his remarks that morning and readied himself for the unenviable final time slot. Titled "The Significance of the Frontier in American History," Turner's talk began with a quotation from the Superintendent of the Census for 1890: "Up to and including 1880 the country had a frontier of settlement, but at present the unsettled area has been so broken into by isolated bodies of settlement that there can hardly be said to be a frontier line." During the talk he maintained, "Up to our own day American history has been in a large degree the history of the colonization of the Great West. The existence of an area of free land, its continuous recession, and the advance of American settlement westward explain American development." He closed his address by stating, "The frontier has gone, and with its going has closed the first period of American history." His address became one of the most famous interpretations of American history; however, few heard it that day.

A number of the historians who were supposed to be at the conference attended the nearby Buffalo Bill show instead.[1]

Buffalo Bill Cody set up his hit show across the street from the exposition and played twice daily in front of a grandstand that held eighteen thousand viewers. The circus-like spectacle included feats of exceptional horseback riding, marksmanship, and real-life characters like American Indian Chief Sitting Bull and a band of twenty of his braves. Performers reenacted the Pony Express and stage coach holdups, and the show often ended with an Indian attack on settlers in which Buffalo Bill would ride in with a band of cowboys to save the day. The show, viewed by millions in the United States and Europe, lasted thirty years. Mark Twain felt that the program "brought back to me the breezy, wild life of the Rocky Mountains, and stirred me like a war song." Twain vouched that the show, "down to its smallest details, is genuine—cowboys, vaqueros, Indians, stage coach, costumes and all."[2]

Many would challenge Twain's claim of accuracy. They maintain that the show excessively romanticized the past, and inaccurately depicted American Indians as always attacking despite the historical rarity of it and the consistent breaking of treaties by the American government. However, all agreed that the show's span represented a significant transition in the American West. It included some "experiences Cody and some of his performers had known," and evolved into a "historical recreation of times gone by."[3]

In the same way that Buffalo Bill's imagery far outpaced any kind of truth, so did Frederick Jackson Turner's thesis overshadow the historical reality more accurately addressed by the new western historians. However, all of these interpretations have power, and to underestimate any of them is to miss out on their ability to tell and shape our collective story.

Clearly the commercialized image of the American West attracts people. From the Marlboro man to the ubiquitous Hollywood westerns, Ralph Lauren commercials, Louis L'Amour novels, and the language of many politicians, the American western image defines much of what is uniquely American. Despite the American frontier being "closed" since 1880, sales from the western image remain high and underscore the national and international attraction to connect with a pre-industrialized past. This West consists of fantasized legends in which the values of individualism, freedom, hard work, and strength of character give meaning to life in contrast with the homogenized, monotonous existence of many in a post-industrialized world.

When President George W. Bush spoke about capturing Osama bin Laden, he used the language of the West to describe that endeavor—"Wanted Dead or Alive." Saad al-Faqih, a Saudi exile and reformist who closely examined Osama bin Laden and his key strategist Ayman al-Zawahiri, extended this language and metaphor of the West. "The American mentality is a cowboy mentality," al-Faqih maintained. "If you confront them . . . they will react in an extreme manner. In other words, America with all its resources and establishments will shrink into a cowboy when irritated successfully." In this process Americans will actually "elevate you, and this will satisfy the Muslim longing for a leader who can successfully challenge the West."[4]

President Bush is merely the most recent among presidents ranging from Theodore Roosevelt to Ronald Reagan to employ western themes, language, and images as central to the projection of their presidency. Indeed, even compared with the crops, animals, wealth, religions, music, fast food, and countless other elements included within the transnational exchanges of the Old World and the New, the American western image remains powerful.

Use of the imagery and language of the "imagined" West, however, also begs the question of the "real" one: where and what is "the West"? Although this continues to be debated, writers, historians, and filmmakers gradually identified it as the land west of the 100th meridian. In reality, the western border continued to move, as settlers occupied Native American lands and removed them to reservations. In the field of history, Frederick Jackson Turner branded the identity of this westward moving "frontier."

Historian John Mack Faragher deemed Turner's "Frontier" essay "the single most influential piece of writing in the history of American history." In it, Turner identified the importance of the frontier to the formation of American character. The frontier marked "the meeting point between savagery and civilization, the line of most rapid Americanization." In this space each generation of Americans developed "that coarseness and strength combined with acuteness and acquisitiveness; that practical inventive turn of mind, quick to find expedients; that masterful grasp of material things . . . that restless, nervous energy; that dominant individualism."[5]

According to Turner, these individuals—self-reliant, courageous frontiersmen with the strength to stand alone even in the most trying conditions—operated in a land of freedom, a wide-open range with few constraints and bountiful opportunity to live off the land. There democracy flourished—with little governmental authority where grassroots, popular sovereignty ruled. These conditions allowed for the noble American character to be created and regenerated: a place separate from ethnic and sectional rivalries, where the primitive pursuit of taming the frontier depended on violence. American characteristics of egalitarianism, democracy, aggression, and innovation originated from the frontier experience. What happened when the frontier closed? What defined America and Americans without it?[6]

Turner's thesis dominated the historiography of the West until, beginning in the 1970s, new western historians such as Patricia Limerick, Donald Worster, and Richard White successfully loosened the straitjacket of his interpretation. According to Limerick, the West is more accurately described as not merely a place where Europeans became Americans, but rather a meeting ground of Indian-, Latin-, Anglo-, Afro-, and Asian-Americans. Conquest tied these groups together in a continuing story of drawing boundaries, changing definitions of land from matter to property, and a struggle for cultural hegemony.[7]

Worster, and many other historians, wrote about the role of the environment in history. "Hasn't the natural world been a powerful influence on society?" he asked. "How could you miss the significance of the soil, the significance of weather and climate and the skies?" White challenged Turner's emphasis on the individual and the freedom of the frontier. "The armies of the federal government conquered the region, agents of the federal government explored it, federal officials administered it, and federal bureaucrats supervised the division and development of its resources," he argued. "The West itself served as the kindergarten of the American state. In governing and developing the American West, the state itself grew in power and influence."[8]

Historian Richard Brown argued that "governmental structure was a key factor in western violence." When miners, prone to violence under the "permissive rule of the American federal system," migrated to Canada with its centralized, stricter government intolerant of violence, they became "peaceable and law-abiding." He maintained that core beliefs "mentally programmed westerners to commit violence." These included: "the doctrine of no duty to retreat; the imperative of personal self-redress; the homestead ethic; the ethic of individual enterprise; the Code of the West; and the ideology of vigilantism."[9]

In his work *No Duty to Retreat: Violence and Values in American History and Society,* Brown claimed that the gradual legal reinterpretation of an English common law from retreat "to the wall" at one's back before killing in self-defense to a right to "legally stand fast, and without retreat, kill in self-defense" helps explain "why our country has been the most violent among its peer group of the industrialized, urbanized democracies of the world." Brown claimed that the attitude of no retreat, most evident in states west of the Appalachians, "has long since become second nature to most Americans and has had a deep, broad impact with a significant, although often intangible, effect upon our foreign relations and military conduct. . . . It is an expression of a characteristically American approach to life."[10]

While the work of new western historians influenced academic circles, a broader audience craved the western stories of novels, magazines, books, and movies. The supposed closing of the frontier and the industrialization of the West made the stories that originated there even more important: many became mythologized. In describing their importance Richard Slotkin has written: "Myths are stories, drawn from history, that have acquired through usage over many generations a symbolizing function that is central to the cultural functioning of the society that produced them." The narrative preserves the historical experience, its structures abstracted and reduced to a powerfully evocative collection of "icons" like the Alamo, Custer's Last Stand, and the California Gold Rush. History becomes a cliché that with each new narration expands the range of reference to it because the telling "implies a metaphoric connection between the storied past and the present." In this process the myths become part of the language, "a deeply encoded set of metaphors that may contain all of the lessons we have learned from our history, and all of the essential elements of our world view." The "lessons" of these myths then form into the "basis of universal rules of understanding and conduct" as they transform "secular history into a body of sacred and sanctifying legends."[11]

These stories both grew out of and heavily influenced people of the Owyhee Mountains of southwestern Idaho where the first three episodes of this book took place from 1868 to 1918. These chapters reveal the incongruences between the myth and reality. Throughout this period, the government acted as a protector, mediator, and/or facilitator of western settlement and expansion. The second series of stories range from 1981 to the present, and offer examples of how mythology and the role of the federal government evolved and clashed with each other. By that time the state and federal governments had gained such power that they no longer acted as facilitators of private development but as regulators, competing developers, and then ultimately back to mediators. The western myth had evolved as well, and its strength is evident in the central role it played in the outcome of these later episodes.

Chapter 1 provides a brief overview of the history of Owyhee County and its people. The geographic, economic, political, and religious makeup offers context for the conflicts denoted in this book. Chapter 2 examines how competing mining claims in 1868 resulted in an underground battle between warring corporations. The early prospectors, miners, and settlers created a capitalistic culture of opportunity and mobility at the cost of Native Americans. Settlers set precedents: violence and conquest prevailed—over people and land. Individuals secretly sought, claimed, owned, and fought for their property rights. Reality often conflicted with stories later told. Mining strikes brought diverse people from the East and throughout the world, yet this rarely was depicted. Rather than competition creating efficiency, in this case it led to expensive court costs. Values of individualism, self-sufficiency, and democracy bowed to corporate and governmental control.

In the shootout analyzed in chapter 3, settlers "massacred" Native Americans or imparted justice—depending on one's perspective. This episode represented one last attempt for Native Americans and settlers to coexist. The violent ending and its later depiction remind us of the power of popular narrative, the increasing and rival roles of government in the West, and the competing values that shaped American identity and resulted in a narrower way of life and land use. A particular understanding of "honor" triumphed over "conscience" and helped frame a popular "American" story retold by generations to justify behavior and policy. With Native Americans removed, "white" settlers targeted other groups.[12]

Chapter 4 recounts how a violent milieu between cattle and sheep owners moved into the courtroom where cattlemen exercised squatter rights and more acceptable settlers trumped newcomers. The prejudiced comments about and discriminatory actions toward Basque immigrants revealed their status within the racial and ethnic hierarchy in the West. This attitude, coupled with policies like the Immigration Act of 1924, narrowed the opportunities for Basques and other immigrants. Their exclusion in popular western novels, artwork, and films supported this restricted definition of American identity.

The first three chapters challenge western mythical images and demonstrate how the government facilitated western expansion and mediated conflicts. The next three chapters trace how these forces evolved to play central roles in the ongoing development of the region. Chapter 5 serves as a bridge chapter between these sets of stories. It outlines the evolving role of government and the marketing of western mythology in order to understand their dominating role in the "New" West of the late twentieth century. Americans, and many others throughout the world, attached to the western frontier the imperishable ideals of the national epic: individualism, self-reliance, democracy, and a defined sense of right and wrong.

Chapter 6 shows how the myth came to life and went on trial with the 1981 murder case of two Idaho Fish and Game wardens by Claude Dallas. Raised on Louis L'Amour and Zane Grey western novels, the Midwest-born Dallas moved west to live the life of the cowboy. As society marched forward into the twenty-first century, Dallas increasingly sought the traditions and values of earlier times in the West. The court case exemplified deep divisions between those who supported Dallas and saw him as a hero with western core values and those who thought his values and actions anachronistic, warped, and tragic.

Chapter 7 shows how in the decade from 1989 to 1999 contrasting visions clashed again. This time, instead of settlers against Native Americans, or sheepmen versus cattle ranchers, normally competing entities fought together against the government's desire to build the Saylor Creek Bombing Range. This modern range war allied an unusual coalition of ranchers, Native Americans, and environmentalists against the very institution that established reservations and encouraged settlement. These battles again took place in the courtroom and were fought with press releases and between governmental entities. Although nonviolent, the outcome paralleled earlier conflicts—those with the greatest economic and political advantage won. The governmental bureaucratic battles wore people down and mocked the notion of the West as the bastion for renewing democracy. Some retreated further into romantic stories of the West, while others learned to take matters back into their own hands.

After the federal government dictated the outcome of the Saylor Creek Bombing Range, both officials in Owyhee County and environmental groups realized they needed to go on the offensive. The expensive decade-long court battle convinced these parties to try local collaboration to settle the ongoing environmental clash. Chapter 8 outlines how these normally contentious counterparts engaged in a painstaking process of give and take. This challenging collaboration shifted the role of the federal government from central actor back to facilitator and mediator, its original role in the West, while it modeled new procedural possibilities for other contentious land-use battles.

As settlers entered the Owyhees, the sociopolitical elite used whatever they could to exploit resources. Besides the implements of modern capitalism, they employed control of the government and the western image to consolidate and maintain their position. These battles involved intense confrontation that at times turned violent. During each episode the land served as the interactive backdrop. Owyhee County in southwestern Idaho rarely has been written about. Turner argued that in 1880 the frontier closed, but it did not close in Owyhee County. It is the most remote and wide-open space in the lower forty-eight states and still meets the 1880 US Census Bureau's frontier definition of less than two people per square mile. This dramatic landscape plays a crucial and connecting role throughout these stories and it is there that we begin.

The dramatic walls of the Owyhee Canyonlands. (US Department of Interior, Bureau of Land Management.)

The snow-capped Owyhee Mountains beyond a homestead.
(US Department of Agriculture.)

The arid high desert country with mesa in background. (Courtesy of Owyhee County Historical Society Museum and Library.)

CHAPTER ONE

The Owyhees

In the Owyhees the land mattered, as did what people imagined it to be. One example is the county's name. In the early 1800s British trappers and explorers traveled throughout the Northwest looking for economic opportunities. In 1819, Donald Mackenzie led representatives from the North West Company, which included three Hawaiian workers, into this area. Mackenzie dispatched the Hawaiians to trap for beaver along a large stream, but when they failed to return he investigated. Mackenzie found one of the Hawaiians murdered and no sign of the others. As a tribute, he named the area in their honor, and over time that became known and spelled as "Owyhee." Nothing about this land reminds one of Hawaii.[1]

The land itself makes it easy for the imagination to run. While many imagine a pine-filled mountainside when they think of the West, the vast landscape of Owyhee County, Idaho, defies that description; it remains high desert country, a craggy land made of broken lava and filled with sagebrush and tumbleweeds. Most vistas in the county remain unobstructed by any signs of human development. Reporters have described it as "The Heart of Nowhere." Adventure writer Ted Trueblood called it the "Big Quiet."[2]

Geologists theorize that the area became that way approximately seventeen million years ago, when a meteorite slammed into what is now southeastern Oregon. This collision pierced the earth's upper mantle, the layer of hot rock beneath the continental crust. Consequently lava flowed from this crater and formed the Columbia and the Owyhee Plateaus of southwestern Idaho. These lava flows dammed up an enormous lake, whose streams and rivers wore deep, sharp, sudden canyons into the plateau and created one of the largest concentrations of exposed rhyolite canyons in the world. Archaeologists also found unique arrays of fossils, from saber-toothed salmon to Pleistocene wolverines and scimitar-toothed cats.[3]

Evidence of human inhabitants dates back at least six thousand years, revealed by digs that have uncovered abundant evidence of chips from the production of stone tools along the Pole and Camas Creeks north of the East Fork of the Owyhee River. The most active settlement dates between 600 and 1200 CE. These discoveries led one archaeologist to identify this region as "the most complex mosaic of prehistory in the state due to the vast number, size, and distribution of these sites."[4]

Native Americans tribes, most notably the numerous divisions of Shoshone and Bannock Indians, inhabited this area. While most settlers grouped them together, the Shoshone actually divided themselves into diverse groups: the Lemhi Shoshone, Sacajawea's people, lived north of Fort Hall in the Salmon River Mountains; west along the Boise and Bruneau Rivers were other tribes of Shoshone named after these rivers. As many as eleven different bands of Shoshone lived from the Gosiute territory in northern Utah past the Ruby Mountains and along the Humboldt River to the Winnemucca region of Nevada. Movement west toward California took one into Northern Paiute territory.[5]

European settlement began with the small numbers of British trappers and explorers, but by the mid-nineteenth century a portion of the Oregon Trail passed through Owyhee territory. Although shorter than its northern counterpart, this South Alternate Route, or "dry route," further challenged tired and parched travelers. They commonly reached this section in late summer through September, with the choking dust billowing up from their oxen's hooves and wagon wheels. Even today, while looking out from an air-conditioned car, the barren backdrop and dry, crackly climate warns travelers of the dangers of breaking down.[6]

In May of 1863, explorers discovered gold in rich placer deposits in the Owyhee Mountains, and the rush was on. The abundance of gold and high-quality silver ore eventually made the mining district world famous and drew prospectors worldwide. Owners displayed ore specimens from

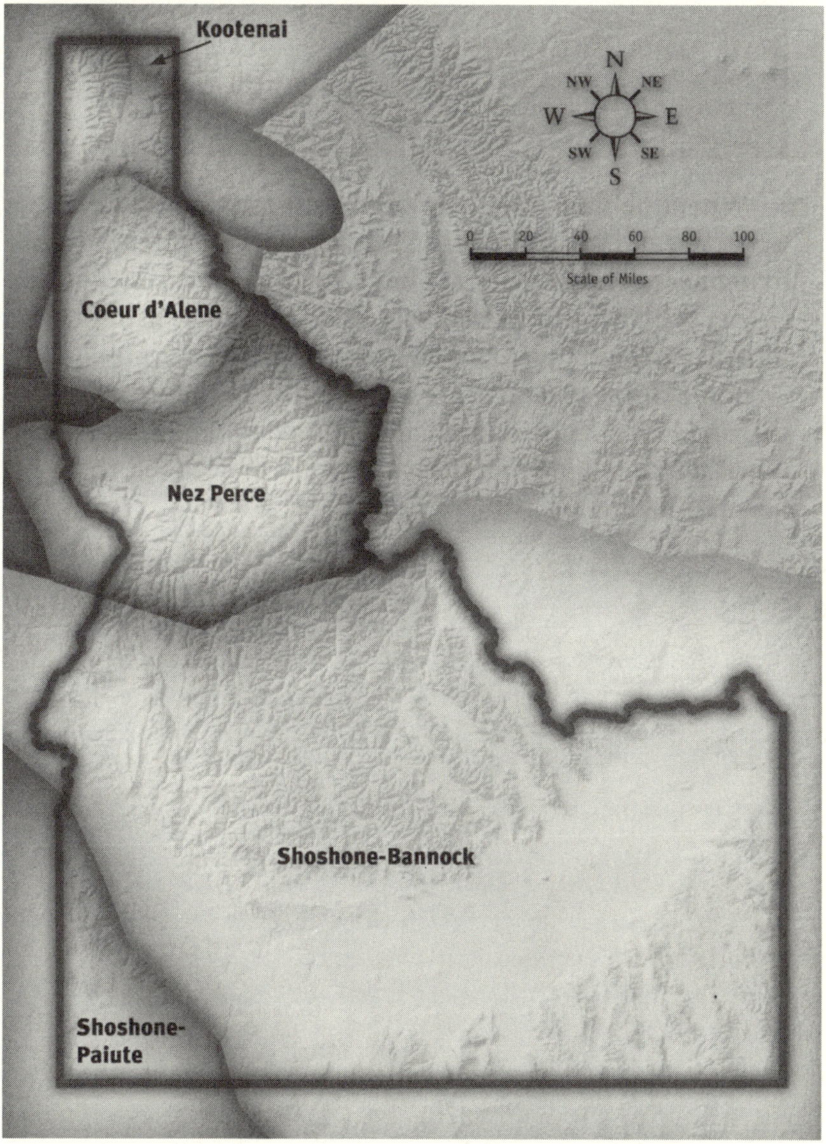

Map of Native American tribes in Idaho. (From ***The Idaho Adventure,*** by Nancy Wilper Tacke and Todd Shallat. Used by permission of the authors and publisher.)

Shoshone-Bannock Indians at the Fort Hall Indian Reservation near Pocatello, Idaho, 1885. (Courtesy of Special Collections and Archives, Eli M. Oboler Library, Idaho State University.)

the ironically dubbed Poorman Mine in the US Congress and at the 1867 Paris International Exposition, where the Poorman exhibit won a special gold medal. The appropriately named Booneville, Ruby City, and Silver City grew up to meet the miners' needs.[7]

Westward migration brought settlers through Native American territories, which led to conflict and violence between the groups. On September 9, 1860, Native Americans attacked travelers on the Overland Trail, one of the rare instances in which Indians assaulted encircled immigrant wagons. Stories from this episode, known as the Utter Party Massacre, remain legendary. In the attack twenty-eight of forty-four immigrants died. It was the greatest loss of life in the Snake River country of what became eastern Oregon and southern Idaho from 1843 until permanent settlements came into western Idaho in 1863.[8]

The Native Americans' seasonal migratory lifestyle ended as settlers, with government assistance, gradually took control of the land. In 1877 the US government established the Duck Valley Reservation and insisted that these Native Americans (specifically the Northern Shoshone and Bannock groups) become self-sufficient farmers. However, these groups felt betrayed by violated treaties, and they were deprived of food sources as settlers dug up the camas prairies and devastated the buffalo population. Fed up, Native Americans fought back. One of the epic battles took place in Owyhee County in 1878, as Bannock chief Buffalo Horn led Native Americans to return to lands they had previously inhabited in eastern Oregon territory. The chief never made it; he died in battle.[9]

Owyhee County

In 1863, President Lincoln named Idaho a territory, and the newly formed legislature in turn designated its first county: Owyhee. It originally consisted of all the land south of the Snake River and west of the Rocky Mountains. In 1864 and 1879, officials carved out Oneida and Cassia Counties from Owyhee County, which reduced it to its present limits. The Snake River forms the northern boundary, with Oregon to the west, and the state of Nevada to the south. Its area is 7,665.51 square miles, somewhat larger than Massachusetts. High desert country dominates the topography, with sagebrush and basalt canyons most plentiful. Hayden Peak (8,403 ft.) in the Owyhee Mountains marks the highest elevation; from there the terrain slopes down toward the Snake River in the northwest where the lowest level of elevation (just above 2,000 ft.) coincides with the Oregon border.[10]

Politically, Owyhee County came of age during the Civil War. Initially, the Idaho mining area supported the federal government's efforts against the insurgent Confederates. However, Confederate refugees from Missouri migrated to Idaho, and these Southern Democrats and their allies strongly contested Idaho's Radical Republican territorial executives and kept Idaho within the Democratic camp for the better part of two decades after the war.[11]

Feeding the growing population created opportunities for cattle and sheep ranches, which had one of the largest and most lasting impacts on the area. Cattlemen drove herds from California settlements, and by 1868 new construction of railroads in Utah and Nevada transformed cattle ranching practices in Idaho, Oregon, and Washington. Long cattle drives to railroad shipping points prompted the cowboy to be one of the dominant figures of the era. In the fall of 1869, cattlemen brought fourteen hundred head up from Brazos, Texas, which diversified ranch stock. The completion

The Bannock tribe of the Northern Paiute are an indigenous people of the Great Basin. (Wikimedia Commons.)

in 1884 of transcontinental rail service from Portland to midwestern Union Pacific lines further expanded markets, and ranchers took advantage of closer shipping points. By 1892 Owyhee County had 24,559 cattle, 15,150 sheep, and 2,046 horses, which accounted for nearly half of the county's total economic value. At its peak in the early twentieth century, one hundred thousand head reportedly grazed the hills of Owyhee County.[12]

While cattle ranching flourished, an 1898 directory of residents and businesses lists "wool grower" or "sheep herder" as the occupation for fifteen of twenty-two individuals. Some ranchers combined operations, but most worked either cattle or sheep. Cattle drives to rail points dominated practices in that industry, whereas sheepherders seasonally migrated with their herds on "open range." Clashes over grazing rights became legendary in the West, and Owyhee County suffered its share.[13]

Cattlemen claimed that sheep ruined the range and contaminated the water. They took to patrolling the range to fend off migratory sheep outfits that hired foreign herders who allegedly "no savvied" the language,

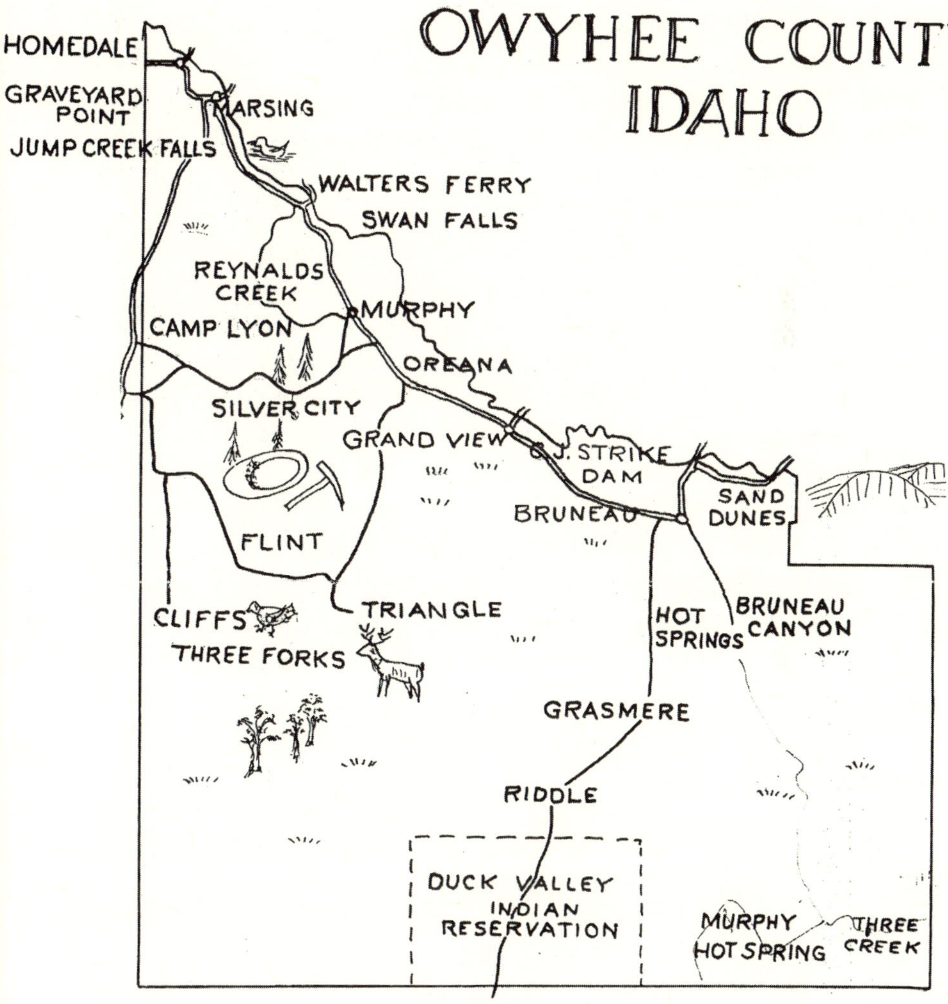

Map of Owyhee County, Idaho. (Courtesy of Owyhee County Historical Society Museum and Library.)

although cattlemen suspected they knew much more than they let on. The local newspaper noted the power of local cattlemen: "I doubt that any jury picked in Owyhee County would go against cattlemen." The sentiment endured into the 1970s. When retiring Basque sheepman Floyd Acarregui shipped his last lambs to market, some cowboys reportedly came to help. "These cowmen won't give you a party," Acarregui claimed. "All the cowmen are here for is to be sure all the sheep leave the country—kinda like goin' to your enemy's funeral."[14]

Besides the raising of livestock, farming became the single most important sector of the economy. Since rainfall in Owyhee County varies from four to eighteen inches a year, farming depended upon irrigation. As early as the 1880s, families drew water from the Snake River for their small farms. In 1902, Congress created the Reclamation Service to "control and spread the benefits of the waters of the West." However, competitors vied for the valuable resource of water, the "new gold of the West," and responded with investment and calls for assistance from the federal government. In 1900, the Trade Dollar Consolidated Mining and Milling Company built the first hydroelectric dam and power plant in Owyhee County on the Snake at Swan Falls. After mining peaked, farmers who needed electricity to power irrigation and drainage pumps increased the demand. By 1913, pumps lifted water 170 feet from the river onto the land.[15]

No individual or groups of family farms or businesses had the means to fully respond to the need. For that, they called on the federal government. In 1928, construction began on the largest federal investment in irrigation, power-generating dams, flood control, and recreation in the area. By the time of its completion in 1932, the concrete arch-gravity dam on the Owyhee River claimed the title of the tallest of its type in the world and served as the prototype for the larger Hoover Dam on the Colorado River. President Hoover sent "greetings and [his] hearty congratulations to all those in attendance at the dedication exercises commemorating the completion of the highest dam in the world, the Owyhee." He called it "another great monument to the skill of American engineers." But the dam would become another example of the clash over land uses in the county. Its devastating effects on salmon runs never entered the conversation at that time but later became one of the rallying cries of environmentalists.[16]

Profiles of People

The people who made Owyhee County range from bankers to those hiding secrets. They provide examples of the diverse lot attracted to this area and represent some of those who made significant contributions to the economic, political, and social development of the county. Christopher Wilkinson (C. W.) Moore migrated from Toronto to the newly discovered gold strikes of 1863 in the Owyhees, where he eventually provided supplies and banking services to miners. Moore went on to earn the second national bank charter west of the Rockies, established ranches in Silver City and Boise, and became known as the "father of Idaho banking."[17]

William "Hill" Beachy was born in Lebanon, Ohio, in approximately 1819 and worked as a steamboat pilot on the Mississippi River, baked and sold bread to soldiers in Mexico during the war there in 1846, migrated to California for the gold rush, and in 1864 headed to Owyhee for the mining strikes. Beachy established a major new mine on War Eagle Mountain called the Golden Chariot, but his true contribution came in transportation. His Railroad Stage Lines connected Boise and Silver City to the Central Pacific rail line in Virginia City, Nevada. One historian wrote that Beachy's transportation contributions were "probably the most important single factor in the early growth and development" of southern Idaho and northern Nevada.[18]

While Moore came from the north and Beachy from the east, others entered from the west. Most newcomers arrived by horseback, covered wagon, or even by boat in northern Idaho territory. William Dewey walked. He traveled four hundred miles by foot from Virginia City, Nevada, to the Owyhee Mountains with $27 [$403 in 2014] in his pocket. He later sold mine holdings for $1 million [$21 million in 2014] and became known as "probably the most widely known capitalist and promoter of Idaho."[19]

James M. Guffey, born in Pennsylvania and closely allied with the powerful Mellon family, came to Idaho in 1891 and quickly consolidated various mining interests into the Trade Dollar Consolidated Mining Company, which generated nearly $500,000 [$13.9 million in 2014] in profits in 1897. Ever entrepreneurial, Guffey invested in a railroad extension into Owyhee County and helped construct a hydroelectric dam at Swan Falls that became one of the cornerstones of the later Idaho Power Company.[20]

Owyhee Dam near Nyssa, Oregon. (Oregon State University Special Collections.)

Perhaps one of the most influential people of Owyhee County was not a man but a woman—Permeal French. She moved to Silver City in 1896, worked as a teacher, and eventually became state superintendent of public instruction, the first woman to be elected to statewide office in Idaho. French established state standards, and drafted a code that required teacher exams and certificates. "She may have had more impact on young people of that era than any other Idahoan," one historian concluded.[21]

While some made their mark in education or business, others were known for their marks on animals or rarely known at all. Livestock owners Matt Joyce used the brand *M J* on the right side of the ear for his cattle; John H. Hart branded a *J* and heart on all his stock; John Mitchell a spur on the left hip. They represent some of the established ranchers and livestock interests in the area. Alongside them worked a diverse group rarely featured in later westerns depicting this era. For example, a top ranch hand referred to as "Nigger" Bill Hearst worked for Con Shea, a very successful rancher. Hearst "apparently punched cattle and broke horses in the Owyhees for years." A "Mexican," Ramon Rodray, herded sheep for another minority in the area, a Basque outfit named the Archabal Sheep Company.[22]

Besides these, a number of very hard-working and tough women succeeded as well. Jean Heazle, born in Bray, Ireland, in 1879, reportedly suffered from a lung ailment, and her doctor prescribed a drier and warmer climate. Heazle migrated to the American West and found work delivering goods and groceries, then ran a dairy, and eventually ranched on her own. "Whenever she entered the nail driving or wood cutting contest, she usually emerged the winner." Owyhee County even had its version of "Calamity Jane." Jane Mason became infamous as a cattle rustler in the rough-and-tumble Juniper Mountain country, an area known for cattle rustlers and horse thieves. The editor of an area newspaper reported that "a tough woman . . . with a boulder in her stocking, most unmercifully beat Wes Rickard while a member of her clan held her victim under the muzzle of his gun."[23]

Then there's the story of "Little Joe," who during the early mining years in the Owyhees took a job as a miner and on the side raised chickens, hogs, and milk cows. Joe became a ranch hand for a number of outfits before buying a small ranch. Joe, who was listed in the 1898 Rockville, Idaho, directory as "Joseph Monohan, Cattleman," took on other odd jobs that were available, such as shearing sheep or driving cattle, and served on juries and voted in elections. Nevertheless, Joe largely refrained from the social life of the community. In 1903, Joe caught pneumonia and died within days: locals were surprised to find out that Little Joe was actually a woman.[24]

Horses played nearly as dominant a role as the people in Owyhee County. Any ranch would have had horses—at least for local use. Kitty Wilkins, known as the "Horse Queen of Idaho," took it further; she drew world acclaim and challenged many of the prescribed gender roles of the time. Kitty gained notoriety as an excellent horsewoman who "rode the range with her buckaroos, overseeing the roundups." However, her greatest fame came for the outstanding quality of horses that she provided throughout the United States. An Omaha newspaper wrote in 1892, "Wilkins is . . . the independent, self-made woman. She is at the head of one of the largest horse raising ranches in the world," reportedly managing a herd of four thousand horses. Wilkins sold her diamond-branded horses as far away as New Orleans and Boston and regularly sold her stock to the US Cavalry.[25]

Owyhee County Today

Snapshots of Owyhee County today reveal the development of economic, social, and political issues as well as the continued attraction to western images. Although early settlers and the federal government forced Native

Historic mining community of Silver City, about 1867.
(Courtesy of Idaho State Historical Society.)

Americans onto reservations in 1884, tribal leaders successfully fought off a proposed transfer to the Fort Hall Reservation in eastern Idaho. Today, the Duck Valley Indian Reservation measures twenty miles long and seventeen miles wide and straddles the Idaho/Nevada state line with almost equal land division. Only two tribes are represented on the reservation, the Western Shoshone and the Northern Paiute. In 1934, under the Indian Reorganization Act, these two tribes formed a government through a constitution and bylaws. Over this same period educational opportunities included boarding schools both on and off of the reservation and day schools on the reservation, which were later consolidated into a combined school district. Farming and ranching became the mainstay of the economy, assisted by construction in 1936 of the Wildhorse Reservoir and subsequent irrigation projects. Membership consists of two thousand people, with over seventeen hundred living on the reservation.[26]

Beyond the reservation, the economy evolved as well. From 1863

Murphy Outpost Days, 2013. (Courtesy of Owyhee County Historical Society Museum and Library.)

through 1942, miners extracted 1,058,694 ounces of gold alone from the area. But the mining boom played itself out, and except for sporadic ventures all that remains are "hundreds of mines [that] pock-mark and honeycomb the mountains" with "upwards of seventy miles of tunnels laboriously hand-dug" in just one of the mines. Today, only Silver City survives and attracts tourists to "its well-preserved buildings, a silent testimonial to the lively mining days." "Visiting Silver City is like going back into history," claims the town's Web site.[27]

Owyhee County maintains many of its early characteristics but also developed new ones. Power production and irrigated agriculture continue to today, and approximately eighty thousand acres receive one or more irrigations per year, which support a variety of crops, including alfalfa, sugar beets, potatoes, onions, corn, mixed grains, and orchard crops. It's still a resource-based economy in which agriculture, forestry, fishing, and hunting account for 36 percent of the most common industries, with construction next with 15 percent. While 70 percent of Owyhee County self-reports as white, nearly 25 percent identify as Hispanic or Latino, a number that has steadily increased. Politically, the Democratic stronghold after the Civil War quickly gave way to the Republican Party, and over 75 percent voted Republican in the 2008 and 2012 presidential elections. At the turn of the nineteenth century, religious denominations included Episcopalian, Methodist, Presbyterian, Baptist, and Roman Catholic, "all of whom [were] owners of fine and substantial church buildings." Today, statistics reveal only 30 percent of the population as religiously affiliated, significantly lower than the 50 percent national average. Of the twenty-six religious congregations reported in the county, Mormons constitute 42 percent, with 25 percent identified as Roman Catholics, the second largest congregation. The percentage of foreign-born residents in Owyhee County is double that of the statewide average, with the majority coming from Mexico.[28]

Today, events like the Murphy Outpost Days attract tourists and preserve many of the traditional western ways no longer commonly practiced. A news story about the event invited readers to "Watch as young cowboys rustle the herd into town at an authentic cattle drive. Listen to famed cowboy poet Art Honey as he weaves the fabric of Western life into words. Experience the lost arts of past generations." According to Jan Alexander, bookstore manager at the Owyhee County Historical Museum, "Outpost Days is our biggest fundraiser of the year, but more importantly it teaches and preserves the rich heritage of the people and traditions of Owyhee County. . . . It explains a little bit more about our county, its history . . . spanning from Native Americans to miners, to cowboys and farmers." Honey's original works of cowboy poetry "personify the message of Outpost Days—to preserve and celebrate western traditions." Reenactors present demonstrations on a wide range of "lost arts from gold panning and fast-draw shooting to blacksmithing, saddlemaking, caning and silversmithing."[29]

While the area remains rich in tradition, the rugged terrain with its especially arid climate has never attracted a large population. Although it contains 4.8 million acres of land, there is still not a single stoplight in the county. It is one of the few places in the United States that still meets the US census definition of frontier that Frederick Jackson Turner made famous: the county's 2010 population of 11,526 computes to one resident per

1.5 square miles—well below the frontier limit of 2 people per square mile. The town of Homedale, whose name was drawn from a hat at a community picnic, is the largest in Owyhee County with a population of 2,633 in 2010. "We're about as far from 'town' as you can get anymore in this country, outside Alaska," commented one fourth-generation rancher. "We're right on the border of southwest Idaho, 100 miles from Boise, 500 miles from San Francisco, 400 miles from Portland, and 400 miles from Salt Lake." And most residents live in remote areas further isolated from the few population centers of this region.[30] Today only two paved roads traverse the land—Highway 78, which runs along the Snake River from Bruneau to Homedale, and Highway 51, which runs south from the Snake River to the Duck Valley Indian Reservation. Owyhee County, Idaho's second largest, has more cattle than people and remains 82 percent federally owned. Despite the western myth of little government presence, the federal government's extensive holdings underscore its omnipresent role in the region.

It's precisely this presence that many in Owyhee County fear. In 1878, locals formed the Owyhee Cattle and Horse Growers Association to protect herds from "rustlers and Indians." Still in existence, the Owyhee Cattlemen's Association claims to be "the oldest cattle group in Idaho." In a commemorative publication honoring the association's 125th anniversary, organizers touted that "rustlers seldom plague the cattle industry anymore and the threat of an Indian uprising is a thing of the past," but challenges remain. Today, cattlemen gather to "fight for their rights . . . against the federal government, environmentalists and those who preach cattle ranching is a thing of the past."[31]

Other interests vie for access to this area. In 1942, the US military established Mountain Home Air Force Base in Elmore County, which neighbors Owyhee County. As fighter pilot training runs increased, the desire for greater air space grew, and the military sought bombing ranges for target practice. However, the increase in population in the Boise and Treasure Valley area of southwestern Idaho that enjoy rafting, hiking, and other outdoor activities, combined with the many advocates of the environmental movement, resulted in greater demands on this area. Many seek the "Big Quiet" for exactly that: the solitude and ability to recreate away from the pressures of modern living.[32]

•••

In the Owyhees, competing visions of land use collided from the beginning; the land itself countered with its own constant changes, reacting to mining ventures, efforts to irrigate, large-scale livestock ventures, and efforts to preserve it. Ecological changes, adaptations, and introduction of new species serve as reminders that this region remained and remains a highly unstable place that reacts to natural forces as much as culture, never to become fully "settled." Historian Donald Worster argues that "a history of the West that does not start from that dialectical perspective . . . is both naïve, simplistic, and arrogant."[33]

The movement of the Owyhee County seat parallels the economic interaction with the land. In 1863, officials named Ruby City as the original county seat, but as mining activity moved, Silver City took over in 1867. By 1934, mining had declined while livestock and agricultural sectors of the economy grew, and the county seat shifted from Silver City to Murphy, where it remains today. Each economic enterprise created opportunity and also provided context for conflict. Government played an increasingly active role throughout. Snapshots of settlers provide a sampling of the characters who made this history.[34]

In 1849, seven-year-old Joseph DeLamar stowed away on a ship bound from his native Amsterdam for the Dutch Indies. After an eighteen-month journey, authorities returned him to his parents, but DeLamar sought adventure and the sea. He sailed throughout the world, earning substantial contracts to salvage sunken ships and trading in Africa, and in 1878 he came to New York and then went west to the mining boom. He bought claims in Colorado and eventually in a mine named after him in Silver City that extracted $8,500,000 [$207 million in 2014] in gold and silver. DeLamar served as a state legislator in the first legislature of Idaho, and when he died in 1918 he left much of his estate to be divided among "the three best medical schools of the day—Johns Hopkins, Harvard, and Columbia."[35]

Other influential settlers include W. L. Lewis, an African-American business leader in Silver City; Ralph McDowell, who built an early irrigation ditch in the early 1900s still in use today; and members of the Austrian community who settled just outside Homedale in 1914.[36] These samples remind us of the diverse groups of people who collaborated and endured conflict on the western frontier. Despite attempts by new western historians to unlock the West from Turner's "frontier thesis," the idea survives. The notion of the frontier provides the space for American stories of individuality, freedom, democracy, and character. If the frontier is gone, are we?

The Owyhees is still the largest and least inhabited land in the lower forty-eight states. While it remains untamed, the lure of opportunity consistently drew those searching for possibilities. The Idaho state seal reflects this. Against the backdrop of the Snake River and the Owyhee and Bannock Mountains, the seal contains a shield filled by an antlered elk's head hanging above a sheaf of grain, with two cornucopias of plenty supported by Lady Liberty and a miner. The motto reads "Esto Perpetua" (This Forever). This is what miners and early settlers imagined when they first came to the Owyhees.[37]

CHAPTER TWO

The Eagle's Silver Heart

Charles Peck wanted to keep it a secret. A mining prospector, in 1865 he discovered a very rich "pocket" or "chimney" of ore about one thousand feet south of the Hays and Ray shaft. The Hays and Ray, unearthed earlier in the year on August 5, had become the most prominent claim of the War Eagle Mountain lodes of the Owyhee Mountains. While eight two-hundred-foot claims already existed on the property, Peck sensed that this vein would prove the most promising. He said nothing; instead, he concealed the pocket and researched ownership boundaries. When it became clear that his find fell within the Hays and Ray claims, Peck offered to purchase the property. The owners refused, and so he gambled and left the area. Peck hoped that by leaving he could bluff the others into questioning the property's value and then return later to purchase the land at a decreased price.[1]

However, the secret got out. This time D. C. Bryan and his small company of prospectors claimed the spot, called it the Poorman, and began to extract extremely high-grade ore. Bryan reportedly gave the mine its name, "Poorman," since, like many independent prospectors, he lacked the capital necessary to develop this great strike. Nevertheless he proceeded, and located and recorded seven two-hundred-foot claims in the area.[2]

As the Hays and Ray owners realized what was happening, they claimed

Poorman Mine on War Eagle Mountain, 1867–68. (Courtesy of Idaho State Historical Society.)

the land for their own, but the Poorman Company refused to acquiesce. In the meantime Peck returned, but this time he joined the Hays and Ray owners' venture, and together they worked as quickly as possible to remove ore. In six days they unearthed some of the richest quartz and sent it to Portland. One correspondent reported: "There is no use describing the richness of the Poorman. No one will believe it without seeing it." The ore amounted to nearly $500,000 [$7.1 million in 2014], assaying at 80 percent gold and silver. "In the history of silver mining," reported one newspaper, "neither Mexico nor Peru furnished anything which can be successfully compared with it."[3]

The Poorman owners anticipated litigation on the conflicting claim, and therefore combined with the Oregon Steam Navigation Company to get the financial backing they would need to defend their case. Meanwhile, the Hays and Ray owners, while confident the law would be on their side, elicited George C. Robbins and the New York and Owyhee Mill Company to secure the financial resources they might need. However, tension over the claims heightened between the two parties and circumstances evolved from legal considerations to potential lethal actions.[4]

On September 24, 1865, forces for the Poorman mine squared off against their rivals from the Hays and Ray. A nearby brush and grass fire raged, which blanketed the area with smoke and dust and provided an ominous backdrop. In anticipation of this conflict, the Poorman defenders had erected what they called Fort Baker—a fortress of logs, with mounted artillery, portholes, and other means of defense. Armed with shotguns and six-shooters, these defenders stubbornly fought the Hays and Ray forces adjacent to the richest part of the Poorman.

With the volatile situation primed to explode, both sides assessed the situation and, instead of going to battle, went to court. Judge Milton Kelly ordered additional excavation at the Poorman site to expose the vein structure. When the diggings revealed the vein to be on the Hays and Ray property, Judge Kelly granted an injunction against the Poorman. Despite rumors that the judge had been bribed, his ruling temporarily halted work at the Poorman while development went ahead on the Hays and Ray vein. The Poorman resumed production in July of 1866.[5] Despite capitalism's claims to efficiency, one mining engineer noted the waste. "A large amount of unnecessary work has been done on this [the Poorman] mine; one shaft sunk near the office would have been all that was necessary; but when claims are in litigation much useless work must be done to prove identity of a vein."[6]

The Poorman is one small episode in the process of corporate consolidation in the West and America during the mid-nineteenth century. Backed by large amounts of capital essential for development and to fight the ensuing legal disputes, corporations battled it out in court—and at times, in the mines. This resulted in litigation expense, a ravaged land, and loss of life. As disputes increased in volume and violence, government intervened to referee and consequently grew in power.[7]

While the West enjoyed an image of being wild, in reality parties increasingly relied on government for assistance. At each juncture along the process of extraction, various levels of government acted as facilitator and mediator, which often defined the contours of the expansion. From assisting with the removal of the Indians to deciding the outcome in cases like the Poorman, government involvement significantly impacted the events and the lessons taken from them.

But government did not fill prospectors' dreams—gold did. It was simply too appealing. As with the modern-day lottery, many knew that the odds were against them, yet they remained confident and willing to take the chance that they would hit the next bonanza. However, even if they did discover a major strike, prospectors needed corporate investment to do anything with it. Very few succeeded; instead, large corporations earned handsome profits and assumed minimal responsibilities.

Conflict over Resources

Elementary students in social studies classes still study the California gold rush. "It all began on January 24, 1848, on the South Fork of the American River, near what is now the California town of Coloma," the story goes. John Sutter wanted to build a saw mill and hired workers, including James Marshall. On that fateful January day, Marshall "saw tiny pieces of gold in the runoff millwater. He collected some of the gold pieces and showed them to Sutter, who swore Marshall to secrecy." But the story got out. Within weeks a well-known publisher walked up and down the streets of San Francisco holding a jar full of gold. By August a major East Coast newspaper reported Marshall's discovery, and on December 5, 1848, President James K. Polk informed the nation in an address to Congress. Before long, the rush was on, and " '49ers, as they were called, descended on California by the tens of thousands." The first year drew 80,000; by 1856, "more than 300,000 people had followed their gold dreams."[8]

Versions of this story played out throughout the American West. In 1859 in Nevada and Colorado, thousands flooded to the Comstock and Leadville lodes. Three years later prospectors discovered large mineral deposits in what would become the Idaho Territory, with the Boise Basin initially drawing the greatest attention. The eight seasons from 1862 to 1869 resulted in a major western mining rush that attracted miners to a variety of districts throughout Idaho. The stages repeated: from prospecting, to discovery, to stampede, and, if mineral quantities warranted, development of a new mining district.[9]

This process played out in southwestern Idaho in the 1860s. On August 2, 1862, the George Grimes party ventured out from mining towns in eastern Oregon and discovered gold in the Boise Basin. Enticed by this latest claim, other mining parties founded Idaho City and Centerville. The discoveries in this district eclipsed anything previously found in the Pacific Northwest, and attracted an influx of population to these new mining regions that continued unabated for two years. By September of 1863, 6,267 people lived in Idaho City, which outpaced Portland to become the largest town in the Northwest. Early mining efforts proved successful; by the end of 1863 the total basin yielded $4–$6 million [$74–$111 million in 2014].[10]

That same year restless prospectors hoped to anticipate the next strike, and a party departed in the spring from the Boise Basin in a southwesterly direction. On May 18, they arrived at a place that they named Discovery Bar, about ten miles south of the later site of Dewey, where they found good placer diggings and staked their claims. Content with their findings, they named their adjacent spot "Happy Camp" and the nearby flowing water "Jordan Creek" after the leader of the party, Michael Jordan. Later the local paper dubbed them the Lucky Twenty Miners, heralded them as heroes for their "valuable discovery of the Owyhee mines," and listed their names "that they may be handed down as the pioneers of Owyhee County." Furthermore, the paper touted their early success: "Hardly a man in camp was to be found, but had enough to settle all of his bills and from $300 to $1,000 [$5,500 to $18,500 in 2014] besides."[11]

These mining opportunities in the West attracted people from all over the United States. William Black, born in South Carolina in 1802, journeyed west with the gold rush to California in 1849 and followed the strikes until he landed in Idaho. John Holgate of Ohio moved and worked in Oregon and Washington. When opportunities arose in Idaho, he pioneered mining efforts in the area. In 1863 he worked in the Boise Basin and moved southwest to Owyhees the next spring as he heard of early opportunities. Mining attracted more than half of the members of the territorial legislature that convened in 1865; they had first gone to California and then made their way to Idaho.[12]

Two of the most successful prospectors and miners in Idaho were David Fogus—reportedly the first person to find gold in the Owyhee country—and J. Marion More, who later became Fogus's partner. On June 28, 1862, Fogus found traces of gold in a creek in the Owyhees; however, after assessing the find to be minimal, he focused his attention on the most active strike of the times—Boise Basin. There he enjoyed exceptional success with discoveries at Pierce, Florence, and the Powder and Burnt Rivers. With the momentum of these ventures, Fogus decided to return to where he first found traces of gold in the Owyhee Mountains.[13]

Fogus's partner, J. Marion More, enjoyed significant success in his own right. A Tennessean by birth, More migrated to California with the hordes of '48 and '49. He lived the life of a prospector, experienced the boom-bust cycles inherent in the venture, and relocated accordingly. In 1861 he joined the Clearwater rush in the northern Idaho territory and represented the miners in the Washington legislature that same year. He became a well-respected leader in that community, a role he maintained when he ventured to southern Idaho and helped found Idaho City. More became a member of a variety of fraternities and lodges, including the Royal Arches, Masons, and Fenian Brotherhood. Like Fogus, he enjoyed success in mining ventures in the Boise Basin and set up his headquarters in Idaho City. More then decided to join forces with Fogus, and the two set their sights on the possibilities in the Owyhees.[14]

They would first have to deal with the Native Americans tribes who had inhabited this land for centuries. In July 1864, ranchers accused Native Americans of stealing cattle, driving off horses, and killing some prospectors working in the area. A group of twenty volunteers gathered in Silver City and pursued the Native Americans to the mouth of the Bruneau River, where a battle ensued. The newspaper reported that the fighting sent "twenty bucks to the 'happy hunting grounds'" and claimed that the consequences of this battle meant clashes with Native Americans would decrease.[15]

Early conflicts had occurred with Indians as settlers made their way along the Oregon Trail, and as mining interests increased so did the number and size of battles. One of the most significant battles took place when Colonel P. E. Connor, with a detachment of California volunteers patrolling near Battle Creek (Idaho), encountered approximately 175 Native Americans (75 of whom were women and children). A battle ensued: fourteen federal troops died and eight more were wounded, while all but ten of the Native Americans perished.[16]

The end of the Civil War left large numbers of soldiers available for duty, and as greater numbers of settlers headed west the government established more military posts to protect settlers. Near the Idaho/Oregon border in Owyhee County, authorities established Camp Lyon in 1865, and to guard the road to California founded Camp Three Forks on the southwest slope of South Mountain. In addition to the federal military presence in these forts, other private companies and volunteer vigilante groups worked to protect the growing population and their own economic endeavors.[17]

Diverse Attraction

Despite the presence of Native Americans, stories of atrocities, and the hard life of mining, the legends of wealth held great sway. Years after the fact, David Fogus still remembered a story that had drawn him to the Owyhees. He met a man who reported that his nephew had found so much gold that they pounded it into weights and used it for sinkers while fishing. The location where Fogus first found gold gave Sinker Creek its name.[18]

Government leaders further fueled the fever. In 1864, President Lincoln appointed Caleb Lyon as the second territorial governor. Ever controversial, during his tenure the capital shifted from Lewiston in the north to Boise in the southwest. The northerners argued that he stole the capital. On November 20, 1865, Governor Lyon addressed the citizenry of Ruby City and spoke of the tremendous value of the diamonds that had allegedly been found in the area. His words helped touch off a stampede; many stormed to the Owyhees seeking their fortune.[19]

Another famous story centered on an 1845 discovery in central Oregon by a misguided immigrant party. When children went in search of water they returned and reported bright "shiny stuff" in the creek gravel—enough to fill their blue water buckets full. Although trying conditions forced the party to push on, their mythical discovery fueled the relentless search for this gold. Michael Jordan and his fellow prospectors reportedly migrated to this region to pursue this legendary find. Ineffective in their bid for the elusive Blue Bucket, they nonetheless successfully appropriated the best mining ground before much of the rush to Owyhee even got under way.[20]

While some claims produced large yields, a number of the miners left empty-handed. When word of the new Owyhee mines reached the Boise Basin, hundreds of miners scrapped their plans and ventured to the red-hot Owyhee placers. The rush left many "disappointed, and some hardly off their horses, but joined with the balance of the disaffected newcomers to

Mill buildings at the Oro Fino Mine on War Eagle Mountain in 1866. (Courtesy of Idaho State Historical Society.)

curse the country, the camp, and the party that found it." The local paper reported the seasonal end to the great quartz rush. "An eager and expectant crowd, who attracted by the golden stories of Idaho, sought to better their fortunes, but they did not find gold on the surface; and now they wind their way homeward." The reality of the situation sharply contrasted with popular stories. This returning wave discouraged many others from migrating to the area, which caused equipment suppliers to divert resources and left Owyhee miners short of tools and mining gear in their initial season.[21]

While some turned back, the general success of the area continued to attract newcomers. In 1863, besides the finds of the Jordan party, two other major discoveries surfaced: in August the Oro Fino lode located near Silver City, and the Morning Star find on October 14. Interest grew in both finds when miners extracted nine ounces of gold and silver from a rock weighing just over a pound. These few sites produced in less than eleven months what comparable mining districts produced in two to three years. The local paper asked, "Who can tell the amount that in all human probability will be put in circulation within the next year to come?"[22]

Within two years, the Owyhee rush surpassed the national fame of any of the earlier southern Idaho gold discoveries. Between 1863 and 1865, officials recorded 250 mining locations. Albert D. Richardson, a noted newspaper correspondent who traveled throughout the West, claimed that Owyhee had "the most abundant gold and silver bearing rock ever found in the United States." He described the War Eagle Mountain mines as "the richest and most wonderful deposit of quartz yet discovered in the United States, even eclipsing the famed Comstock Lode." By 1867, a spectacular sample shipped to the Paris International Exposition won a special gold medal. The use of the Washoe process, previously developed on the Comstock and applied in the Owyhee mines, advanced production more rapidly than in the other quartz districts in Idaho.[23]

In the fall of 1864, A. P. Minear established a custom mill with ten 450-pound stamps used for crushing ore to extract and further process it. Simultaneously, More and Fogus invested handsomely in two properties dubbed the Oro Fino and Morning Star properties. The two also launched the best ten-stamp mill in the district and began operation on October 3, 1864. The rich ore More and Fogus uncovered offset the expense of the large amount of rock that had to be hoisted by hand from company shafts. On November 27 More triumphantly arrived in Portland with $60,000 [$896,000 in 2014] in silver bricks. A month later the Morning Star shaft bore 115 feet down and extracted an even richer ore. Their use of the Washoe process created the highest efficiency, producing nearly $1 million [$15 million in 2014] in the first year alone. The next summer the owners hoped to add 24 stamps. Their success, along with that of many others in the area, contributed to rapid expansion of Silver City. The rush was on to uncover War Eagle's "Silver Heart." By February of 1865, Owyhee boasted a population of one thousand, with some of the largest strikes yet to be discovered.[24]

These mining communities attracted a diverse lot. Chinese immigrants from Canton remained one of the largest groups of immigrant miners to this region. Their earliest presence in Idaho dates to 1864, and their large numbers led the *Owyhee Avalanche* to note that "almost every abandoned claim or gulch in which the color of gold can be found has its gang of Chinamen at work." In 1867, over five hundred Chinese worked Jordan Creek alone. Statistics reveal that out of a territory-wide population of 14,999, nearly a third (4,274) were Chinese. As occurred throughout the West, the Chinese encountered hostile resistance in Idaho, including legislation to exclude them.[25]

Besides the Chinese, large numbers of Irish also worked as miners. In a jailbreak account, a listing in the local paper included each name of the prison escapee and a description of nationality (James O'Brien "is an Irishman"). The listing of eleven included four Irishmen, four Chinamen, a German, and described only one, Ed Stock, as American. This article provides insight into at least one newspaper's understanding of what constituted an American.[26]

Other individual stories demonstrate the diverse nature of these communities and the opportunities that they provided. One account in a local newspaper described an Indian immigrant, Joe Miller, better known as "Black Joe," who worked by "blacking boots around town." Born near Calcutta in 1808, Joe Miller immigrated to America, eventually settling in Silver City.[27] Historian Elliot West's study of mining communities in Idaho found them inhabited by "proportionately more immigrants than the most polyglot precincts of Chicago and the most ethnically diverse wards of cities like South Bend, Indiana." As such they remind us of the diversity that was frosted over in later, marketed versions of the West. The image also portrayed individuals as the backbone of this development, yet the reality was far different.[28]

Investors from throughout the United States and the world infused this area with the necessary capital for large-scale machinery, labor, and transportation costs. East Coast investors remained the most consistent pool, and the latest news from the *Mining and Scientific Press* supported the claims of promoters who traveled east to connect these investors with holders of undeveloped claims. It also left them vulnerable.[29] Comparable to the "dot-com" craze of the late 1990s, the speed, size, and volume of investments, at times, resulted in overambitious projects, fraud, and a lack of local control. For example, in August of 1864, the Morning Star Gold and Silver Tunnel Company of Idaho conceived an elaborate project bankrolled with $5 million [$75 million in 2014] capital stock. They hoped to run a tunnel similar to the Sutro tunnel project for the Comstock. While the scheme gained significant attention in New York, those in Owyhee knew little. The project came up empty and quickly disappeared from the news, another victim to the dreams of overzealous investors. A letter between investors summarized the situation well: "There are many persons turning their eyes towards Idaho and if you have any interests there in mines they quite likely will be salable *whether they are of any account or not*" (italics added).[30]

However, besides the capital necessary for the onsite excavation, the infrastructure required to transport the machinery and unearthed minerals proved to be extremely costly. For example, each mill had to be brought in via the river and then carted three hundred miles by wagon at a cost of 25 cents [$3.75 in 2014] per pound. By 1866, companies had transported ten stamp mills, but it would be another twenty years for the district to reach its maximum production due to the poor transportation infrastructure.[31]

As mining ventures fanned out from California, a parallel transportation grid connected the Owyhees: southwestern Idaho became one of the spokes emanating from points in California. The journey remained long and dangerous. J. M. Hornback left Chico, California, with six heavily freighted wagons on June 23, 1865, and arrived in Idaho City two months later on August 22. One report estimated that a good ten-mule team, with two or more in a company, could haul about eight hundred pounds of freight, along with the necessary six hundred pounds of feed, over this route from Chico to Idaho. It would be decades before an adequate infrastructure existed and the fare dropped to a more reasonable price. Accomplishing these tasks required massive investment of resources.[32]

The tension between individual prospectors and the corporations needed to develop these projects corresponded with a series of dichotomies that existed in the late-nineteenth-century West. Individuals who were moving constantly in search of the next strikes contrasted with those who were ready to settle down and establish a community. The diversity of those attracted to the region challenged the formation of a common identity. Finally, the need for peaceful relations between claimants and laborers belied a culture of conflict and violence that existed between parties living and working in this area. Silver City, Idaho, presents a case study of these clashing interests. A short description of the elements at work in this town provides the backdrop to the ensuing conflict.

A band on the balcony of the Photograph Gallery of the Silver City Wells Fargo & Company office in the late 1860s. (Courtesy of Idaho State Historical Society.)

A Case Study of Competing Interests

From the founding of Silver City, mines consistently served as its lifeline. Reliance on mining meant accepting the boom-bust cycle; and insufficient supplies, inadequate infrastructure, and difficulties maintaining order constantly plagued these early days. Yet, the array of services offered and established community organizations provide evidence that a segment of the population certainly desired to build a sustained community and not merely to scrape off a profit and move on.[33]

In August of 1865, the Wasson Brothers and J. L. Hardin established the local newspaper, the *Avalanche.* Within the next few years a second paper, *The Tidal Wave,* competed for readers. The clothing supplier Oberdorfer's advertised "A Fine Assortment of Gentlemen's Winter Suits and Ladies' Ulsters." Announcements for the War Eagle and Miners' hotels listed their offerings, and the photographer H. E. Leslie promised "all kinds of work in

View of Silver City, Idaho, circa 1885. (Courtesy of Idaho State Historical Society.)

the photographing line in the latest and most improved styles of the art." Community organizations also thrived. Fraternal lodges such as the Masons, the Independent Order of Good Templars, the Odd Fellows, and the Knights of Pythias formed and publicized their meetings and activities. By 1865, the Owyhee school system had enrolled ninety-three pupils. The city also enjoyed a circulating library and a lecture series on topics ranging from temperance to Darwinism.[34]

Itinerant preachers rode on horseback between mining communities and served the people. When Rt. Rev. Daniel S. Tuttle was appointed missionary bishop of the Idaho Territory in 1867, he helped establish Episcopal churches in Boise, Idaho City, and Silver City. However, as the mining region moved and the religious background of miners changed, St. Andrew's Episcopal Church was consecrated as Our Lady of Tears Catholic Church.[35]

Besides ministers, entertainers often traveled a mining community circuit. The Apollo Minstrels reportedly attracted "full houses every night and [made] the people laugh exceedingly." John Kelly, who traveled with a small "Paiute boy" as his assistant, played his violin in mining communities throughout the West. The Silver City Amateur Theatrical Association presented scenes from Shakespeare's *Winter's Tale*.[36]

Silver and Ruby Cities became known as "sober, respectable mining communities," yet they certainly had their share of bars and houses of prostitution. One article said, "We have it on good authority that one 'hunky shebong' shipped $8,000 [$119,000 in 2014] as net proceeds of its July business as the bar gets one half, it makes in all over $16,000 [$239,000 in 2014] in one month. Thus it will be seen that these leaches corral more cash than most quartz mills." The red-light district of Silver City spanned Jordan Street in the vicinity of Long Gulch Creek, with Stella's, Mother Nacks, Big Dick's, The Irish Queen's, and Georgie's among the most popular.[37]

It was a tumultuous and violent time. One newspaper article reported that Jeremiah O'Connor died from an accidental explosion in the Ida Elmore Mine, leaving behind his wife and two small children. A story headlined "Brutal Affair" described two men named Gibson and Hansen who got into a fight in a "hurdy-gurdy" house where Gibson "pounded Hansen in a shocking manner." The *Avalanche* informed readers that "Thomas Wilson [was] stabbed to death in a card game by James Hargrave, alias 'Lucky Jim,' in Silver City, on August 29, 1865."[38]

These actions and editorials paralleled those of many other communities throughout the West. On the one hand, historian Richard Maxwell Brown wrote, a "remarkably open, mobile, and expanding society" existed during the "Western Civil War of Incorporation." Brown argued that "this allowed many of the lower and middle class to not only avoid the battlegrounds but to thrive elsewhere." The early evidence of Silver City supports Brown's claims. However, not all managed to avoid conflict; local disturbances created the desire for greater order and protection in Silver City and other communities throughout the West.[39]

In his studies of violence in the West, Brown concluded that a belief system "mentally programmed westerners to commit violence." Brown argued that the duty to never retreat coupled with a homestead ethic that encouraged individual enterprise and an ideology of vigilantism set up a framework for violence. These principles reinforced a belief in self-preservation, the right of revolution, and popular sovereignty. In Silver City in 1866, a group called the Northwest Vigilantes included prominent members of the community. They aimed to "rid the Pacific Northwest of its toughs." One account maintained that to accomplish their goal they ended up "decorating the trees, rafters, and bridges with cut-throats and killers."[40]

Conflict and violence permeated this environment as various parties attempted to fill the vacuum of control. In the early spring of 1868 these forces clashed on War Eagle Mountain, demonstrating the volatility of situations like this in the West and how government was often involved in their resolution.

Battle over the Silver Heart

Both the Ida Elmore and Golden Chariot mining companies knew the claim held "some of the richest ore ever seen." Locals described it as containing "both silver and gold in it in large quantities, pure native silver held together by leaves and threads of gold." Their success was the problem. Had their find been marginal they likely could have reached an agreement and moved on. But instead of peacefully resolving the competing claims, miners squared off. The battle largely took place three hundred feet underground, with the disputants emptying countless rounds of ammunition in an attempt to gain control of the three-foot-wide vein of silver and gold.[41]

Due to poor or inaccurate cartography, the boundaries of mining claims in the West often overlapped. This is precisely what occurred in March of 1868 on War Eagle Mountain. The two mines could hardly have worked any closer; their hoisting works were separated by a mere seventy-five feet. Owners of the Ida Elmore claimed that the New York vein lay entirely within their mine, while the Golden Chariot countered that the Ida Elmore boundary followed a distinct ledge that excluded the New York vein. While territorial boundaries remained nebulous, both sides clearly claimed this most profitable portion of the vein.[42]

The investors in the Golden Chariot mine—Hill Beachy, Grayson & Company—recognized the potential of their mining venture. In November 1867, the mine began shipping ore to mills in Boise City and averaged $48 to $50 [$762 to $794 in 2014] per ton for each run of their loads. As winter approached and roads closed, mine manager George W. Grayson continued directing work on the mine in order to have stockpiles of ore ready to be freighted with the spring thaw.[43]

The Ida Elmore also enjoyed success, and as each mining group worked farther along the vein they realized they soon would meet. Aware of costly legal battles and contentious disputes that had slowed down or halted other mining ventures, the parties agreed to create an unmined neutral partition—a block of ore. However, the temptation proved too great; in February of 1868 the local newspaper reported that workmen from both mines had broken through the neutral zone.[44]

Tensions mounted. Perhaps a lawsuit could settle the matter, but with so much money at stake a peaceful outcome seemed doubtful. Even the territory's chief justice admitted that "legal proceedings were too slow where a single day's output of ore meant thousands of dollars to the persons taking it." The parties were primed for violence. On Wednesday, March 11, witnesses observed many of the miners "milling around largely idle while other parties with ominous faces hurried back and forth whispering the news and gathering guns and pistols." Some curious parties even ventured down into the mine to get a closer look at the disputed section. However, they quickly scurried above ground when miners extinguished the lights and gunshots rang out through the long passages.[45]

The contours of mining—stopes (steps made by the mining of ore) and drifts—quickly became the battlefields of war as miners fortified their locations. The darkness, the unending echoes of exploding shots, and the ricocheting sounds of bullets bouncing off timber and mining shafts made it nearly impossible to determine who was hit, or who was winning. Above ground, aware of the well-armed combatants, others waited—anxious to learn the fate of friends and family.[46]

Each side possessed cases of rifles, shotguns, and pistols, with a magazine of ammunition. Espionage efforts by smaller parties attempted to identify and capture the munitions of the other. Although neither side succeeded in this, it changed the nature of the contest and forced both sides to post guards and remain ever vigilant. Mostly they waited in the dark, passing the hours until a light appeared on one side, which immediately resulted in a fusillade from the other side. At the most intense intersections of combat, the miners used hand grenades and Greek fire throwers in an attempt to inflict the greatest damage on the enemy.[47]

Both sides succeeded. Timbers from six to nine inches thick in the drifts and stopes stood stublike—sawed in half by a succession of bullets. Strewn splinters and spent shells littered tunnel portions where the fiercest fighting occurred. Yet, some also realized the difficulties of using the guns and munitions of traditional warfare and turned to the tools of their trade to gain an advantage. The Ida Elmore party used hoses to eject hot steam and water to scald and drown their opponents. However, this tactical advantage was short-lived, for the Golden Chariot fighters responded in kind.[48]

Given the underground battles and conflicting newspaper accounts, it was difficult to follow the battle. On Wednesday, March 18, 1868, the *Idaho World* reported that the parties had reached a truce and agreed to withdraw their men from the mines and adhere to a court settlement of the conflict. However, the next day the *Owyhee Avalanche* claimed that at least 150 rounds of ammunition had been fired underground that day. The *Idaho World* printed a retraction of its article on Saturday, March 21, "Bloodshed was predicted as the community braced for the next underground battle." Accounts agreed that fighting had intensified over the week and culminated on Wednesday, March 25, when the underground Golden Chariot party stormed the Ida Elmore works and forced their opponents to retreat to their main hoisting shaft. After securing the area, the miners fortified the shaft by surrounding it with a bunker of gunnysacks filled with sand. They had successfully cut off the exit of the Ida Elmore fighters and left them with only the New York shaft, which lay 400–500 feet north, as their sole means of escape.[49]

After the Golden Chariot party secured the area, they assessed their position and the number of casualties. In their attack they captured one of the Ida Elmore men, disarmed him, and took him prisoner. Two others remained penned in a stope and refused to relinquish their arms, but later realized the futility of their position and surrendered. Yet, as the situation stabilized, the Golden Chariot men realized to their horror that they had lost one of their leaders and mine owners: John C. Holgate lay dead from a gunshot to the head.[50]

Fighting continued intermittently throughout the night, and by the next morning the combatants carried out a miner suffering from a gunshot wound. A Jewish miner who was a veteran of the Confederate Army and a member of the Ida Elmore party named Meyer Frank died about two o'clock that afternoon. Witnesses reported others injured, among them James Howard, another member of the Ida Elmore group, who emerged from the mine with his right arm shattered between the elbow and shoulder by a bullet.[51]

Despite the injuries and fatalities, the "War on the Mountain" continued, with the Golden Chariot gaining the advantage. They stabilized their control of the ground they had seized and sent a group to work, taking out as much ore as possible. As the miners feverishly excavated the ore, the battle continued around them. With the Golden Chariot's bold action of ore extraction, Fogus and his forces from the Ida Elmore shifted the battle aboveground in offensive operations. While both sides had recruited miners from other communities to fight, Fogus sent for further reinforcements in the area and prepared his strategy.[52]

Meanwhile, community members implored local government authorities to take action. "Is our sheriff not invested with the power required by law to stop such proceedings?" the *Owyhee Avalanche* asked. In Boise City the *Idaho Statesman* described the lack of response as "deplorable" and "disgraceful." It admonished the sheriff for not arresting "every man found threatening the public peace."[53]

The *Owyhee Avalanche* came to the defense of the heavily criticized sheriff. It published a response from Sheriff A. C. Springer with his denial of a duty to interfere. In an editorial the newspaper asked: "Cannot these people, who pretend to know so much about the Sheriff's duty, distinguish between the affair in question and a public disturbance of the peace?" Since both sides felt that the valuable mining ground was theirs, they were simply defending their property, something that everyone has a legal right to protect. "In what manner can the Sheriff prevent them?" the newspaper asked, recognizing the futility of the lone officer against more than a hundred involved in the battle taking place primarily underground.[54]

Territorial officials recognized the danger and potential precedent of the chaotic situation and decided to act. Governor D. W. Ballard dispatched district attorney E. J. Curtis, famous Indian fighter and US Deputy Marshal Orlando Robbins, and later even territorial chief justice John R. McBride to address the situation. As Fogus rallied his men for an aboveground offensive, Curtis attempted to persuade each side to halt the violence and let the tensions subside. Later that day, Saturday, March 28, Robbins arrived with a proclamation for peace from Governor Ballard and word that federal troops had been called out from Fort Boise.[55]

Accompanied by Sheriff Springer, Robbins read the proclamation to representatives from both factions. In his message the governor acknowledged the conflict and the deaths that occurred and warned that these actions were "imperiling the public peace" and fomenting "terror in the minds of peaceable citizens." He then outlined how these actions defied the law and "command[ed] all armed parties to disperse peaceably to their homes without delay." Moreover, he warned that engaging in any further action "subjects them to heavy punishment, endangers the public peace," and reminded the citizens that this action "tarnishes the fair name of our Territory." He pledged that the "whole power of the territory will be used by the executive" to ensure the restoration of peace.[56]

In reality the mining war further stretched Ballard's fledgling government. Since its establishment in 1863, the territorial authority had struggled to gain control. No one except the territorial secretary knew the civil and criminal codes, since the published volumes remained in San Francisco awaiting payment for the printing bill. With communication between the northern and southern portions of Idaho Territory extremely slow and cumbersome, and with troubles with Native Americans in large numbers and financial abuse and discrepancies, the survival of the government in Idaho seemed in doubt.[57]

Governor Ballard attempted to establish order, but this remained especially tenuous in the post–Civil War years. A large influx of Confederate refugees from Missouri, along with other Southern sympathizers, made Idaho a strongly Southern territory. Consequently, the Republican governor and other territorial officials appointed by the president of the United States clashed with the legislature. In 1866 and 1867, the situation grew so intense that the governor called out US Army troops for personal protection. Despite remaining a target of secessionist sympathizers, the governor survived in office and worked to curtail events—such as this mining war—that threatened governmental authority. He decided to travel to the Owyhees himself.[58]

In the meantime his proclamation gained the attention of the combatants. Perhaps weary of a protracted battle, both sides indicated that if a suitable agreement could be reached they would be "willing to give up their arms and submit to the authority of the United States." Again lawyers and judges rather than soldiers resolved the conflict. The negotiated compromise meant that Wilson and Company, the controlling interests of the Ida Elmore, would hold fifty feet of the mine south from the north side of the main shaft; meanwhile Grayson, Beachy & Company, owners of the Golden Chariot, would be allowed to retain the remaining portion of the vein south of that point. After the boundaries had been clearly defined and deeds exchanged, both sides put down their arms and began to clean up all the damage for their return to work. The governor arrived just in time to witness the end of the hostilities. The paper reported the "general gladness" felt throughout the community with a peaceful resolution and prevention of greater loss of life.[59]

Government Stays the Course

However, the relief was short-lived. After the conflict subsided, J. Marion More traveled to Silver City to ensure the order of his affairs in the Owyhees before he returned home to Idaho City. One evening he joined Ben White, Jack Fisher, and some other friends for dinner. According to newspaper accounts, More drank liberally, recounted the recent controversy, and described his dissatisfaction with the outcome. After dinner the group made their way through town and passed in front of the stage office in the Idaho Hotel. Sitting there was Sam Lockhart, one of the adversaries in the dispute, and "hot words passed between them." According to one account More was unarmed and carried only a cane in his hand. He reportedly raised the stick as if to strike Lockhart, who backed away a few paces and fired his gun. Six to eight shots rang out. Fisher took a bullet through his left thigh, while Lockhart suffered a severe flesh wound to his left arm. More ran toward the Oriental Restaurant about fifty yards away. He fell in front of the restaurant severely bleeding from a bullet wound near the center of his chest. To witnesses More said, "They have stolen the mine and now their man Lockhart has killed me." He died the next afternoon.[60]

The sound of the shootings quickly drew a crowd. Lockhart's friends Hill Beachy, G. W. Grayson, J. M. McQuaid, and Gus Simondi ran into the hotel lobby and found Lockhart with blood dripping from his arm. They quickly loaded their firearms and rifles, secured positions, and prepared for revenge. Outside, many of More's friends gathered "wild with passion and loud with threats and cursing." "Bring him out; Hang him!" they screamed, apparently believing Lockhart's culpability.[61]

Just before the situation erupted again, territorial chief justice McBride made his presence known. He convinced both sides to allow law enforcement to take over. Sheriff Springer gathered an armed posse of deputies and stationed them inside and outside the hotel. Lockhart quickly left the area, which led many to believe he was probably more responsible for the difficulty than anyone else. Later, Lockhart's arm was amputated, but gangrene set in and, after several weeks of suffering, he died.[62]

Governor Ballard again decided to take swift action. He dispatched Orlando Robbins to Boise and requisitioned troops for Silver City. Ballard stopped short of establishing martial law but firmly addressed the citizens of Owyhee County. He assured people that "the parties implicated in the late occurrence are now under arrest." The governor pledged that "no failure of justice will occur" and announced that he would not hesitate to use all power to enforce order. Finally he appealed to all citizens to remain in their homes and avoid public assemblies. True to Ballard's word, Brevet-Colonel James B. Sinclair and First Lieutenant Charles Byrd arrived with ninety-five troops and a cannon. The soldiers bivouacked just outside of town for the next few days and backed up Ballard's claims.[63]

The presence of the troops, Chief Justice McBride, and Governor Ballard himself calmed the situation. The territorial government and federal troops shored up local law enforcement and convinced the parties that acts of violence would not be tolerated. By April 5, 1868, the "War on the Mountain" had ended, and the situation appeared calm enough that the soldiers returned to Boise. That same day, J. Marion More, prominent pioneer, founder, and community member, was buried in Idaho City.[64]

Conclusion

As ministers conducted services for More and the other casualties of the mining war, the miners returned to work. Despite rumors that those killed haunted further excavating efforts, the mines succeeded. By the end of 1869 five companies—Orofino and Morning Star, the Poorman, Ida Elmore, Ainsworth, and the Golden Chariot—had shipped nearly $5 million [$86 million in 2014] in bullion from the Owyhees. Estimates of production figures place the total take as high as $30 million [$517 million in 2014] extracted from the "silver heart" of War Eagle Mountain.[65]

Competing interests continued to battle over these valuable resources. The *Owyhee Avalanche* reported, "Last Wednesday a shooting affray, originating in a dispute about a mining claim, took place between the [well-

J. Marion More portrait. (Courtesy of Idaho State Historical Society.)

known and prominent citizens] John Taylor and John McMahon, resulting in the latter receiving a pistol bullet through his left leg . . . producing a frightful wound."[66]

As the battles continued, the financial costs mounted. The accounting books for the Ida Elmore revealed that of the $600,000 [$10 million in 2014] produced in the first year, one third or $200,000 [$3.4 million in 2014] went to pay the cost of the war and litigation. Due to the conflict, the Golden Chariot shut down and installed new hoisting works, which meant that all $200,000 [$3.4 million in 2014] it had realized in the year's production went toward the expenses of the battle.[67]

Other unusual elements stand out in this episode. The coalitions needed to defend the mining claims realigned more commonly held associations. Miners and owners regularly fought each other; in fact, miners formed their own cooperative and organized a union in order to gain greater profits and control. However, in this instance the loyalty lay along company lines; miners gathered with owners to battle a common enemy. While no doubt some involved acted as mercenaries, the loyalty of these armies indicates a motivation to protect their allotment and way of life. As historian Daniel Herman notes, not all can be defined by the "three great drawers" of history—race, class, and gender. Many things motivate. This seems to be one of those instances.[68]

Ironically, this filthy, monotonous, and dangerous work that ravaged the environment extracted something beautiful and highly sought after—gold, silver, and other minerals. The opportunity attracted a mobile and diverse lot, who battled for control. The violence of their conflicts reinforced a western ethic commonly portrayed in books and films. However, the conflict primarily provided an opportunity for government to mobilize, and the shortage of local government officials meant that the territorial and federal government intervened. In the process, government involvement extended from facilitator for the developers to conflict mediator, and set the precedent for an ever-increasing role in the West.

Individuals such as David Fogus staked initial claims in the Owyhees, but development of mines ultimately required substantial corporate investment. Despite this reality, the largely mythical individual prospector capitalizing on his claim became the lasting image of this era, and books, television, and films reinforced this ideal. Evidence of the staying power of the image and the ability of large corporations to manipulate it through favorable legislation linger to this day. Despite the efforts of many to update legislation, the 1872 mining law (dubbed the Homestead Act for miners) remains on the books. This nineteenth-century piece of legislation allows companies, the majority of which reside outside the United States, to extract minerals in large quantities while paying relatively little for claims. In fact, mining corporations extracted more gold in the mid-1980s than during the California gold rush of 1849.[69]

Besides the scarred land, poor health, and deaths resulting from these conflicts over control of resources, one must also remember the group that paid the greatest price of all—Native Americans removed from their lands. The following poem by Esther Brubacher summarizes some of that sentiment, as we turn our attention toward their story.

Silver City's Mountains
Far across the desert
The Blue Mountains Glow
Silver City's mountains
Of our Idaho.

Like vast mounds of turquoise
Shining in the West;
Holding in the night time
Stars upon their breast.

High above the others
Big War Eagle stands;
Monarch of the desert,
and the lone sage lands

Brooding now and silent
Lonely and apart
Since they came and took away
the Eagle's silver heart.[70]

CHAPTER THREE

The Battle of Shoshone Mike

The end of the first decade of the twentieth century marked significant changes in the world. Albert Einstein theorized his relativity postulate; construction began on the Panama Canal; aircraft had been used as an offensive weapon for the first time in the Turkish-Italian war; and the French invented the first photocopy machine. In the United States, Thomas Edison introduced the Kinetoscope, which made talking movies a reality; the Boston Red Sox won baseball's first World Series, Henry Ford developed the first Model T automobile; and in New Haven, Connecticut, a restaurant served a beef patty on two sides of toast and introduced the hamburger.

For many Idaho communities, this push toward the future meant connecting to the railroad. By 1874, population growth in southeastern Idaho meant that the Utah Northern ran a line into the Mormon community of Franklin. Within a decade the Union Pacific crossed southern Idaho. In northern Idaho rich deposits of silver ore attracted thousands, and by 1884 the Northern Pacific served the northern part of the state. In 1889, territorial officials prepared a constitution, and Idaho entered the Union on July 3, 1890, with a population of 88,000 citizens. The state grew fast. By 1900 the population had nearly doubled to 161,772, and a decade later had doubled again to 325,594. By 1910 in Idaho, the largest sawmill in the United States had opened at Potlatch, and the Miller Dam on the Snake River enabled large-scale irrigation; and in 1914 Idaho elected the first Jewish governor in the United States.[1]

Yet, while society modernized, in the southwestern corner of the state of Idaho a small band of Indians attempted to live a different lifestyle. Although the US government established the Fort Hall Indian Reservation in eastern Idaho in 1869 and the Western Shoshone Reservation (later named the Duck Valley Indian Reservation) in 1877, this small band refused to reside on either of these sites. Instead, they lived a seminomadic life that took them from Idaho, across the northern portion of Nevada, and all the way to California. Well known by the settlers of this region, each year they returned to their base camp in Rock Canyon near what became the town of Twin Falls, Idaho.[2]

Frank and Guy Tranmer also enjoyed this area. Their father, the well-respected Judge Tranmer, had jumped off a wagon train bound for Oregon in the 1870s and established himself in the Snake River Valley. Known for fair-minded legal decisions, officiating of marriages, and generous participation in civic matters, Judge Tranmer enjoyed a sterling reputation. However, the same could not be said about his sons Frank and Guy; they always seemed on the periphery of trouble. For their main source of income they herded wild horses and sold them to area ranchers. Some questioned how they managed to bring in such stock.[3]

One day, according to Guy Tranmer, he and his older brother Frank, along with a gangly youth from Twin Falls named Nimrod Urie, trotted down a hill and came upon an Indian named "Mike" and his family. As the Indians branded horses in a corral, they directed the riding party to not stop at the corral but to move toward the camp. According to the Tranmers, along the way an armed Indian stopped them and said, "I am going to kill you." Surprised, Guy Tranmer asked why, since "they had always been friends." The Indian replied that he had "no friends and was like a wild horse." The Indian then allegedly shot over the head of the Tranmer party, who scampered for cover behind some rocks. The Indians also sought protection, and the two sides began to shoot at each other. The majority of the shots ricocheted off the rocks, but the Tranmers hit one of the exposed Indians and wounded him badly. A young boy from the nearby camp emerged to gather spooked horses, but he quickly fell to the ground with a direct hit.

As the volley of shots gradually subsided, the Tranmer party successfully escaped to the camp, happy that they had suffered no casualties in the exchange. As the Indians rode off, the Tranmers noticed them circling around the top of the hill where they later found the dead body of the boy.[4]

On Thursday, May 12, 1910, the *Twin Falls Times* placed the story in a broader context. According to the article, a "marauding band of Shoshones" had stolen considerable stock from cattle and sheep ranchers in southern Idaho and northern Nevada, and the ranchers had appealed to the sheriff of Elko County, Nevada, for assistance. The sheriff investigated and concluded that the Indians had stolen approximately eighty horses and run them over the state line. The sheriff reportedly sent word to citizens to "kill all the Indians, and every Indian that may be found roaming the Idaho country." In the ensuing battle, the Indians killed a member of the Tranmer family. When the news spread, "all the rifles [that] could be mustered were secured and some 60 ranch men and cowboys formed a posse." The members of the posse planned to "strictly obey" the instructions of the Elko County officer. The paper predicted that by the time this was over "quite a number of Indians will have been sent to their happy hunting grounds."[5]

For years, both the Tranmer family and Mike's band had traveled the Shoshone Basin and south to Gollaher Mountain across the Nevada line. Many blamed the Indians for lost cattle and horses in the spring of 1910. They assumed that a band of Indians got caught trying to steal horses and killed the young boy. It never occurred to most that someone from their own community—especially somebody from the reputable Tranmer family—might have done it.[6]

Others remained unconvinced. In thirty years no one had ever accused the Indian band of horse or cattle theft. Instead, they surmised that Mike had strayed upon the Tranmers as they altered brands on a group of corralled horses. Since one of Mike's daughters had married the foreman of the well-known Shoe Sole Ranch, the Tranmers feared Mike's reaction and decided to attack first. To dispose of the evidence, the group later drove the horses off into the desert sage, then shot and buried them in long parallel trenches to keep the buzzards from revealing their location. In later reporting, Mike's daughter Heney maintained that while Mike's son, Jack, brought some horses into camp, the Tranmers ambushed, shot, and killed him. When the Indians came upon the body, they sought revenge and went after the Tranmer pack, killing a member of the party in the fight. The rest of the group managed to escape. When they got to town the Tranmer party blamed Mike for stealing the horses and for the killing.[7]

Regardless of what actually happened, the perceptions created from newspaper articles and fueled by word of mouth resulted in a guilty verdict for Mike and his family. In a scene repeated in the nineteenth century but rarely in the second decade of the twentieth, a posse formed to capture the band. This episode represents one of the final chapters of a battle that originated with the earliest settlers: radically different visions of land use and ways of life collided. The power assumed by the settlers in these conflicts with Native Americans and the stories appropriated from these episodes far outlasted the events themselves.

For many, these conflicts and the accompanying stories fortified the civilizing mission of the settlers and justified the many sacrifices of their ancestors. However, few recognized the way the pursuit of a common enemy blurred differences of race, religion, ethnicity, and class. In some instances, Indians played critical roles in the capturing of other groups of Native Americans. As historian Patricia Limerick writes, "The idea of an Indian war as a conflict of whites against Indians seldom had much to do with reality because Indians were usually on both sides of the conflict." Moreover, some of the settlers viewed the Indians as friends, and the two helped each other. Such collaboration demonstrates that confrontation was not inevitable.[8]

Nevertheless, the outcome of events confirmed positions of authority. Settlers maintained their advantage, and the involvement of the local, state, and federal governments reinforced their role as facilitators of western development. The events became the core material of legends and myths, and the central theme of countless Hollywood movies. For many the myths confirmed a heroic and honest past. But with time the stories revealed the destruction and death caused by settlers and represented a challenge to the veracity of these myths. Both sides claimed their version of the stories for their purposes.

Native Americans and Settlers

The dearth of reliable documentation makes Mike's date of birth difficult to pinpoint. Estimates place it in the early to mid-1840s, when Native Americans came in contact with a few non-Natives, mostly trappers and explorers. While these relatively few invaders brought with them devastating diseases and killed larger numbers of big game, their effects paled in comparison to those of the later waves of settlers. These arriving thousands brought more disease, hunted big game to near extinction, and staked an ever-widening range of prime land for farming, ranching, and mining. Moreover, the herds of cattle and sheep that they brought devastated the grasses that served as an essential element of the food supply. Mike and his band's lifetime experience consisted of this unending loss, which is critical context for this last episode of conflict.[9]

Mike was only one of thousands of Native Americans in the region who experienced this loss. Migration patterns make it difficult to identify all Idaho Indian tribes, whose territories do not conform to state boundaries; nevertheless, the Nez Perce, Coeur d'Alene, and Pend d'Oreille dominated the north, while divisions of Shoshone and Bannock inhabited the south. The Lemhi Shoshone, Sacajawea's people, lived north of Fort Hall in the Salmon River Mountains, while west along the Boise and Bruneau Rivers lived other tribes of Shoshone. As many as eleven different bands lived from Gosiute territory in northern Utah, past the Ruby Mountains, and along the Humboldt River to the Winnemucca region of Nevada. As one moved farther west toward California, the Northern Paiutes dominated. Most settlers rarely identified or understood the distinctions between these groups; they tended to lump them together. And by the time of the Tranmer and Shoshone Mike encounter, the Indian populations had been decimated.[10]

Early travelers to the Shoshone region found a friendly and accommodating people. However, as their food supplies dwindled and significant numbers of their tribe died, the Shoshone began to deeply resent the settlers. Contrary to what is commonly thought, the appropriation of Indian lands resulted in violence much earlier and on a much larger scale in the Far West than it ever did on the Great Plains. The settlers' incessant desire for more land, minerals, and wildlife meant disaster in the delicate desert environment of Utah, Idaho, and Nevada. The land simply could not sustain these numbers of settlers and their lifestyle, and wildlife and native plants quickly succumbed to the onslaught.[11]

Indians responded in various ways—at times they negotiated, and at other times attacked. Prior to the gold rush of 1849, few Indians assaulted

Snake River Agency, Fort Hall Indian Reservation, Idaho, 1872. (Photo by W. H. Jackson. Courtesy of Idaho State Historical Society.)

settlers along the Oregon and California Trails, but after the rush Shoshone, Bannock, and Northern Paiute warriors killed as many as four hundred people along the Humboldt and Snake Rivers. In 1854 and 1860, the Boise and Bruneau Shoshone reportedly staged attacks on immigrant parties in what became known as the Ward and Otter Massacres.[12]

In the mid-1860s, the *Owyhee Avalanche* chronicled instances of violence and retaliatory actions. On October 26, 1867, the paper headlined "Shocking Massacre": "Again it is our painful duty to record one of the most terrible Indian massacres that has ever taken place in our midst." The story recounted an Indian attack on a stagecoach headed to Fort Boise. That same edition reported, "William Black . . . was shot and fatally wounded by Indians. . . . He died yesterday morning." On March 14, 1868, the paper reported: "A Mr. Jarvis, from Boise Valley, was bringing a wagon load of vegetables . . . [when] he was killed by Indians in the Canyon." The *Ava-*

lanche reported others who suffered "savage atrocities" and had been "brutally murdered."[13]

Occasionally, the paper noted governmental attitudes and actions toward Indians and the settlers' desire for more protection. On November 25, 1865, the *Owyhee Avalanche* reported the arrival of territorial governor Caleb Lyon to Ruby City, where he addressed a large crowd. The editors looked favorably on his Indian policy to "either fight or feed them, and for this purpose [I have] requested, with all hopes of success, two regiments of cavalry." The governor anticipated "offering them the terms of peace or death; and if they will not quietly accept the one, the other will be forced upon them." "This is good talk," the article concluded.[14]

On February 18, 1866, the *Avalanche* reported on "two more victims of those bi-ped hyenas." These were "good men who had given their lives in pioneer pursuits." This loss supported the "arguments painfully multiplied in favor of more troops and the utter extermination of the Indian tribes." The author asked, "Can it be that we are much longer to record the humiliating facts that the Government will not protect her pioneer citizens?" Are these pioneers, "who more than any others are bringing to light the hidden wealth of the nation and living a life approximating torture, . . . to receive no encouragement?" In inflammatory rhetoric the writer asked whether "the savages who delight in stealing and burning [the pioneer's] property, taking his life, scalping his lifeless corpse, cutting his heart out, etc. are to be fed and clothed for so doing? As they do nothing else." The editorialist asked, "How long? Ye red rapists, how long?" The fight against the Native Americans certainly served as a rallying cry for the settling population.[15]

However, at times, culprits came from the settlers themselves or the soldiers sent to protect them. On October 7, 1865, the *Owyhee Avalanche* reported that "a gang of thieves visited Reynold's Creek and Bernard's Ranch, and at the Sawmill." While Indians initially drew the blame, investigators identified "certain whites" as culpable.[16] On November 28, 1865, in a letter to the editor, a local blasted visiting soldiers. He wrote of a visit by "a band of cutthroats (commonly called New York wharf rats) in the shape of U.S.A. Regulars." The soldiers "stole everything they could get their hands on about the ranch, flour, rice, sugar, coffee, potatoes." They had consumed all the liquor they could find, stolen hay to sleep on, and "robbed the corral of the fence poles and wood pile for fuel." When challenged about their behavior, the commanding officer replied, "They were going out to fight the

Indians and that [the author] should not begrudge the soldiers a little draw." He refused to compensate the owner for stolen goods and even hesitated to castigate one of his men who had recklessly shot a loaded gun in the rancher's house. The author concluded that "these men are more to be dreaded than the native Indians of the country and I also believe New York has sent them out here to get rid of them."[17]

Nevertheless, many settlers realized that soldiers were necessary to protect their endeavors. On September 2, 1865, the *Owyhee Avalanche* reported that connections with California and Nevada were impossible without federal assistance to combat Indians. They applauded the stationing of soldiers along the route and predicted that the "harsh though musical notes of the steam whistle will be heard from a score of mills, yielding monthly their tons of bullion."[18]

However, the isolation of the region meant government attention reached there last. Initially the Shoshone dealt with trappers and fur traders from both the British and American nations. In June of 1846 the forty-ninth parallel provided a northern boundary, and in March of 1849 federal officials created the Oregon Territory, with its capitol at Oregon City. This designation placed all of the Indians of this vast region under the superintendent in Oregon City, which meant that the bands of the Boise, Bruneau, and other Shoshone tribes, situated hundreds of miles away in the far eastern corner, were left alone. However, in 1861, federal officials created the Washington Territory, and the district superintendence shifted to Olympia until 1863, when the territory of Idaho was assigned its own superintendent of Indian affairs. The increased attacks on wagon trains and on settlers in this area caused federal officials to establish Fort Boise in 1863 and to remove the Boise and Bruneau bands to the Fort Hall Reservation in 1869.[19]

Along with the establishment of Fort Boise, two other events proved pivotal during the decades of friction between Indians and settlers in this region—the Bear River Massacre of 1863 and the Bannock War of 1878. On January 29, 1863, in one of the bloodiest massacres of Indians in the history of the Far West, Colonel Patrick Edward Connor and his California Volunteers killed two hundred and fifty Northern Shoshone, many of them women and children. After the four-hour battle, the soldiers looted the Indians of all valuables. They found belongings of wagon train immigrants, which they later used to justify their actions against the Indians. The rest of the day soldiers spent in abhorrent behavior. Severely wounded Indians "were killed by being hit in the head with an axe." One report wrote of a soldier finding a baby still alive in the arms of a dead Indian woman. The soldier, "in mercy to the babe killed it." Several of the women were "killed because they would not submit quietly to be ravished, and other squaws were ravished in the agony of death." Furthermore, rather than take the time for burials, federal troops left the bodies of the Shoshone to decay where they fell.[20]

In the battle with the Bannock, federal troops were on the defensive. The Indians had not adapted well to the sedentary life on the reservation, and in 1877 a visiting General George Cook commented, "Starvation is staring them in the face, and if they wait much longer, they will not be able to fight." In the late spring of 1878 the Bannocks, under Chief Buffalo Horn, left the Fort Hall Reservation and started out along the Snake River. As they made their way west, they killed some settlers and destroyed some property. The first real battle took place just over the Idaho border in the Owyhees near Jordan Valley, Oregon, on June 18, 1878. Volunteers from local mining communities such as Silver City gathered and met the Indian forces, but quickly retreated when they suffered casualties. The Indians continued in a westward route and joined forces with some members of the Paiute and Umatilla Tribes. Despite early momentum, the rebellion quickly collapsed when they lost their leaders. Federal troops under the direction of General Howard routed the Indians and returned them to the reservation. The Army Adjutant General reported in 1880 that nine soldiers and thirty-one citizens were killed and fifteen soldiers and three citizens were seriously wounded. Seventy-eight Indians had been reported killed and sixty-six wounded, although many estimated Indian losses to be much greater. The government spent $556,636 [$12.6 million in 2014] fighting the war.[21]

As the US government protected settlers, it also reinforced its presence as the authoritative power of the region, even beyond local and state entities. Despite early beliefs in radical individualism and unfettered government involvement in this region, the danger of these situations meant settlers sought governmental protection.

Between Lifestyles

Shoshone Mike's name reveals how settlers defined him. Mike's Indian name is not known, and even if any settlers did know it they never referred to him that way. His full English name was Mike Daggett, although it is also not clear how he received his surname. Some argue that, as was common in this era, an Indian agent gave him the name in the same way they randomly identified others throughout the region. Since a Daggett served as the superintendent of the Duck Valley Indian Reservation, perhaps he gained his name this way. Others argue that Native Americans commonly took on the names of settlers for whom they worked or whom they had befriended. These names offered some protection and a superficial sense of the acculturation of Native Americans.[22]

Others referred to Mike as Salmon River Mike, Rock Creek Mike, Idaho Mike, Indian Mike, and finally Shoshone Mike. This last moniker came from members of the posse, who reported that when asked, "What kind of an Indian are you?" he responded, "Shoshone Mike." Also, this name played well in the media, since Mike Daggett, Idaho Mike, or Rock Creek Mike all sounded like "an Irish emigrant fleeing the potato famine" instead of an independent Indian leader attempting to defend his family.[23]

However, some convincingly argued that Mike was not Shoshone at all but rather a member of the Bannock Indians. Shoshone Indians of the Elko, Nevada, region identified him as Bannock, and Mike's style of dress, his family relations, and the language he spoke further support this identification. Mike wore traditional clothing with buckskin moccasins and his black hair shoulder-length in two braids. His headdress found after the attack bore an exceptional resemblance to that of a Bannock chief in the area. Furthermore, Mike's wife derived from the Ute Tribe, which had closer relations with the Bannock than did other bands. Despite the uncertainty about Mike's name, its most significant detail remained: the conquerors named the conquered.[24]

The Americanized names of other family members also indicate how Mike and his band lived in both worlds. For example, Mike's wife went by the name of Jennie, and his sons were named Charlie and Cleve. However, not all of Mike's family stayed with him. One daughter married Lige Harris, described as a "dark Texas Negro." Harris's brother Henry had worked his way from cook to foreman of a group of "Negro" cowboys who worked on the Boar's Nest Ranch. Later he worked as foreman over the entire crew, and these connections no doubt helped Mike and his family if they needed to trade for goods or wanted to work for money. We do not know how the broader community viewed this interracial marriage, but it further dispels myths of a "white" West; and the marriage probably helped Mike's family in difficult times.[25]

Most likely we will never fully identify Mike's origins, or why he chose not to live on the reservation. Despite the difficulties, members of his band maintained their migratory patterns. For centuries, Indians of this region had migrated. During the spring they went north toward the large fields of camas blossoms. There the Indians only had a few weeks to harvest the short-lived crop of bulbs, followed by a march toward other opportunities. They might venture east over the mountains to buffalo country, travel south to gather pine nuts in the pinion forests, or venture west toward the jackrabbit havens of Nevada. Historians later identified the Indians of this region as "one of the most ecologically efficient Indian groups in North America." However, settlers changed everything.[26]

They so altered the terrain in which the Native Americans lived that Indian sources of food changed as well. Settlers cut down the pinion pine orchards and used the wood for fence posts to divide property. This forced Mike and his band to proceed cautiously, being ever diligent about where they crossed to avoid conflicts with those who had claimed the land. Settlers dammed and diverted streams, which resulted in fewer fish migrations each year. The newcomers' hunting practices made the buffalo nearly extinct and drove other species high into the mountains. Even the jackrabbit, a ubiquitous source of nutrition, declined in numbers.

In place of the jackrabbit, ever-increasing numbers of sheep and cattle chewed the grass to the nub and polluted nearby watering holes. Cheatgrass and inedible species of brush replaced valuable native forages. Mining ventures meant towns popped up rapidly, and disappeared just as quickly when the claims ran out. This meant that the Indians had to dodge new mining ventures, and the scarred and polluted land was no longer viable for hunting or producing food. As settlers controlled more resource-rich land, Mike sought sparsely populated regions.[27]

In a territory that stretched from the southern hills of the Snake River Valley in Idaho, southward over the Nevada line to Gollaher Mountain and San Jacinto, Mike and his band temporarily succeeded. Settlers had not yet dammed the Snake, and therefore the river provided a plentiful supply of water and outstanding salmon fishing below the great falls. Steep canyon walls secured an area plentiful in small hidden valleys and buttes, with mounds of rocky domes and sections of thick forests interspersed throughout the terrain.[28]

For Mike and his band, the variety of plant life meant harvests changed in succession and offered a continual source of nourishment, while animal life remained plentiful: grouse, varieties of rabbits, and even deer and elk in large numbers. Also, the relatively few farms and ranches in the area aided Mike and his band. Nonfamily labor was in short supply for farmers and ranchers, so they often welcomed the help that Mike and his band could provide with seasonal jobs like haying, herding, and branding cattle. This work also allowed Mike a supplemental income to offset any shortfalls.from the wild harvest and hunting.[29]

This arrangement required mutual trust. The stories of area farmers provide evidence of shared work and friendships forged. The Crockett and Wieghall families settled in the Rock Creek Canyon lands and raised crops and cattle in the area. Both families held within their family lore their first contact with Mike and his band.

Not long after moving to the area in 1880, the Crocketts sighted smoke coming from an area near their new cabin. When they explored, they observed an Indian hut with war drums, spears decorated with eagle feathers, bows, quivers of arrows, baskets for gathering food, and jackrabbit nets. The Crocketts panicked and spent the next few nights sleepless, listening to drumbeats and chanting, terrified of what might happen when they encountered the Indians. When they finally went to town and raised the subject with the local storekeeper, he laughed and told them: "Why, that's only Indian Mike, back from his summer wanderings. Their camp has been in that bend of the river for years. Better be neighborly. You can't find a better family for neighbors than the Mike Daggetts, and if he moves away, some bad Indians might take his place."[30]

Before long, the two families became friends. Their children played together, and taught each other their customs. When one youngster from Mike's band learned how to hunt, he passed on this newly acquired knowledge to the Crockett boys. He showed them how to shoot with bow and arrow, how to set deadfalls of flat stones for rodents, how to trap fish with willow baskets or set snares in the brush for cottontails and white-tailed jacks. Despite language barriers, the parents connected as well. They exchanged food and homemade goods and utensils.[31]

The Wieghall family recalled an even more startling and humorous introduction. While the father was herding cattle, Mrs. Wieghall was working in the kitchen when she felt someone's eyes upon her. She looked up and nearly fainted upon seeing a "broad-shouldered Indian brave grinning at her from the kitchen door." She summoned her courage and asked what he wanted. Mike sought essential supplies, so Mrs. Wieghall quickly poured out small amounts of sugar, tea, coffee, flour, and dried prunes in small pieces of brown paper on the kitchen table. She also included a box of her husband's precious tobacco.[32]

As she did this her husband entered and, although initially alarmed, he realized that the situation was amicable. As Mike prepared to leave, he asked in broken English what he could exchange for payment. The husband made sweeping motions over his head with his hands in hopes that Mike would understand his desire for venison. Mike seemed perplexed but shrugged, mounted his horse, and rode off to his camp. The next day he returned dragging an enormous rack of deer antlers. When Sam Wieghall realized what had happened and began to laugh, he made chewing motions with his mouth, and when Mike got the message they both roared with laughter. The two families continued to visit each other.[33]

One of the Wieghall children remembered this custom. "Jennie [the mother] always sat in the front of the buckboard while Mike and the older boys came in to eat. My mother took food out to the women waiting in the wagon and always gave them baked cookies." She described the family as "fairly neat and clean," and said that Mike treated his children "as though he really enjoyed them." After dinner they listened to Mike tell and mime stories of the Indian legends and superstitions of the territory. She recalled gifts that Mike brought the family, including Indian dolls made of sagebrush and hairbrushes of "wire-grass roots, dried, cleaned, and tied together with buckskin like a tiny whisk broom." The two families remained close. Mike even named one of his daughters Hattie after one of the Wieghalls.[34]

John Hansen, who had emigrated from Copenhagen, Denmark, operated the general store in the area. Mike traded there for flour and sugar, coffee, and ammunition. The two became friends, and Hansen claimed Mike never defaulted on his bills or loans. To balance his account at the store and for trade with other settlers in the community, Mike braided reatas, hackamores, rolled reins, romals, and fashioned other cowboy trade goods that became well known in the area. One cowboy bought a reata from Mike that measured over ninety feet long. Mike's wife, Jennie, also made moccasins and gloves that gained a reputation for their quality. Cowboys continued as loyal clients for many years. During drought years, Mike and his family relied on trade and good credit. The experiences of sharing during difficult times tightened the bonds between Mike and the settlers at Rock Creek.[35]

Relations between these families remained positive over the years even though they lived quite different lifestyles. When Mike and his band arrived in the area each fall, the Native American children continued to ride horses, play games in the meadows, and explore the numerous caves in the area. Meanwhile the settlers' children went to school, an unwelcome place for the Native Americans. Despite this, the children played together, and by the spring or early summer when the band prepared to leave, both sides found it difficult to say good-bye. The months apart made them appreciate when the smoke above the Crocketts' willow trees reappeared, signaling the arrival of Mike and his band. "Everyone around here like[d] Mike," claimed a member of the Crockett family. Although he had every opportunity, "We knew he wouldn't take any of our calves." Given the climate of Indian/settler relations, "I guess Mike's being here close kept stray Indians away, and we were glad to have one here we could get along with." This cycle became the expected pattern of life in the canyon and continued from the 1870s until 1910. Despite the constant stories of Indian attacks or army battles, these groups forged a common bond and understanding—a sampling of how Indian/settler relations could have evolved. However, increasing population and a contentious turn of events threatened this peaceful coexistence.[36]

In Pursuit

Even though Mike enjoyed the friendship of the Hansens, Crocketts, and Wieghalls, relations between settlers and Indians remained hostile throughout much of the region. Fortunately, Mike successfully evaded these groups over the years. In the spring of 1910, Mike and his family continued with their annual pattern. They broke camp, loaded their wagon with baskets full of tools and hunting supplies, along with large quantities of staples such as dried camas, sego lily bulbs, wild onion, rose hips, and dried fish and jerky. As usual, they headed west out of the canyon and over the rounded, timbered hills.[37]

Not long after they began to migrate, the episode with the Tranmers occurred and the chase began. In order to cover more ground, the posse divided into smaller groups but never located Mike and his band, only some of their camps. Some members of the posse grew discouraged and went home. In the meantime, stories surfaced that further complicated the matter. Not far from where Mike and his band fought the Tranmers, employees of the Shoe Sole Ranch discovered trenches where the horses had been buried. This cast further doubt on the culpability of the Indians, since it seemed out of character.[38]

Other events called into question the guilt of Mike's band. On January 9 and 11, 1911, headlines in the *Humboldt Star* of Winnemucca, Nevada, read: "Urie Makes Complete Confession of the Foul Murder of the Quillicis' Atrocious Double Murder at Imlay—Masked Bandits Hold Up Saloon And Shoot Proprietor And His Wife—Murderers Are Captured." In what was described as one of the "most atrocious and brutal crimes ever committed in Humboldt County," storeowner Jean Quillici was shot dead and his wife mortally wounded by three masked bandits in Imlay, Nevada. Humboldt County sheriff Graham Lamb eventually arrested a twenty-three-year-old named N. R. Urie and J. F. Tranmer for the murders. Both were found guilty. For defenders of Mike and his family, Tranmer and Urie's guilt in this crime supported the innocence of the Indians. They hypothesized that if Tranmer and Urie had committed murder, then stealing horses seemed even more likely.[39]

It is not clear whether or not the posse learned of the Quillici murders; in any case, the hunt continued. For Mike, keeping his band fed and free from capture remained never-ending problems. They ate whatever they could find along the way, including rabbit and dug-up bulbs. At times they resorted to rattlesnake, squirrels, and a paste made from ants. To further minimize the risk of being captured, they often traveled at night with unshod horses to cover their tracks. According to Mike's daughter, they met up with Jennie's sister near the Nevada and Utah border, where they drew supplies, money, and information about the posse. Occasionally they came across sheepherders, hunters, and miners and heard rumors of other fights between Indians and settlers in the area.[40]

On good days they covered as much as thirty miles, but on days with difficult terrain or security concerns, they barely completed five. The more distance they covered and the longer they evaded the posse, the better their chances of survival. After initially heading south, they turned west and passed just north of Ely, Nevada, then Hamilton, and traversed Little Smoky Valley and up and over the Diamond Mountains to the town of Austin. Next, they worked their way through the Clan Alpine Mountains, where they stopped for a few restful days and hunted deer in the Silver Range. However, fearing area ranchers might recognize them, they packed up and headed toward Wadsworth, then ventured north, passing by Pyramid Lake and Lake Winnemucca, before they reached the open, flat, alkaline Black Rock Desert.[41]

There the heat bore down on them unrelentingly. They could not find water for themselves, let alone for the horses, many of which died along the way. When a horse collapsed, black buzzards immediately circled the body and signaled the party's location. With worn-out moccasins and bandaged feet, they limped on. And finally, as they struggled to survive, they drew some luck. They came upon a well-protected canyon, with fish in nearby lakes and plentiful supplies of antelope and quail. For the first time since they left, they had surplus food, and so they relaxed for a brief time and revived themselves.[42]

But the need to move remained ever present, and by late June they left their established camp in Little High Rock Canyon and traveled west all the way to Cedarville, California. There they boldly ventured into town and bought essentials at T. H. Johnson's general store and moved on. For the next few weeks Mike and his family successfully found food in the lower hills until they had to stop to welcome a new member of the band—one of Mike's daughters had a baby. The new life gave momentary hope for a more promising future, but everywhere they traveled they ran into settlers. They continued migrating throughout the summer months, perhaps traveling as far as where the Sacramento River empties into the San Francisco Bay. Having left the posse behind them and feeling relatively secure, they even took on jobs in the hay fields and fruit harvests. These were the relatively good times.[43]

However, as the cold of winter blew, the band suffered. Endless sun reflection off the snow temporarily blinded them, so they covered their faces with rags and squinted through narrow slits. The traveling took its toll, and before long the baby's mother could no longer produce milk, so they had to feed the infant a paste of pine nuts. As they passed through mountains just north of where the Donner party perished, they lost horses, but they continued on and eventually crossed over into the gray green of the Nevada sage. There they gambled with their little ammunition and killed some deer and rabbits. They returned to their previous camp in Little High Rock Canyon and prepared for the worst of winter.[44]

After they established and secured their camp, the snow came and buried the canyon. Tired and hungry, Mike and his band made a decision that further complicated their situation; perhaps they had no other choice. Their lookouts spotted three cows moving toward the shelter of the canyon. The Indians decided to kill the cattle and had nearly completed butchering them when their dog barked and drew the attention of a Basque sheepherder in the area also looking for shelter. The Indians quickly left the carcasses and ran up into the rocks of the hillside as the herder moved closer. He had nearly passed by when his sheepdog smelled the blood and moved toward the butchered meat. The herder paused, surveyed the area, and then drew his horse and headed toward the Denio ranch.[45]

Mattie and Will Denio, a young ranching couple, had just started in the area. Mattie's sister Laura was engaged to Harry Cambron, who managed the Humphrey-Moffat cattle ranch that operated in the Little High Rock country. On the evening of January 17, 1911, Mattie Denio recognized Bert Indiano making his way through the storm toward their ranch house. Since she had few visitors, she welcomed the herder, who she knew worked for two other Basques, Peter Erramouspe and John Laxague. Besides Indiano, Erramouspe, Laxague, and Cambron took shelter at Denio's. In the course of their conversation, Indiano relayed his sightings of the butchered cattle, and the group agreed to investigate the matter after the storm subsided.[46]

On the morning of the eighteenth, the four rode toward the canyon where Indiano had found the cattle. They never returned. When the men failed to report within the week, Mattie Denio began to worry, and as the wedding date drew closer her sister Laura began to panic as well. The Erramouspe and Laxague families also feared the possibilities. When no news came, a search party formed consisting of area family and friends. On Wednesday, February 8, the party left in the midst of another blinding snowstorm and headed east in the same direction as the earlier four.[47]

Rumors surfaced in area papers. Initially one reported that "a bunch of outlaws from across the border in Oregon attacked and killed them and made away with their horses and camp equipment." However, they also mentioned that "recently a party of nine hostile Indians who were said to have murdered a white boy some time before was seen in the area." The Indians supposedly had been piling up stones and "placing signs as warning of death" to any followers, so "there was the possibility that the renegades might have trapped the stockmen and killed them."[48]

About the same time, Warren Fruits, an area rancher, was working his way through a draw when he noticed an alarming sight—what appeared to be a human hand sticking up out of the snow. When he scraped back the flakes he found the bodies, neatly placed in a row with the head of one body at the feet of another. They had been stripped of their clothing, ammunition, and valuables, and left frozen in the snow, with Erramouspe's lip and moustache cut off. Some reports stated that the murderers had even mutilated the bodies by cutting off their genitalia and prying gold teeth out of their mouths.[49]

Slain Basque sheepherders, Little High Rock Canyon, Nevada, February 1911. (Courtesy of Nevada Historical Society.)

Although there were no eyewitnesses, the public blamed the Indians. Even the most ardent supporters of Mike's band figured the group had reached its limits. They surmised that when the Indians realized their cattle rustling had been discovered, they were left with little choice but to fight. Meanwhile, a record snowfall left four feet and the temperature dropped below zero, which made traveling extremely difficult. Mike and his family broke camp and loaded up as much food as possible on their three remaining horses. Breaking trail through the snow exhausted the horses and band, which left the whole party walking. They bundled up with all of the clothing they could find, even that of the killed men, and were lucky to travel five miles in a day. When they stopped, they built small snow caves for protection and ate whatever they came across, including a thin, half-starved cow near Paiute Meadows. The family inched along. They continued east and plowed their way around the northern end of Black Rock Desert, crossed over a frozen stream, and took the easiest route south toward Winnemucca, Nevada.[50]

As the Indians traveled, the search party discovered the bodies and two members returned to inform families and friends. Later, word spread that possessions of the murdered men were found in Mike's camp, and this bolstered the cry for revenge. Law enforcement officials were notified at Alturas in Modoc County, California, and the coroner, county physician, and police in Reno of Washoe County, Nevada. The parties even sent a telegram to the secretary of war and requested that troops be sent to Nevada. As these notices went out, a special chartered train transported officials to the crime scene. There they found remnants of the butchered cattle and the trail of the Indians.[51]

By a horse-drawn sleigh, they transported the bodies out of the canyon to wagons for the long ride to Eagleville, California. As word of the event spread, hundreds from the area gathered along the route as the procession made its way to the church. There they thawed the bodies enough for them to be placed in caskets. The bloodstains left on the church floor remained for decades and add to the lore of this event. On February 14, 1911, two separate funeral services were held—one Roman Catholic for the Basques and a Protestant service for Harry Cambron. Later that day they were buried in the Eagleville cemetery.[52]

A search party formed and sought revenge for the deaths. The emotion

Captain J. P. Donnelly's posse that pursued Shoshone Mike, 1911.
(Courtesy of Nevada Historical Society.)

of the events coupled with the $15,000 [$366,000 in 2014] reward brought together quite a collection—from government law enforcement to those living out cowboy-and-Indian fantasies. The nature of the crime and the Indians' migration meant the involvement of law enforcement officers from a variety of regions, including Captain J. P. Donnelly and his staff from the newly formed Nevada State Police, along with the sheriffs from Modoc County, California, and Washoe County, Nevada. While the initial interest drew bombastic rhetoric and large numbers, about twenty-five actually ventured off into the winter search. Unlike the Indian band, this group sported a large support team with fresh horses and sizable amounts of food, ammunition, and supplies. On February 15, 1911, the posse left Eagleville for the Denio ranch, and the next morning departed Little High Rock Canyon to pick up the trail of Mike and his family.[53]

The winter conditions made traveling and tracking difficult; nevertheless, the posse found campsites, and at most every location discovered possessions of those killed—Harry Cambron's fine white horse, leather from his saddle, and scraps of their clothing. The evidence spurred them on. The leaders feared that if Mike "was able to reach the brakes of the Owyhee, he would be safe forever in that tortured jumble of inaccessible canyons."[54]

The concerted effort to trap the Indians meant coordination and cooperation from a variety of sources. It also revealed the rivalries between them. It was not clear how it occurred, but somehow well-known Sheriff Graham Lamb, of Humboldt County, Nevada, was given a message that took him far off the trail. Some felt that the rivalry over the reward money and the jealousy between the upstart Nevada State Police and the reputable and powerful sheriff's office resulted in the misdirection. As with later state-federal government tensions, local law enforcement entities feared the increasing power of the state. Nevertheless, Sheriff Lamb received a message, supposedly from Captain Donnelly, that indicated the Indians' location to be at the end of the Jackson Mountains. Actually Mike and his band were a hundred miles east of this location.[55]

As the hunt continued, one area newspaper expressed its attitudes toward the Native Americans and the lack of sufficiently stringent punishment. "The average Nevada Indian has no scruples about committing murder," the article stated. Furthermore, the laxity in administering punishment meant, "they have no particular fear of being compelled to suffer the death penalty as punishment for the commission of murder." The writer blamed the action of the Nevada Board of Pardons, who he claimed had commuted the sentence of "nearly every Indian who has been condemned to death." "There have been plenty of murders committed by Indians, but very few Indians have been hanged in the history of the state," the writer added. He predicted that if the murderers of the sheepmen were Indians, then they would be likely to surrender "rather than make a fight and be shot to pieces by the posse. They would rather take the chance of being hanged than to stop any of the posse's rifle bullets."[56]

Papers began to convince public opinion of the guilt of the Indians and their imminent capture. Sheriff Ferrell of Washoe County stated, "The murder was committed by a band of Shoshone Indians, composed of one old man, three young braves, two old squaws, one young one, 17 years of age, and three children." Emphatically he continued, "That these Indians committed the murder there is not the slightest doubt, for at several of the camps we found remnants of the clothing taken from the murdered men, which the squaws were undoubtedly changing to fit the men in their party." He also connected the murder of the sheepmen with the murder of the boy in northern Elko County earlier and spoke with the jailed Urie and Tranmer to get details of the story. Ferrell also added that Sheriff Lamb and his associates had returned from the diversion and rejoined the posse. The men believed that the Indians were headed for the Owyhee country but were making slow progress. Sheriff Ferrell concluded, "There is no doubt but that they [the Indian band] will be overtaken and captured."[57]

In the meantime, Mike and his family continued to slowly make their way. They suffered severely from lack of food in the area and from having to expend more energy to make it through the mountains. Although they saw familiar ranches in the area, they knew better than to approach, especially in this wide-open zone. By sheer determination they arrived at Paradise, Nevada. However, in such sorry shape and so low on food, they gambled and sent two of the boys to town to secure supplies. The suspicious storekeeper served them, but they could not carry enough to feed the whole band for very long. Also, the horses' condition meant frequent stops. It was an anxious rest, as they remained ever fearful of being spotted, and after a few days Mike directed the band to move on.[58]

What was their goal? It is difficult to determine. Most members of the posse felt they were headed toward the Owyhees where they could hide away in one of the many canyons. They were not far away now. As they inched up the ascent of Soldiers Pass and saw the valley below, they realized only one major summit separated them from probable safety. Since a daytime crossing would be too dangerous, they made a quick camp and waited until night, when they hoped they could gather their energy for one last climb.[59]

While Mike prepared for his last dangerous crossing, those in pursuit had different plans. In effect, they had encircled him and gradually tightened the noose. To the north, officials in the Duck Valley Indian Reservation patrolled the area in case Mike slipped onto the reservation to gain sympathetic support. From Elko, Sheriff Ferrell and Private Buck formed a posse to head northwest and closed off any possibility there, while Constable Dean H. Young gathered a group of miners and cowboys who knew the terrain well and could keep Mike and his band from escaping through the mountain passes. If necessary, Governor Oddie authorized the Nevada State Police Inspector A. W. Cablan to send police to Elko. Finally, all local, county, state, and Indian officials had been alerted. Even the media joined the act, with a variety of newspapers from around the West sending reporters.[60]

By Sunday, February 26, 1911, the posse had been traveling for sixteen days and nearly two hundred wintry miles from Little High Rock Canyon. They too were exhausted and ready to complete their mission. Then, according to one account, Indian scout Skinny Pascal and George J. Meyers spotted a column of smoke, heard a dog bark, and zeroed in on the camp. What happened next depends on whose story you want to believe.[61]

What Happened?

"We took trail 6 o'clock Sunday morning. We follow trail . . . about 20 miles," remembered Skinny Pascal, the Indian scout of Sheriff Lamb's party. "I saw smoke in Indian camp first in little canyon just edge of valley." Another posse member, Mort West, chimed in: "We are apt to get shot up in there, Cap," he said to Captain Donnelly as he pointed toward the deep, narrow canyon under a great cliff. "You had better send in scouts. I volunteer to be one of them." Suddenly another hollered, "There they are!" "Down there," pointing to a group of horses and figures running down the canyon through the snow.[62]

As members of the posse rounded the cliff and made their way down the canyon rim, they shot at the horses a "young squaw" was attempting to drive from the camp. The Indians scurried to prepare for battle. Mike, their leader, put on his feathered war bonnet while the rest smeared their faces with green and yellow paint. "The bucks jerked off their shirts and bared themselves to their waists. The squaws tucked up their skirts to their knees, and the dance to whip up their courage began. The children joined their parents in the intricate dance."[63]

Members of the posse heard the beat "as the squaws began to drum and to chant the fever-raising rhythms and courage-exciting incantations of the Shoshone war-dance ritual." The posse paused and for a few minutes merely watched them dance. Inspired by the drum beats, the songs, and the dances, the Indian warriors retreated to protective cover, where "they started to load and fire." Captain Donnelly ordered the posse forward. Skinny Pascal was told to inform the "renegade Shoshone" that if they surrendered they would not be harmed. "Old Shoshone Mike" hollered back as he fired five shots at Pascal, who returned them, hitting Mike. As Donnelly rushed up to the body, the Indian leader struggled to raise himself up and reached for his rifle, and Donnelly shot him. As the toothless, white-haired old chief lay dying, his proud war bonnet fouled in a mix of mud, blood, and snow, he screamed out:

"Me Shoshone Mike! Me Shoshone Mike!"[64]

Ben Cambron, the brother of one of Mike's alleged victims, rode up to where Mike lay and also took a shot at him. As this scene faded, the "spine-chilling yells" and "high pitched screams" of the Indians combined with the "whoops and hollers" of the cowboys to create a cacophony. The cowboys unleashed their fury. Since February 8, 1911, they had dreamed of this moment to avenge the "mutilated bodies of their friends and relatives."[65]

With the central fighting around Mike ended, "his braves" fought independently in scattered areas as "squaws" attempted to distract attention from "their bucks" and draw the fire of the posse toward them. A member of the party, Ed Hogle, became transfixed by a young squaw who "went into a sinuous-swaying dance" as she chanted in her high-pitched thin voice. Ed held his rifle at his side as the woman moved closer to him. Within feet of him she flopped to the ground, and "a young buck" poised on the ground behind her rose up and "got the drop" on Ed, putting a bullet directly in his heart. Hogle staggered toward another posse member and gasped: "Look out fellows, he's got me!" The posse later learned that Ed Hogle had been killed by the last bullet of Harry Cambron's gun. "When Ed's comrades saw him fall, they went into the 'kill' for good." They targeted the "buck," and as he moved from his protected cover the nine members of the posse shot him; he staggered, then fell with a thud.[66]

The posse was appalled at the fighting tactics of the Indians, with "the bucks" in the rear while "the squaws and children ran ahead." Nevertheless, Captain Donnelly had shouted, "Don't shoot the squaws' boys!" Yet, since the squaws assisted the braves and even the children threw rocks and sand, they were left with no choice. "Unavoidably the little children were killed as they clung to their mothers." Even "Mike's squaw" got involved, beating the war dance rhythm on her drum. One stray bullet struck the "Old Squaw," who immediately fell, her drum going silent. Her daughter, the "Scout Squaw," screamed, dropped her spear, and ran to her mother's side, throwing her arms around her. A few of the children also gathered around, and "all began wailing over her."[67]

Not far from this scene, another "squaw with a bow and arrow" approached one of the posse. He ordered her to drop the weapons. Instead, she prepared to shoot. As he looked "into her piercing enraged black eyes, [he] saw a dark spot suddenly appear on her forehead," and she "plunked down like a log." Another cowboy had shot her to "save his comrade's life." As the battle waned, Heney, the "scout squaw," grabbed one of the young boys and ran off into the sagebrush. After evading their pursuers by running through the brush "like rabbits," the Indian boy was finally caught, although not without kicking and screaming with all his strength. Heney had to be "lassoed," pulled to the ground, and then bound at her hands and feet.[68]

The posse members thoroughly enjoyed themselves. One member boasted of the posse laughing throughout the battle as people were killed. He remembered the battle as the defining moment in his life. "No! Joy unbounding to us youngsters. That day and the summer that followed was the crest of our lives; and few of us will ever be so happy again, for that year we were heroes entertained and sought after by all."[69]

Or did the event happen this way:

The Indian band was exhausted. Weary from the unending movement and the hard labor of being on the run, they took pains to carve out a camp from the cold, snowy floor of the canyon. They had very few provisions—only a small sack of dried food and two skinny rabbits they had recently caught. As always they stayed to themselves, out of the way, trying to avoid any trouble. However, this last location left them exposed and vulnerable to attack. After a long day they finally got the opportunity to sleep. Suddenly their dog sensed something and barked. The posse heard the sound, spotted smoke, and discovered the camp.[70] Heney, one of the Indian women, noticed the posse and went to drive the horses to the camp to allow the band to escape. Meanwhile, the posse stampeded down the wash in a "wild, undisciplined charge, a mob of shooting, shouting, laughing, whooping cowboys." They killed as many horses as possible, one of which partially landed on Heney, knocking her down. The Indians scrambled from their slumber and scurried for some kind of cover in the chaotic confusion. They heard gunfire, saw Heney running toward the camp, and prepared to protect themselves from the onslaught. Heney claimed, "White man shoot first. Indian had gun. Maybe one, two. Maybe not many powder."[71]

They were grossly outmatched, four men, some women, and children, against nearly twenty-five experienced shooters. For weaponry they had only Harry Cambron's pistol, an old black powder shotgun, an ancient Colt cap and ball, and bows and arrows. These paled in comparison to the posse's new high-velocity repeating rifles and sidearms. Nevertheless, they were accustomed to being at a disadvantage and did their best.[72]

Mike realized he had few options. He was their primary focus; if he could draw the attackers' attention to him and run away from the camp, it would give his family their best opportunity to survive. With all his strength he ran away. Immediately bullets riddled his body, and he fell. Ben Cambron, Harry's brother, rode over to Mike as the old Indian was gasping his last. Cambron said, "What kind of damn Indian are you, anyway?"[73]

And Mike replied, "Me Shoshone! Me Shoshone!" Mike did not have an opportunity to speak further since Cambron then pried open the dying man's mouth with his rifle barrel and said, "Wonder how old he is. Let's have a look at the son of a bitch's teeth." He had to be pulled off Mike's body. Then Cambron shot him. As Mike lay there, virtually every cowboy "emptied his gun at him until his body was half shot away." By the time the posse finished, Mike "looked like a sieve," with a part of his neck shot away and blood oozing from his chest and stomach.[74]

The attackers fired at any target, whether it was a man, woman, or child. One thirteen-year-old Indian boy, panicked in the confusion, started to run away, and a posse member shot him. His brother scurried to the fallen body, and another posse member took aim, fired, and the two dead bodies tangled together in the bloody snow. Mike's wife, Jennie, tried to crawl toward Mike but never made it; posse members shot her as well, and she died in the arms of her daughter.[75]

In the battle, Ed Hogle was killed, and an arrow wounded another. After the posse learned of Hogle's death, they "went berserk." They unleashed their fury on the few remaining Indians, who by now had very little with which to protect themselves. Like a pack of wolves the posse hunted down the only two remaining young. Eventually they trapped them in the bottom of a dry streambed where they shot and killed them. Heney's nineteen-year-old sister "Snake" huddled in the brush with a baby strapped to her back. She had been the family clown, always laughing and making others smile. Posse members shot her and later found the baby strapped to her dead mother, crying and screaming with mud and snow all over its face.[76]

Heney tried to remove the children to a safe location, but they wanted to help the band. They picked up small rocks and sand and tried to throw them at the attackers. As one of the boys ran toward cover, the posse roped him and dragged the boy back. Despite their noble intent, the efforts of the children matched those of the entire band. It was futile; they simply were outmatched. By the end of the battle, three children and Heney were all that remained. Long after the Indians had stopped returning gunfire, the posse continued to circle the area and shoot. In the aftermath, the only noise from the Indian side came from their dog, a tricolored collie frantically searching for its owner.[77]

Aftermath

While the posse celebrated their victory throughout the night, Heney attempted to console the children while she herself sobbed and wailed over their loss. The next day Sheriff Lamb arrived on the scene. Upon seeing the dead mustangs and bullet-ridden women and children, the reputable officer roared, "What the hell has been going on here?" No one answered. In later years many wondered why police diverted Lamb and his party to another supposed location of Mike and his family. Regardless, a central question at the time that has remained through the ensuing years is: Were the Indians truly given an opportunity to surrender?[78]

After the night of celebration, the posse dynamited a hole in the frozen ground and buried all the Indian bodies in one mass grave. Then, from the closest ranch they secured a wagon to transport the captives and the body of Ed Hogle. Despite the snow and cold, hundreds of curious onlookers gathered to give their heroes a warm welcome. Even a railroad worker took a handcar out to meet the procession. Pumping the car along the tracks, he cheered with the rest of the crowd. The posse triumphantly rode down out of the hills with "the hog-tied bodies of the prisoners" in front of a spring wagon solemnly bearing the body of Ed Hogle. From there they continued on to Eagleville, California, and on March 8 arrived to "the wildest homecoming celebration in that town's history." The town showered their heroes with dinners and drinks. "When anyone of the fighting men tried to buy anything at a counter, a dozen men sprang to their feet to buy for him."[79]

Although feted as heroes, their financial compensation failed to equal their warm homecoming. The promised sum of $15,000 [$366,000 in 2014]

Location of slaying, Little High Rock Canyon, Nevada. (Courtesy of Nevada Historical Society.)

became $4,700 [$115,000 in 2014], whittled to a mere $126 [$3,073 in 2014] per man after litigation costs. On the trail they had dreamed about how they would spend their allotment, but after receiving their reward some realized they could make more selling items from Mike and his band for souvenirs; others kept them as prize possessions.[80]

The posse placed the prisoners—Heney, Cleve, Hattie, and the baby—in a jail cell. Heney grew tired of the stares of onlookers and covered herself and the children with a blanket whenever possible. One can only imagine the scrutiny as they waited for the case to be tried. It proceeded largely as a formality; their guilt was concluded by their possession of the sheepmen's horses. Authorities dropped charges against Heney and sent her along with the three surviving children to Fort Hall on November 17, 1911. There the Mosho family adopted them. Unfortunately, disease quickly took its toll, and that spring "Hattie Mosho" died of spinal meningitis. On July 26, 1912, "Henie Louise Mosho" died of tuberculosis, and six months later "Cleveland Mosho" died of the same disease. Only the youngest, the baby "Josephine Mosho," survived. Although she was diagnosed as tubercular, authorities removed her from the reservation, and eventually Superintendent Evan W. Estep adopted her. She grew up as Mary Josephine Estep.[81]

While the event had ended, in many ways the story had just begun. From that point forward, stories continued to be told that exaggerated the entire episode. One must question the validity of Heney's "confession" as remembered by Mort West over twenty years after the event. According to West, after initially arguing that the Indians killed the Cambron party because "they thought they were officers," Heney admitted that they had wanted their horses and outfits. The spectacular confession included admitting to stealing numerous other horses, and at least six other murders—including "a Chinamen to see him jump." Allegedly, after the Indians tortured him and finally robbed him, they were upset that he had only six dollars and killed him. West claimed Heney said they also "killed a Mexican and four other men." As they made their way across the Pyramid Lake Reservation, they "bulldozed the Paiutes into letting them have anything they chose." Heney reportedly then told of how Mike led his band through the Gerlach, Nevada, area, "robbing every sheep camp or cabin they came to." She supposedly told her audience of the "wonderful way Shoshone Mike had pillaged, plundered, killed and tortured his victims."[82]

Although the validity of this confession remains highly doubtful, the story took on a semblance of truth. News stories about this episode and the long shelf life of the stories told later helped to create the legends and myths that have lasted until today. Throughout this episode the media played a key role in advancing these images. Many of the leading newspapers in California and Nevada carried news of the story of the capture of the Indians. The *Nevada State Journal* commented: "The men who helped to run down and capture the assassins of the four Washoe County stockmen have performed such a signal service to the State as can hardly be estimated and the credit due them cannot be measured in words." The newspaper maintained that "these murderous Indians" had threatened the lives, the property, and the peace of the entire state. They not only opposed the law, but also were "savages knowing no law but the resort to treachery." As long as they were "free to move about, no man in all that wide open country might feel safe to leave his ranch or to follow his occupation."[83]

It did not take long for the legend to develop. The article continued: "The service the pursuers rendered was a most arduous one. It involved the facing of such physical fatigue, the manifesting of such fortitude and the exhibition of such tenacity of purpose as has seldom been described." The members were to be exalted for their courageous performance of duty in the face of death, and their efforts "should be made the subject of a story to be retold by many a fireside for many a year." Captain Donnelly and his men were "equal to that emergency and throughout it all, comported themselves with credit and honor to the best traditions of the race." They followed the trail. They went clear through, they "fought the good fight and if there is to be any special honor conferred, they should not be forgotten."[84]

The description in this article fits well with the formation of mythology that Richard Slotkin describes in *The Fatal Environment.* He claims that myths enlist us, "morally or physically, in the ideological program." They derive "usable values from history, and [put] those values beyond the reach of demystification." The primary appeal of mythology is "ritualized emotions, established beliefs, habitual associations, memory, nostalgia." Their symbols and metaphors depend on the audience's intuitive recognition and acceptance. As if on cue, on March 8, 1911, the *Nevada State Journal* reported that "negotiations were already in progress to make the survivors of the band, nearly exterminated at Kelly Creek, the central attraction in a big vaudeville and moving picture project." While negotiations continued, "urgent requests have also been made to ascertain on what terms and conditions the four captives might be secured."[85]

Conclusion

In the Owyhees and northern Nevada, talk of Indian reprisals continued all the way until World War I. The popular interpretation of the Shoshone Mike event became the truth for the majority of people in the area. But the event has far greater significance. This episode revealed the rival roles of government in the West, provided an example of how competing values shaped American identity, and demonstrated how this clash resulted in a more narrow way of life and land use.

The dominant role of the government in resolving the issue reaffirmed its increasing presence in the West. From the protection of settlers to the formation of reservations, governmental policy defined the contours of western development. However, the friction evident between different governmental entities (local sheriffs, state police, and federal officials) also previewed an ongoing tension in the West over which level of government would be involved and to what degree.

This incident also represents a period when particular definitions of "honor" and "conscience" battled, as Daniel Herman describes in his book *Hell on the Range.* Herman argues that a plebeian version of an Old South honor code emerged in the nineteenth-century American West, epitomized by "physical courage, loyalty to kin, and fierce defense of family and personal reputation." Honor "trended toward assertion, strength, fierceness, combat." Conscience, meanwhile, "placed moral courage above physical courage; individual piety above family reputation," and "exhortation and rehabilitation above punishment and shaming." It leaned "toward restraint, modesty, sympathy." We will never fully know what happened in this standoff. However, the evidence of the feeble condition of Shoshone Mike and his band coupled with their lack of resources for defense points to this being a case where "honor" trumped "conscience."[86]

The definition of Indians as a threat and an "other" parallels the way Anglo-Americans of this same period characterized Mexicans in the southwest of the United States: an "alien presence rather than as part of 'American' history."[87] Moreover, the defeat of the Indians and the continual telling of that story became the "American" history. In the process of placing the Indians outside of the story, Anglo-Americans framed who could be inside of it. At least in this episode, the "family" for whose honor they fought included a diverse group. Even with the Indians removed, there were more battles to come over borders of "us" and "them."

If Mike and his family had been able to return to the Snake River Valley, the land would have looked unfamiliar, for irrigation dramatically changed the entire face of the region. What had been primarily high desert country and a hunting ground of Native Americans became a productive farming region. Row upon row of green covered the land in a homogenized and strict pattern very different from the diversity the region had possessed. This management of the land paralleled the settlers' treatment of the Indians. On top of an indigenous population and a diverse ecosystem, settlers enforced a rigidity of structure, pattern, and homogeneity.

Mike and his band offered one last attempt at coexistence, but the settler society rejected them. After the settlers' victory, the absence of a common enemy exposed the fault lines of the emerging culture in the American West. Whether acting against Chinese miners, Mexican laborers, African-American cowboys, or Basque sheepherders, "American" settlers in the West at times were as racist in attitude and action as those in any other section of the country. This chapter's events expose the attitudes toward Indians. After their removal, other groups increasingly became targets.

CHAPTER FOUR

"An Asset and Not a Liability": *Omaechevarria v. State of Idaho*

Did he know what he was doing? Was he just following the boss's orders? Did he understand the officer when he got arrested? Who paid the fine and court costs? What happened to him after he was arrested? Did he spend time in jail? Could this poor Basque immigrant ever imagine that his name would be cited in a court case in the US Supreme Court? There are these and many more unanswered questions. Here's what we do know.

On August 15, 1914, Owyhee County law enforcement officers cited Basque sheepherder Secundino Omaechevarria, an employee of R. F. Bicknell of Boise, for a misdemeanor offense of grazing a band of sheep on land "previously occupied by cattle." George Swisher filed the complaint on behalf of a number of cattlemen in Owyhee County.[1] Omaechevarria was arrested and found guilty on September 3, 1914, and fined $150 [$3,500 in 2014] plus court costs. However, the defense challenged the decision all the way through the court system until it argued its case before the US Supreme Court on December 20, 1917.

Secundino Omaechevarria was stuck in the middle. Sheepherding provided an opportunity for impoverished Basque immigrants, thousands of whom came west, yet at times it left them sandwiched between sheep and cattle interests on the range. Those connected with cattle ranching often seemed "more American" than Omaechevarria and others like him: spelling and pronouncing the name alone left many tongue-tied. Proceedings often sided with cattle interests largely because of a notion of squatters' rights and the low socioeconomic class of many sheepmen, which often gave cattlemen disproportionate influence in state legislatures and over early grazing regulations.[2] *Omaechevarria v. State of Idaho* emerged in the midst of a xenophobia that crested with the Immigration Act of 1924 (or Johnson-Reed Act), which closed America's ports to open immigration and instituted a quota system.

Just as the government limited immigration, it also dramatically impacted development in the West through land policy and court decisions. The range wars climaxed with the passing of the federal government's watershed decision, the Taylor Grazing Act in 1934, which forever altered grazing practices.[3] With this legislation the federal government carved out grazing districts on much of the public domain and placed them under the administration of the Bureau of Land Management. However, the passage of this controversial legislation came only after countless disputes: ongoing disagreements between cattle, sheep, and agricultural interests; legal proceedings attempting resolution; and a number of violent clashes. *Omaechevarria v. State of Idaho* resides within this contentious context, just past the chronological midpoint between the emergence of large-scale sheep and cattle interests in the latter half of the nineteenth century and passage of the Taylor Grazing Act.

In the midst of these range battles, court decisions, and policy precedents, what happened to laborers like Omaechevarria? What did he think of all this? What did he do as the court case made its way through the system? Was he involved? Did he continue working? Sadly we know precious little about his story outside of the proceedings of this court case. But to understand him and others like him, we have to identify what brought them here.

Sheepherding in the West

Given the present state of our land and the animals that graze upon it, it is hard to imagine that when Columbus arrived, fifty million buffalo grazed from Canada to Mexico. Many tribes of Indians built their culture around the animal. Similarly, the settlers' way of life centered around cattle and

Ranchers have worked the Owyhee range since the 1860s. (Courtesy of Jake Putnam.)

sheep. Columbus brought Spanish cattle that bred with English stock and would eventually become known as "longhorns." As populations increased in the 1800s, so did greater markets for these longhorns and other breeds of cattle. The railroad opened even larger opportunities, and livestock owners drove cattle to railroad heads in Kansas and Nebraska where they "found" large, grassy plains ideal for grazing cattle. However, since the 1862 Homestead Act allowed settlers up to 160 acres of land in exchange for cultivating and living on the land, some livestock owners continued to push west and often ended up on arid and fragile "leftover" land. This terrain typified the land of what would become southwestern Idaho and eastern Oregon, where cowboys drove thousands of longhorns in the 1860s.[4]

Cattlemen strove to meet the increasing demand for meat of the trappers working in the area and the miners who combed the Owyhees. By the 1870s many settlers turned to raising cattle as a lucrative alternative to other ventures. The numbers grew quickly from 24,559 head in 1882 to 100,000 by 1888. Ranches in Owyhee County included such large-scale operations as Grayson and Company, with sixteen thousand head, medium-sized outfits such as those of Con Shea and the Hardiman Brothers, which ranged around five thousand head, and many smaller operations. One local author commented: "All of Owyhee County was a huge pasture at that time. There were no range restrictions and cowboys followed the herd . . . wherever grazing was good."[5]

While Columbus had introduced cattle in the East, Spanish missionaries established sheep and goats throughout the northern reaches of New Spain during the seventeenth and eighteenth centuries. Additionally, immigrant parties trailed sheep west across the Mississippi as early as 1841, and markets grew greatly after the discovery of gold in California. By 1850, over five hundred thousand sheep ranged in mostly small flocks on private lands in the West. The profitability of raising sheep attracted investors and the industry exploded; by 1880, nineteen million head of sheep grazed in seventeen western states. Whereas cattle ranches operated from a local base, absentee investors regularly hired migrant herders with transhumant practices and cashed in on the profits.[6]

In the decade of the 1850s, herders brought nearly half a million sheep from New Mexico to California, and by the mid-1860s these bands supplied mining towns in Nevada, Idaho, and Montana. Besides being attracted by mining markets, grazers sought the open range available in the Idaho Territory. On April 23, 1867, the *Idaho Statesman* reported: "We are credibly informed that there are five thousand head of sheep now on the way from Honey Lake to this and adjoining markets. They are coming over the Chico routes."[7]

However, railroad expansion changed Idaho from a thoroughfare for migrating flocks to one of the industry's hubs. In 1890 the state counted 501,978 head of sheep; by 1910 that number had exploded to 3,010,478. With the demand from mining camps, Owyhee County emerged as one of the largest grazing centers, and, within fifty years of the entry of sheep, held the largest number of assessed head within any county of the state, 191,544. Even though these sheep owners recognized the profitability of owning sheep, they often ran cattle for respectability; the employer of Omaechevarria, R. F. Bicknell, did exactly that.[8]

As opportunity expanded for owners like Bicknell, the demand for herders grew accordingly; yet few aspired to shepherding. Settlers described herders as "outcasts and ne'er-do-wells, shifty characters too undependable to be hired in the mines or by cattlemen." One author noted that the sheepherder, the once-honorable figure of the pastoral ages, now "has only one consolation left, and that is the secure knowledge that he is working on rock bottom." A common adage held that "you could not fire a shotgun into the average crowd in the range country without hitting a man who had at some time herded sheep, but it would probably take the charge in the other barrel to make him admit it."[9]

Sheepherders did not have the luster and prestige of cowboys, who broke and rode horses, roped cattle, wore six-shooters and boots, spurs and chaps. Herders, in contrast, walked and had pack mules and more closely "resembled the *peons* that Americans read about after the Mexican-American War of 1846–48." Compared to cowboys, they seemed "meek, impoverished, mix-blooded men, incapable of social improvement and unwilling to seek it."[10]

Nevertheless, they were needed. Sheepherders immersed themselves in the bloody, messy work of the lambing season during winter months when they helped deliver thousands of lambs and then divided them into bands. They sheared the sheep in March and April and trailed them to the foothills to feed on spring grasses. During the summer, herders drove the bands into the mountains, and steered them from one meadow to another, and descended only to ship the lambs. They began to trail down to the valleys before the first snowfall, and by December they held the sheep in corrals. Herders then began to prepare for the birth of the first lambs, and the process started again.[11]

Besides the continuous movement required, mortal dangers frequently threatened. Spotted fever from ticks, snakebites, and lightning or snowstorms forced herders to remain vigilant. One herder wrote home to say he had been lucky to lose only forty sheep in a snowstorm; another herder had lost fifteen hundred. During the summer months in the mountain meadows, wolves, coyotes, cougars, or bears often attacked the herd. If the herders lost large numbers, they might be fired and have difficulty finding work again. All this occurred in isolated settings where often no one knew of a herder's health or situation. An Idaho paper reported that a sheepherder drowned while attempting to draw water from a creek. Searchers later found an axe, a bucket, and his sweater; it was presumed he slipped in while cutting a hole in the ice.[12]

Indeed, beyond the physical challenges, maintaining mental and emotional stability was often the most difficult task for herders. The intense

Basque sheepherder on horse. (Courtesy of Basque Museum and Cultural Center.)

isolation and loneliness, especially in the summer when herders went for weeks without seeing another human being, took its toll on many. "I remember when I got my first letter from my mother," one Basque herder said. "I had to go behind the trees to read it because I was crying like a baby." For some, this extreme isolation became too much to bear and they went insane or became "sheeped" or "sagebrushed," as the herders referred to it. In 1908 the courts tried a Basque herder in Mountain Home to determine his mental health. After hearing the results of an examination by a local doctor, the court declared, "He was so far disordered in mind as to endanger health, person and property," and the court committed him to an institution. In fact, early Basque immigrants to Idaho formed a health insurance organization, and part of its coverage included return passage to the Basque Country for any member who suffered from mental illness.[13]

Opportunity for Basques

Although held in low regard by most Americans, sheepherding offered one of the few jobs for young Basque men emigrating with few skills and no knowledge of English. As one immigrant claimed, "The worst is no can talk." Another asked, "What the hell else was I going to do, work in an office?" Sheepherding in the American West represented the latest chapter in the ongoing migration of Basques from Europe to points throughout the world. From mariners to merchants to missionaries, Basques participated in each step of the discovery and settlement of the New World. As early as the seventh century Basque whalers built an industry they monopolized until well into the sixteenth century. The continuous search for whales meant longer voyages, and evidence documents Basques fishing for cod off the Grand Banks near Newfoundland long before Columbus's arrival.[14]

As Spain colonized vast lands, Basques also seized the opportunities and spread throughout the colonial empire. They assisted in the formation of communities in what became Mexico, Uruguay, Colombia, and Venezuela. One Basque explorer founded the northern Mexican province of Nueva Vizcaya, naming its capital after his Bizkaian birthplace, Durango. Another Basque descendant gained even greater fame: Símon Bolívar, the liberator of South America. The Basques' most famous religious figures, Ignatius of Loyola, the founder of the Jesuits, and Francis Xavier, the well-known missionary, and many other members of the order played instrumental roles in these colonies.[15]

Given this long tradition of migration, Basques' movement into the American West represented a relatively minor part of Basque worldwide settlement over several centuries. Yet, whereas other migrations attracted individuals from diverse economic backgrounds, this latest one consisted almost exclusively of lower-class laborers. Many of the Basque immigrants who came to Idaho at the turn of the twentieth century came from subsistence-level farms growing a variety of crops in the wet maritime climate. Since their farms were small, usually consisting of between six and ten hectares often carved out of the side of hills, Basques traditionally practiced primogeniture: they selected one son or daughter as the sole inheritor of the farm to avoid fragmentation of family property. The other siblings of the traditionally large families maintained a place on the family homestead as long as they remained single; some chose to enter a religious community or went to town for work.[16]

For many Basques, travel to another part of the world for temporary work offered one of the few ways for them to create a better life. For centuries they had seen and heard of Basques succeeding in these ventures, particularly in South America, and returning home to a far better life. Therefore, while Basque industrialists drew workers from distant corners of Spain, young Basques emigrated to work throughout the American West.[17]

Basque family in front of farmhouse. (Euskal Museoa Bilbao Museo Vasco. Courtesy of © F/ E. Abaitua.)

Determining the number involved in this migration has always been difficult. Starting in the sixteenth century, when Spain and France drew their border and sliced off the three provinces in the north (Lapurdi, Nafarroa Beherea, and Zuberoa) from the larger four to the South (Bizkaia, Araba, Gipuzkoa, and Nafarroa), Basques appeared on official documents as Spanish or French nationals. Moreover, emigration of the lower classes is even more difficult to trace. Therefore, we know few specifics about Secundino Omaechevarria's reasons for emigrating, but by placing him into a general profile we at least gain a contextual understanding.

Records reveal that Secundino (misspelled "Lecundino") Omaechevarria landed at Ellis Island in 1911 at age thirty-one, slightly older than the average for other immigrant male Basques coming to herd sheep. Most early herders to Idaho were single males under the age of thirty with little money and education. On average, the fifty-three Boise-bound Basques who arrived in New York between 1897 and 1902 brought $36.50 [$1,000 in 2014] each. In 1910 only 50.9 percent of the Basques in Idaho could read and write. Of the few who were married, half had left their wives behind. Many intended a short stay, desiring to return to the Basque Country and create opportunities afforded by their savings.[18]

Like 96 percent of the rest of Basque immigrants to Idaho, Omaechevarria followed the chain migration from a small region of the province of Bizkaia to the high desert country. While Omaechevarria emigrated directly from this region, the first Basques who came to California in the midst of the gold rush did not come from the Basque Country but rather the pampas of Argentina and Uruguay. They represented a group ready to risk a second migration, and had experience in large-scale, open-range, sheep-raising practices, which proved invaluable in their move to southern California. Knowledge of transhumance made herding in most of the Great Basin region possible. By the time sheep entered Idaho in greater numbers, Basques such as Omaechevarria migrated directly from the Basque Country.[19]

Contrary to the stereotype of Basques, these newcomers had little or no sheepherding experience. If they herded sheep at all back home, the flock consisted of small bands that provided cheese and wool for the family, a practice that involved none of the loneliness, financial risk, or danger of the large-scale herding in Idaho. Often within days of arriving, these inexperienced herders were responsible for herds of twenty-five hundred sheep. Equipped with their agrarian background and a willingness to take any job, hundreds of Basques became herders in the American West.[20]

While the financial rewards remained paramount, young Basques who immigrated to Idaho in the first years of the twentieth century endured these challenges for a host of reasons. For some, the needs of their families drove them to succeed, while others fought off their fear of failure and deeply desired to earn the respect of their native community. "It was unthinkable," one author stated, "that a Basque emigrant could return to his village without having succeeded in his immigration efforts." After eight years in Idaho one herder reported to his father that he had not made enough money yet to return to the Basque Country; if he returned now, he would be seen around his native village with "holes in [his] pants," and people would call him the "Bad American."[21]

This combination of societal expectations, agrarian background, and financial goals explained how Basques came to be directly linked with herding in the American West. Andy Little, dubbed the "Sheep King of Idaho," hired Basques throughout his life. His biographer wrote: "the Littles are the first to say that Basque herders, managers, foremen and other employees helped build Andy's business as much as anyone." Anthropologist William Douglass added that "sheep ranchers frequently employed Scottish, Mexican, Indian, Portuguese, Chinese, and American herders, but, with a few exceptions in all but the Mormon dominated areas of the Great Basin, by

1900 the Basques were the preferred sheepherders in most outfits." This reputation greatly helped new Basques in the region find employment; however, their herding practices determined how that reputation evolved.[22]

While many employers such as Little and Bicknell preferred Basques, they quickly drew the ire of cattle and farming interests. From its inception, the sheep industry had numerous "tramp bands," which did not operate from base ranches. Rather, the absentee owners of these "tramp bands" hired non-English-speaking immigrants such as the Basques and sent them onto public domain lands. These ventures required little or no investment in buildings or land and often resulted in handsome profits. Yet, precisely because these owners paid no taxes, had no community roots, and hired alien herders, they drew the indignation of landed stockmen. As these bands flourished and as agriculture expanded in the region, itinerant sheepmen sought less crowded range conditions. This nomadic search for grazing opportunities often resulted in friction between livestock owners competing for the best grazing land.[23]

Basque sheepherder with sheep dogs. (Courtesy of Basque Museum and Cultural Center.)

Case Testimony and Context

Testimony in the Omaechevarria case exposed many of these issues. The officer cited the herder for trespassing on land that the cattlemen argued had been used continuously for cattle range, and the probate court agreed. The appeal of this guilty verdict in September of 1914 transferred the case to a twelve-member jury in Silver City. The state called six witnesses to testify. Their argument centered on a squatter's rights appeal, the damage that sheep did to land and water, and the lack of residency of sheep owners in the area. However, comments from particular witnesses revealed a blatant prejudice against the herders.[24]

In his trial testimony, George Swisher, who had initially brought the complaint and represented at least ten other area ranchers, described the boundaries of the disputed range and acknowledged that the "balance of the land is in public ownership, the title being in the United States and the State of Idaho." Yet he claimed, "The range described in my complaint and indicated in State's Exhibit 1 is exclusively cattle and horse range and has been as long as I have known it." He echoed the often-heard claim of the problems of herding sheep and cattle together. "The effect of grazing sheep on a range occupied by cattle is that it runs the sheep off the range—or the cattle. They won't raise together."

Earlier court decisions backed Swisher's assertion. As one judge wrote, "Sheep eat the herbage closer to the ground than cattle or horses do, and, their hooves being sharp, they devastate and kill the growing vegetation wherever they graze for any considerable time." The justice added: "It is a matter of common experience that a large band of sheep to the windward, affects one's sense of smell when a considerable distance away." Statements like these made it difficult for sheep interests to prove the contrary.[25]

Furthermore, Swisher complained of the lack of residency of herders and the effects of the herders' dogs, while emphasizing the ranchers' patience in these matters. "I have known these herders to run cattle off of the salt grounds when they came in with dogs," he said, adding, "I have known the Basques to do that lots of times." Swisher emphasized that no sheepmen lived in the area. "I do not know of any men engaged in the business of raising sheep who live in the territory described in the complaint and indicated on State's Exhibit 1. If there were any there I would know of it."

Swisher assured the court that he and the other ranchers had repeatedly explained to herders that this was cattle range. "We asked them to move out. We interviewed them, and they moved out, with the exception of one man, a Basco, we were quite a while making him understand it, but he never moved his camp, that I knew of."[26]

When questioned under what authority the cattlemen had established the land as exclusively cattle range, Swisher answered, "It was an understanding between us when I went there. We knew it to be a cattle and horse range though I don't know of any agreement we had in particular. We discussed it amongst ourselves." When pressed by the defense, he maintained, "It has been an old understanding between the old sheep men and cattle men." However, in the end he made a legal justification to the land. He stated, "I claim only possessory rights to this land. We claim the right to the range by priority of right under the Code there—6872." This was the law initially used to find the herder guilty of trespassing.[27]

In Idaho, as early as 1872, the territorial government attempted to avert conflicts between sheepherders, farmers, and cattlemen who customarily grazed on the public domain near their dwellings. The legislature, controlled by cattlemen, enacted very stringent trespass laws against sheep but left cattle and horses the freedom to graze at will. They enacted a two-mile-limit law that forbade any sheep from grazing within two miles of "any human habitation and any cattle range." By 1879 three counties had accepted this decision, and in 1887 it became the general law. After the admission of Idaho to the Union in 1890, the statute was reenacted and its validity sustained by the US Supreme Court in *Bacon v. Walker.* To avert further clashes between the sheepherders and cattle ranchers, the state introduced additional legislation, and in 1883 the law (section 6872 of the Revised Code) prohibited grazing "on any cattle range previously occupied by cattle, or upon any range usually occupied by any cattle grower, either as a spring, summer, or winter range for his cattle." Even though the law allowed for the priority of possessory right for both cattle and sheep owners, the cattlemen clearly gained the upper hand in the structure of this law.[28]

The next witness for the state, E. A. Stauffer, reiterated much of Swisher's testimony. He affirmed that this land had been continuously used for cattle range and cited his father's 1888 cattle ranch as evidence. Speaking against absentee owners, he stated, "There is no sheep men live there and own any ranches there. There is no sheep men own any land within twenty miles of this mountain. Everybody living on this mountain are cattle men." Answering questions on boundaries, Stauffer stated, "I never saw Mr. Bicknell until yesterday, but his camp tender has known real well where the lines were." Stauffer maintained that he "did not erect any monuments, in particular, it wasn't necessary." Rather, he insisted that natural boundaries functioned as markers. "It was more bounded by creeks—more than anything else, and mountains. I didn't put up any stakes with notices on them that that was the line of a cattle range. It wasn't necessary. Sheep men respected it without." When questioned about his authorization to set boundaries, Stauffer maintained, "I just took it onto myself, . . . the fact of living and owning land and having a prior right—I would consider that a legal right. I think I have a right to pasture on there." And added: "Sheep men have always respected this." Stauffer testified that newcomers failed to respect these boundaries and that their recent arrival disqualified them from range rights. "And another reason is that sheep men today that are coming into this—to graze their sheep on this territory there—are new men, men who have never been there before, and I wouldn't consider had any right."[29]

Yet in the midst of his testimony he also admitted another core tenet of his argument. "Sheepmen that were in that time were a different class than there is now. They were white men and they could understand English." Besides raising issues of residency and squatters' rights, besides identifying the problems of raising cattle and sheep together, Stauffer's testimony revealed a central issue in this case—race. He distinguished the earlier herders, whom he connected to himself and his fellow cattle owners, from the new herders, whom he depicted as nonwhite, foreign-language speakers of another class.[30]

The defense called only three witnesses to the stand. The owner and employer, R. F. Bicknell, testified that he lived in Boise and maintained interests in both cattle and sheep. He countered the cattlemen's claims that cattle and sheep could not graze on the same range. "Yes, I have handled them both upon the same range at the same time." And later he affirmed that, "Yes, I bought both fat cattle and fat sheep off the same range." In the end, Bicknell maintained it was not the type of livestock placed on the range that made the difference, but rather the grazing practices. "It does not destroy a cattle range to graze sheep upon it unless it is overgrazed. It destroys any range to overgraze it, with cattle or sheep."[31]

The second witness, J. W. Starkey, also a sheep owner who lived in Boise, seconded Bicknell's claim that cattle and sheep could be herded together. "I have seen sheep and cattle running on the same range; the cattle were not particularly fat, but it was the spring of the year. I have seen cattle running on a range that had been grazed over in the spring by sheep." Regarding the ever-increasing pressure for land, Starkey stated, "No, I leased land from the State. I got this land in sheep so that I could lease it. It is the only way that I could hold my ground."[32]

And the final witness for the defense, W. D. Evans, no doubt brought some laughter to the case, at least for one portion of the courtroom. When asked if sheep and cattle could run on the same range, Evans asserted, "I have run mine together." And when asked, "Did they get fat?" Evans's reply was, "I sold the beef to Mr. Stauffer"—one of the ranchers who had earlier testified and was bringing this case.[33]

While the testimony illustrates many of the contending issues, placing it in its historical context helps us understand the agitation among these diverse interests. Numerous papers throughout the western United States regularly reported instances of violence; these often involved Basque herders. The Basque language newspaper *Californiako Euskal Herria* (The Basque Country of California) reported on May 30, 1896, and August 14, 1897, shootings of Basque herders in California and Arizona. In Winnemucca, Nevada, on August 4 the paper reported, "Armed men are visiting the sheep ranches near Disaster Peak, shooting the sheep and stealing horses. It is supposed the invaders were cattlemen, who took this method of driving the sheepmen from the country." On September 1, 1905, the *Nevada State Herald* reported that a man named Wallace shot a Basque herder, Simon Salas, in the shoulder. Reportedly, Salas was herding sheep on a mountainside while Wallace remained on a creek below. Wallace claimed he called to Salas to "come down." Allegedly Salas refused, and Wallace shot at him. Wallace, who homesteaded in the region, had shot at another herder in a separate incident a year earlier.[34]

Court records further reveal the conflict between these groups and help explain the attitudes of those who brought the case against Omaechevarria. The 1911 case *State of Idaho v. Luis Yturaspe* involved an incident in which

James A. Percy sent his dogs to scatter four Basque sheep bands.[35] Later, he chased one of the herders, Luis Yturaspe, with a hammer, and Percy charged that Yturaspe then pulled a gun on him. In 1911, cattleman Harry Hoyt brought assault charges against a Basque herder, claiming that he had asked the herder to remove the twenty-five hundred lambs from property near Boise. When Hoyt began to drive the sheep away, the herder fired his rifle in the air, and according to court records, mustered enough English to say, "Stop you son of a bitch or I will shoot you." The herder was fined $500 [$12,195 in 2014].

Sheepherders were not always the targets. In Hailey, Idaho, sheepman Purefoy Blankenship seriously wounded a well-known rancher, T. F. Murphy. Both were respected residents of the area who quarreled over range rights issues. Allegedly, Murphy threw rocks and advanced toward Blankenship. While backing away, Blankenship slipped and fell, and his pistol accidentally discharged, severely injuring himself. He then drew the gun and shot Murphy, the bullet entering the abdomen and coming out at the back, having penetrated the left kidney. Despite his wound, Murphy rode home. Meanwhile, Blankenship limped two miles, secured his horse, and traveled to town for medical treatment and to notify officials.[36]

The employees of the sheepmen and ranchers battled as well. In New Mexico, cowboys drove one hundred wild horses into bands of sheep as they rode alongside and fired their pistols in the air. It took the sheepmen a week to gather their animals. In another instance, cowboys captured and tied herders to trees and drove their herds into muddy bogs where many became trapped and died. In a branding mark of shaming, cowboys captured one sheepherder and "cut cattle marks into his ears." These conflicts were "as much ethnic as environmental."[37]

One local newspaper revealed this ethnic tension. On June 4, 1915, the *Owyhee Avalanche* reported, "Little Can Be Learned about Tragedy on Account of Nationality of Victim and Associates." County officials held an inquest regarding the body of the sheepherder Domingo Garaitandia, who was found dead presumably from a poor heart condition. He was a new herder who had been in the area barely a month since emigrating from Spain, where he left behind a wife and two children. The paper reported that "it looked as though he had died naturally but he had been shot." While the article acknowledged a possible future investigation by the Spanish consulate, it revealed a lack of interest in this matter. "Nobody knew much about it and since they [Basque immigrants] all spoke Spanish then nobody paid much attention."[38]

Meanwhile, in Malheur County, Oregon, just over the Owyhee County border, no doubt remained about one victim's identity. On May 7, 1910, the *Idaho Statesman* headline read, "Jury Convicts Murderer of Basque." On April 3, Charles Wear shot and killed Domingo Aldecoa in "the most cold blooded [murder case] in the history of Malheur County." The two were fighting over land access when Wear took a rifle and killed Aldecoa, according to witnesses. "Because of the prominence of the defendant in the sheep industry," the case was bitterly contested. One witness testified that when informed that Aldecoa was dead, Wear responded, "That's good; that is seven of them." Although the number reference remained unclear, the attitude rang clear.[39]

Oftentimes, the cattlemen and other sheepmen believed that the herders feigned ignorance when cattlemen attempted to run herders off grazing ground. The herders "would wave [their] arms and say 'no savvy, no savvy,'" but cattlemen suspected that "they 'savvied' more than they let on, acting upon instructions from their employers." While they turned violent on occasion, more commonly ranchers turned to the state for protection of their interests. For example, in Blaine County, two grazing violation cases rose from the fourth judicial district court up to the state supreme court. In another case, Basque herders Peter Bidegain and John Etcychar attempted to repeal a prosecution by the state on charges of running sheep on range reserved for use by the cattlemen. Additionally, the state of Idaho charged Miguel Goitia with a misdemeanor for pollution of water on Last Chance Creek by a band of sheep. Each of these cases strengthened the role of the government as an arbiter in the area.[40]

In the most extreme cases, residents grew particularly irate at these itinerant herders and their apparent disregard for the land. Courts charged two Basque herders with setting fire to range and timber, and bound them over on $2,000 [$47,000 in 2014] to appear before a grand jury. Accounts claimed that the herders habitually bedded their sheep in the timber and protected them from coyotes and wolves by setting fire to several trees around their flocks. This practice eliminated the need for night watching; in the morning they drove the sheep away, but often left the fires burning. Critics claimed that numerous large fires ignited because of this practice, which resulted in the legal action brought by the government. Those subpoenaed to testify in the case included George Swisher, who brought the complaint in *Omaechevarria v. State of Idaho.*[41]

Government Decides

The thousands of disputes, both litigious and violent, underscored the need for ongoing land regulation in the West. The battles fought on the range shifted toward clashes over policy authorship, with the state and federal governments setting long-lasting precedents. At the local level, the Silver City court system became overwhelmed with these legal proceedings, which often went against the herders. On October 1, 1915, the *Owyhee Avalanche* reported "all verdicts in favor of the cattlemen." And another story noted "one case was settled out of court and had a happy ending for everyone except the sheepman."[42]

Sometimes, however, decisions went against the cattlemen. In Washington County, the state supreme court granted sheepman A. G. Butterfield a new trial when it reversed the judgment of the Seventh Judicial District Court, which had found him guilty of grazing of sheep upon range reserved for cattle. The supreme court held that a range that has been used by both cattlemen and sheepmen could not be termed an exclusive cattle range under the meaning of section 6872 of the revised codes.[43]

Meanwhile, pressure on the land increased. The June 5, 1914, *Owyhee Avalanche* reported: "E. B. York foreman of the Fred Palmer sheep outfit with headquarters in the western part of the county was in the city Saturday consulting County Attorney Melvin in regard to instituting the two-mile limit proceedings against another outfit. The range must be getting in a very crowded condition when sheepmen will invoke the two-mile limit law against each other."[44]

National land policy further limited use. The General Revision Act of 1891 established "national forests," and section 24 enabled the president to "set aside as public reservations any timbered section of the public domain." That year President Benjamin Harrison established the Yellowstone Timberland Reserve in Wyoming, and the following year he set aside five more reserves, including the largest in Oregon's Cascade Mountain, which were protected by the first regulations prohibiting the "driving, feeding, grazing, pasturing, or herding of cattle, sheep, or other livestock" within the reserves.[45]

By 1897, the federal government had established another fourteen reserves, and in June legislation placed the administration of all forest reserves under the secretary of the interior. Livestock men went to work. They lobbied Congress to ensure that pasturing of livestock on the public lands in national forests would not be restricted, as "long as it appears that injury is not being done to the forest growth, and the rights of others are not thereby jeopardized." However, sheep grazing, particularly the practices of itinerant herders, continued to be viewed as severely damaging, and reports from fifteen different Idaho foresters concurred. They voiced hostility toward "tramp" sheepmen, especially those bringing in herds from out of state; blamed sheep for the destruction of the range and contamination of water owing to herd size and location by watersheds; and consistently complained that herders started fires. Forest managers supported limiting use, and by 1900 sheep were excluded from almost all US forest reserves.[46]

For sheepmen regulation meant greater difficulty, and for itinerant herders doom. Government policy required sheepmen to purchase permits, and in 1906 grazing fees were set at five to seven cents per sheep, with subsequent increases that fostered even greater resentment. Local livestock associations allotted and administered these parcels, which allowed them to protect their interests and exclude itinerant herders. To give themselves further control, they even proposed that areas that had previously failed to meet the criteria for incorporation into the national forest system be admitted. Furthermore, in 1909 Gifford Pinchot, head of the US Forest Service, ruled that the transient owners of sheep and cattle were not entitled to allotments within the national forests. This decision excluded great numbers of herders, and severely impacted Basques, who had been running significant numbers of transient bands.[47]

Sheepmen countered these attacks against their industry. They initiated court cases that questioned the constitutionality of the Organic Act of 1897, and in 1911 the US Supreme Court concurred and allowed limited grazing for sheep. Nevertheless, as conflict grew the federal government placed army troops to patrol national parks. Tensions increased as succeeding presidents set aside further reserves. Presidents Harrison, Cleveland, and McKinley established forty-one reserves with 46,410,209 acres. By the end of President Theodore Roosevelt's tenure, the federal government had tripled that amount to 158 reserves with 194,505,325 acres.[48]

While this took care of national forests, it left wide open the question of far larger tracts of land in the public domain. Grazing rights continued to be one of the greatest sources of confrontation, as exemplified by Omaechevarria's arrest. Despite the guilty verdict at the probate court and the failure of the appeal, the defense decided to continue with the process. In September of 1915, the case came before the Idaho Supreme Court.

In the appeal the defense argued four main points regarding the case. First, they maintained that the statute in question (6872 of the Idaho code) contravened section 1 of article 1 of Idaho's state Constitution. Second, they argued that it violated section 1 of the Fourteenth Amendment to the US Constitution. Third, they argued that the legislation directly conflicted with the Act of Congress of February 25, 1885. Finally, the defense held that the state had failed to establish the clear territorial boundaries of this land.[49]

Again the sheep interests lost; but they decided to appeal to the US Supreme Court, which took it under consideration in its October 1916 term. The continued commitment of time and money for the appeal indicated the importance of this case and the sheep industry's hope for a favorable precedent. In their briefs, both sides again outlined their central arguments, but the sheepmen stressed the notion that the arrest of Omaechevarria violated the provisions of section 1 of the Fourteenth Amendment because it deprived the herder of property without due process of law and denied him equal protection. Oral arguments were set for December 20, 1917.[50]

"Good" versus "Bad" Basques

The targets of these policies became clear: sheepmen who were citizens and owned land wished to remove itinerant herds and foreign herders—primarily Basques. One *Humboldt Star* headline read: "Sheepmen Get Basques Excluded." In a specific example from the Mono National Forest, nineteen sheepmen and stock owners who had grazed their flocks for the past few years were notified of their lost rights "bearing on the point of citizenship which excludes alients [*sic*] and non-property holders from grazing privileges in the forest." After personally surveying conditions in the West, the chief forester determined "that Basque sheep owners were fast gaining possession of the grazing rights and completely crowding the citizen and property holder from grazing their sheep in the forest." The forester allowed those who had grazed in this area to continue for the year, "but such persons must be citizens of the United States, or, if not citizens, must be bona fide residents of and owners of improved ranch property either within or adjacent to the national forest lands which they have formerly used." He concluded, "Anyone not in the above class will be treated as trespassers."[51]

A 1919 Forest Service report revealed the sentiments of a variety of livestock interests. "[The] public range is fast being destroyed by transient sheep owners who have no thought of preserving the range for future generations. These owners are for the most part Basques, who are not citizens of the United States, and are here simply to get what they can from the natural resources of this country with the least possible expense to themselves." However, the report deemed the few naturalized Basques "good citizens" since they improved the ranch property and developed the country.[52]

By the time *Omaechevarria v. Idaho* reached the US Supreme Court, differences in the amount of time they had spent in America, their economic success, and their future plans created starkly different perceptions of Basques. Some Basques throughout the Northwest enjoyed exceptional economic success; a few in Idaho grew especially wealthy. In 1893, Juan Achabal's ship sunk on the way to America, and he landed with, literally, only the clothes on his back, but by the early 1900s he owned eighty thousand sheep and employed fifty-nine men in southwestern Idaho. Jose Bengoechea emigrated in 1897, worked a few years as a herder, but within two decades rivaled Achabal for sheep ownership; he also worked as vice president of the local bank and was proprietor of the Mountain Home Hotel, the town's finest.[53]

While these Basques gained respect in broader American societal circles, most of their countrymen toiled further down the economic ladder, and many as itinerant herders—the same way that Achabal and Bengoechea got their start. These herders and their practices continued to be targets of animosity. Hypocritically, while most of the settled livestock owners had recently migrated to the area and started their businesses in a similar fashion, they viewed these "tramp" sheepmen as the epitome of anti-American. Their argument held that these rootless wanderers trespassed onto their land, cared little to nothing about local affairs, stripped the land of its value, and returned with their riches to their homeland. On December 5, 1913, the *Humboldt Star* reported that five Basque sheepmen returned to Spain, some of them to visit, but "two of them have sold their bands of sheep and will remain in the old country. Incidentally, these latter took away with them several thousand dollars, which will also remain."[54]

On the floor of the Senate, Key Pittman of Nevada delivered a vituperative description of Basques herders. "[The sheepmen] get that class of labor because they seem to be adapted for sheep herding, and they are lacking in intelligence, independence, or anything else. They are just about as near a slave as anybody could be under our present existing conditions." An Idaho newspaper expressed similar sentiments: "The scale of living and the methods of doing business of the Bascos are on a par with those of the Chinamen. However, they have some undesirable characteristics that the Chinese are free from." The writer described Basques as "filthy, treacherous, and meddlesome. However, they work hard and save their money. They are clannish and undesirable, but," the author warned, "they have a foothold and unless something is done will make life impossible for the whiteman."[55]

These heavily prejudiced statements at the local and national level, when contrasted with favorable comments in newspapers and other reports, revealed the era's criteria for acceptance and respectability. Specifically, land ownership and citizenship represented a commitment that allowed Basques membership in the broader community. The *Humboldt Star* praised a group of Basques as "expert sheepmen" and "an industrious people. Many of them own large flocks of sheep and are landowners and have made this country their permanent home."[56]

The larger numbers that applied for citizenship, although perhaps simply due to greater Basque immigration, may have been a response to this anti-alien environment. In Winnemucca, Nevada, alone, where only forty-eight Basques had filed for US citizenship between 1871 and 1906, an additional 108 Basques did so between 1906 and 1912. In Ada County,

Idaho, only thirteen Basques filed a Declaration of Intention between 1888 and 1903; yet between 1906 and 1909 at least forty-eight Basques filed for citizenship.[57]

However, for many, World War I revealed loyalties. As the war dragged on and the United States became militarily involved, it affected nearly every aspect of life, including the sheepherding industry. Indeed, from the time the *Omaechevarria* case began in August of 1915 to its final decision three and a half years later, much of the world's attention focused on the enormous suffering and societal changes brought by the war. Locally, this meant volunteering for a variety of services and contributing to the war effort. While the economic changes greatly impacted the livestock industry, the societal pressure for particular displays of Americanism further heightened differences in the Basque community.

The war effort substantially increased demand for wool, and thus herders, at the same time that conscription called many into military service. The government projected it would buy sixty million pounds of clean wool for military uses, which represented nearly half the total American clip. On behalf of western woolgrowers, a committee offered to furnish the war department all the wool required at current market prices.[58]

In response to the wartime environment, officers of the Idaho Cattle & Horse Growers' Association urged their members "to cooperate with other live stock interests this season and avoid as far as possible any controversies over the division of range on the public domain." They encouraged their members "to conserve the great range resources to the utmost, to the end that maximum production may be attained at this time." Appealing to their sense of patriotism, they prompted members to "all lead as peaceful lives at home during this world crisis as possible . . . and to cooperate with state officials in their efforts to safeguard public interests." Despite the patriotic plea, they did not miss the opportunity to criticize land policy toward sheep owners. They objected "to withdrawal of 1,000,000 acres for sheep trail purposes and have written to this effect to the state board of land commissioners."[59]

The war also highlighted the differences within the Basque community—between itinerant herders who saw in the war an opportunity for greater financial gain and those who wished to assure the public of their loyalty. On August 26, 1917, the *Idaho Statesman* reported that in some sections of the state, "sheepherders, mostly aliens, . . . have formed a combination and virtually gone on strike, demanding wages of $100 [$1,800 in 2014] a month and board." The president of the Idaho Woolgrowers Association countered that "the industry could not afford this increase in pay, that sheepherders generally were receiving $60 [$1,090 in 2014] and board, and that the item of board was growing large on account of increased costs of food stuff." He warned that "the presence of large numbers of aliens in some of the range counties threw an increasing likelihood of being drafted on the American employees in the industries in those counties, and that these Americans in many instances formed the nucleus of skilled employees for sheepmen, cattlemen, and ranchers."[60]

In the meantime, Basques with residency worked hard to assure the public of their loyalty. In an unprecedented action, prominent members sent resolutions later published in the *Idaho Statesman* to the mayor of Boise and the governor of Idaho, assuring them of their desire to be an asset to the "land of opportunity, unrivaled in all the world." They expressed their desire to "participate [and help fund] any patriotic rally held in this city." Basque community members pledged full support and "loyalty to the government of their adoption during the present international crisis." The resolution acknowledged their absolute confidence in the "wisdom, purity of purpose, and transcendent ability, humanity, and patriotism of the president of the United States and are grateful to him for the unparalleled efforts he has made to avoid war with Germany." They promised to "uphold this government, and to help sustain it in any controversy or armed conflict in which it may engage." They hoped to participate "as freely, loyally and cheerfully as if we were native born citizens, of this, in our estimation, the greatest nation beneath the sun."[61] No doubt responding to the jingoistic and anti-alien sentiment of these times, they strongly asserted their desire to be seen as "an asset and not a liability."[62]

Membership in community organizations also demonstrated Basques' loyalty and desire to appear patriotic. A local newspaper's headline described bond purchasing: "Membership Increased 25 in Saturday's Campaign; Nine Spanish-Americans Help." Each member of the Ada County Limit Club either already owned or pledged to purchase the maximum amount of war savings stamps, with a maturity value of $1,000 [$11,600 in 2014]. The paper praised the enthusiasm "met with from Spanish-Americans, many of them foreign born." The new members met at a small pool hall belonging to John Archabal (note the Americanization of his actual name, Juan Achabal) and agreed to the pledges after a brief presentation by the Ada Limit Club committee, who were especially pleased "that so many of these men were willing to support the government in this manner."[63]

In a separate article, others praised respected members of the sheep industry for their subscriptions to Ada County Liberty Bonds. "Two well known Ada county sheepmen, Sam Ballantyne, and Jose Mendiola, each bought $10,000 [$233,000 in 2014] worth . . . bring[ing] those representing the sheep industry to well past $80,000 [$1,860,000 in 2014]." Moreover, the article highlighted Mendiola as "the third sheepman of Spanish extraction to respond with a large loan, but there are many who have taken smaller loans and intimated that they may take more later." The chairman of the Liberty Bond drive stated, "It is gratifying to see these representatives of a great industry respond so freely in the country's hour of need, there isn't a class of people anywhere who are more loyal."[64]

Finally, the Americanization and loyalty drive did not only involve men; women and children also participated. A paper reported, "Entertainment Begins Boise Organization's Attempt to Get Acquainted with Other Races." To get familiar with the foreign-born women of the city, the Americanization Committee of the Good Citizenship Club invited "about 20 of the Basque women" to gather with leaders from the Columbian Club, the Catholic Women's League, and the state regent of the Daughters of the American Revolution. The paper reported that "the success of the party was due to the enthusiastic co-operation of the teachers of Lincoln and Central schools, who drilled the Basque children in songs and dances, which they gave in the afternoon on the stage at Carnegie Hall."[65]

The Decision

These activities continued in towns such as Boise and demonstrated the Basque community's desire for acceptance. However, the court case continued as well and exhibited the experience of another segment of the Basque population. On March 18, 1918, over three and a half years after

US Supreme Court Justice Louis Brandeis. (Harris & Ewing Collection at the Library of Congress.)

Omaechevarria had been cited for trespassing, Justice Louis Brandeis issued the decision affirming the conviction and again handing a victory to the cattlemen.[66]

Regarding cattle and sheep grazing on the same land, Brandeis wrote that "in arid and semi-arid regions cattle will not graze, nor can they thrive, on ranges where sheep are allowed to graze extensively." Whereas Omaechevarria's attorneys argued that the statute used in this case remained inconsistent both with the Fourteenth Amendment and with the Act of Congress of February 25, 1885, Brandeis held that "the police power of the State extends over the federal public domain, at least when there is no legislation by Congress on the subject." Moreover, on the issue of defining trespassing on the boundaries of the range, Brandeis again sided with the cattlemen and claimed that "men familiar with range conditions and desirous of observing the law will have little difficulty in determining what is prohibited by it."[67]

The defense had also argued that the statute in question directly conflicted with the Act of Congress of February 25, 1885, which had been designed to prevent illegal fencing of public lands. They maintained that the cattlemen's assertions amounted to claiming exclusive use and occupancy of the public lands, which the 1885 act prohibited. Again, Brandeis favored the state. "No case has been found in which it was even urged that these state statutes were in conflict with this act of Congress." He asserted: "Congress has not conferred upon citizens the right to graze stock upon the public lands. The Government has merely suffered the lands to be so used." Furthermore, "It is because the citizen possesses no such right that it was held by this court that the Secretary of Agriculture might, in the exercise of his general power to regulate forest reserves, exclude sheep and cattle therefrom." With this Brandeis concluded: "All the objections urged against the validity of the statute are unsound. The judgment of the Supreme Court of Idaho is Affirmed."[68]

Conclusion

While we know the outcome of *Omaechevarria v. State of Idaho,* we do not know what happened to the defendant. What did he think of the decision? Did he return to the Basque Country or stay in America? Did he wonder why the court heard testimony from everyone involved in the case except him? Omaechevarria's story serves as a metaphor for countless western laborers stuck in the middle of power disputes.

While this court decision affirmed the cattlemen's position, the true termination for the itinerant herder came with the passing of the Taylor Grazing Act in 1934. It closed the open range. Anthropologist William Douglass has commented that Basques mark this legislation as an Old Testament–New Testament division of their time in the American West. The *Omaechevarria* case represented one more step toward that landmark legislation. In this case, when cattle, sheep, and Basque interests converged, cattle interests won.[69]

One cannot separate land policy from the other seminal piece of legislation that drastically impacted Basque immigration—the Immigration Act of 1924. In the buildup to passage of this legislation, "ethnicity got linked with disability." One quota supporter stated of immigrants: "In every face there was something wrong. . . . There were so many sugar loaf heads, moon faces, slit mouths, lantern jaws, and goose bill noses that one might imagine a malicious jinn had amused himself by casting human beings in a set of skew-molds discarded by the Creator." Historian Barbara Young Welke argues that "where white men's status as lawmakers protected the borders of belonging, the structure of law masked the breadth and depth of able white male privilege as well as the subordination of disabled persons, racialized others, and women."[70]

Basques were a later immigrant ethnic group that attempted to do what earlier immigrants had done—exploit resources for financial gain. The prejudiced testimony about and discriminatory actions toward Basques denoted their status within the racial and ethnic hierarchy in the West. They revealed a nativism that supported squatter's rights. Anthony Mora explains in *Border Dilemmas* that this occurs when a group uses "imaginings of geography and ancestry as a means to claim a native identity."[71]

For Basques, acceptance required land ownership, naturalization, and assimilation into American culture. Those Basques willing and able to meet these standards adapted, and the Basque-American identity evolved with it. It paralleled the experience of other groups. In 1924, Native American Coleman Byrd declared, "The time has come to show that we are more than just Indians, but good Americans." Substitute the word "Basque" for "Indians" and the sentiment is the same. This era marked a division between Basques who accepted this notion and others who viewed the price as too high and returned to the Basque Country.[72]

While there was much actual physical violence in the sheep and cattle battles, *Omaechevarria v. State of Idaho* played out in a courtroom. Daniel Herman argues that in the 1880s and 1890s cattlemen "tried to control the violence and shift the battle to the range associations, courts, and state legislatures" where they enjoyed "favorable influence and control."[73] This movement away from the gun in an attempt to appear more civilized ultimately increased the government's power. But then the battle was fought over who ran the government and which branches gained influence. This increased government influence ran contrary to the rugged individualism that many considered an essential element of the American West.

This chapter and the two preceding ones have delineated the borders of belonging in the West. The reality challenged mythical images and demonstrated how the government facilitated western expansion and mediated conflicts. The next three chapters trace how these forces evolved to play central roles in the ongoing development of the region. At times various forces clashed as diverse interests attempted to co-opt the mythical story and influence government decisions to favor their interests. The weight of the western myth and role of government shifted considerably in the seventy years between the two sets of episodes of this study. Stories told from the first era generated the American western mythology that so heavily influenced the thoughts and behavior of those in future episodes. Tracing this shift makes evident how the myth moved from story source to active character and how the government became its interpreter.

CHAPTER FIVE

The Power of Myth, Marketing, and Government in the West

It was an experience from when I was twelve years old and living outside of America that first drew me into the field of American western history, although at the time I did not understand the impact of this event.

It was recess, and swarms of kids buzzed the playground. Students had recently returned for the new school year in the fall of 1974. My father, a university professor, directed a study-abroad program and moved our family from Boise, Idaho, to live in the small, remote (Spanish) Basque town of Oñati for a year. After we got settled the first month, school began. My parents and I, along with a local administrator from the university, packed into his white matchbox-size car, wound our way through the narrow medieval cobblestone streets, and parked in front of the town square's gazebo, facing the school. As I exited the automobile the students swarmed around me like gnats to light on a summer evening. I was the first American they had ever met. The students tugged at my sweater, grabbed onto my arms, rattling nonstop Spanish. The only word I understood was "Americano! Americano!" And then, interestingly, all of the children began playing out cowboy-and-Indian scenes.

It happened twice more that day. I climbed the outside steps with my teacher, and we made our way to the fourth floor. Behind a door, chaotic noises exploded. When I opened the door, silence descended, all movement stopped, and forty pairs of eyes burned holes through me. Although I was a foot taller and fifty pounds heavier than any other student—a twelve-year-old seventh grader—I was placed in the fourth grade because my parents were convinced it would be easier for me to learn Spanish there. As I waited, an oversized desk was brought in and placed in the middle of the room, and there I sat, a giant in the land of Lilliputians. (I could almost read the bubbles above their head: "They really do grow them big in America.") "Americano, Americano," the boys shouted, again making the gestures of cowboys and Indians. Disoriented, not understanding a thing, and unable to communicate with anyone, my mind wandered throughout the morning. When the plaza clock struck twelve, students began grabbing coats and getting ready to go. Not knowing what to do, I blindly followed and gradually understood that it was lunchtime and we were headed home. Like the Pied Piper I made my way down the main street with all my classmates who lived in my half of town in tow behind me. They laughed and giggled and tugged and spoke to me. The only words I understood were "Americano, Americano," and again came the cowboys and Indians.

This was the first time in my life I had been called an American. What did it mean? I had never really thought about it. Whenever anyone in America asked, "What are you?" I responded with my ethnic ancestry. But thinking about it later, I wondered why the students immediately chose cowboys and Indians as their identifier for me? I grew up four blocks from the Idaho state capital and knew nothing about cowboys and Indians. I later learned the source of their perceptions. American westerns dominated the offerings in the local theater, and the popular western television show *Gunsmoke* appeared daily on one of the two channels they received. But what was the appeal for them, and so many others?

Despite attempts by historians to tell a more accurate history of the West, the masses yearned for the myths. Even though very few miners actually made money in the gold rush, and successful claims generally resulted in the invasion of big capital and the creation of wage earners, the crowd cheered for the solitary prospector to hit it big. Although many ranches evolved into large corporations—a number of them foreign owned—and cowboys actually worked as poorly paid wage laborers, the public loved tales of the range and romantic stories around the fire. Why did western legends resonate so deeply with Americans and millions of others around the world?

They found in the western frontier of the 1800s the setting for the national epic, a scene of excitement, romance, and inspiration. The western story provided a unique set of imperishable core values: individualism, self-reliance, democracy, and a defined sense of right and wrong. It became America's Trojan War, her Arthurian cycle, her Song of Roland. The British writer Jenni Calder described the belief in the American West "not as historical fact but as historical force." In 1900, ten million people lived west of the Mississippi, and sixty-six million lived east of it. The large percentage of Americans who lived in the East witnessed in the thirty-five years after the Civil War mass industrialization, urbanization, and concentration of wealth. Certainly these factors more directly shaped their lives than the frontier experience.[1]

However, easterners created western stories in the hope of transferring to the West what had already been lost in the "city on the hill" of the East. The West offered Americans the sense of a common heritage and mission. When a nation cannot resolve inherent conflicts by rational analysis, myths become the glue to bind it together. While other societies reaffirm themselves through religious rituals and other traditions, Americans have accomplished this, at least in part, through a return to faith in the land of the West. Southwest literature and history scholar Carl Sonnichsen argues that the creation of these stories grows out of a "natural and normal hunger for a heroic past." The western story filled a gap for Americans, who did not have a thousand-year history. The imaginative journey to the primitive West rehabilitated modern values and reoriented Americans toward a version of progress that supposedly avoided "over-civilization" and decadence. Life in the West could restore authenticity, moral order, and masculinity.[2]

Yet the dissonance between myth and reality meant that marketers sanitized real-life characters. "Wild Bill" Hickok was actually a cold-blooded killer who spent most of his time gambling and chasing prostitutes. Martha "Calamity Jane" Canary lived as a sad transvestite alcoholic, reduced to exhibiting herself as a sideshow freak. If no actual archetype existed, then it could be created; show managers fabricated the history of Phoebe Anne Oakley. Born in Ohio, she had never been in the West before she joined Buffalo Bill Cody's show.[3]

One of the quickest events to be mythologized was "Custer's Last Stand." In his *Complete Life of George A. Custer,* published the same year as Custer's defeat in 1876, Frederick Whittaker depicted Custer as the "brave cavalier, the Christian soldier," and valiant defender of civilization against savage hordes. He stood as a martyr to the weak policy that appeased savages, and embodied the subordination of race and class of all kinds. Because no whites survived, the encounter became a metaphor for the conflict between whites and nonwhites, capital and labor. In the hands of James Gordon Bennett, owner-editor of the *New York Herald,* "Custer's Last Stand" became a story useful for denouncing all kinds of enemies of the social order. Bennett denounced the Sioux as "communistic"; he compared Indian violence with that of labor radicals; and he made lower-class tramps and vagrants the equivalent of savages.[4]

At times myths even shaped reality. In 1849, Kit Carson ventured out with a search party to rescue a woman providentially named Mrs. White, whom Jicarilla Apaches had captured. By the time the party caught up with the Indians, it was too late; they had killed Mrs. White. But Carson discovered a surprising souvenir: "We found a book in the camp," he reported, "the first of the kind I had ever seen, in which I was represented as a great hero, slaying Indians by the hundreds." The real Carson struggled to live up to his fictionalized literary persona; it became his standard of comparison. Yet, the story does not stop there. We learned of this episode from a book written by the actual Carson to capitalize on the market for the mythic Carson. "The mythic Carson shaped the actual Carson in his image."[5]

But perhaps nothing depicted the western stories and legends to a wider audience than did the Buffalo Bill Show. The intertwining of his life and the show tell us much about the power of western stories. Born in Iowa, on February 26, 1846, William F. Cody went west to seek his fortune as a prospector in the Pikes Peak gold rush in 1859. Largely unsuccessful, Cody joined the Pony Express and later fought on the Union side in the Civil War. After the war, Cody hunted buffalo to feed the construction crews building the railroads, where he reportedly earned the nickname "Buffalo Bill" in a shooting match. By Cody's count, he killed 4,280 buffalo during the seventeen months he hunted.[6]

In 1868 Cody returned to the army as a chief of scouts for the Fifth Cavalry and fought in numerous battles against Native Americans. While

Poster of Buffalo Bill's Wild West and Congress of Rough Riders of the World. (Library of Congress Prints and Photographs Division.)

his reputation for skill and bravery grew in real life, his true fame came from the dime novels of Ned Buntline (pen name of the writer E. Z. C. Judson). Beginning in 1869, Buntline created a part factual, part fictional Buffalo Bill who "ranked with Davy Crockett, Daniel Boone, and Kit Carson in the popular imagination." Buntline later convinced Cody to assume this created role in his play *The Scouts of the Plains.* Cody proved a natural showman and stayed with the show for eleven seasons, while he also produced the first edition of his wildly popular autobiography.

In between seasons Cody returned to the West, escorting rich easterners and European nobility on hunting expeditions. In 1876, the army called him back for the campaign that followed Custer's defeat at the Little Big Horn. Cody added another chapter to his legend with a "duel" with the Cheyenne chief Yellow Hair, which he characteristically "embroidered into a melodrama—*Buffalo Bill's First Scalp for Custer*—for the fall theater season."

Finally, in 1883, Cody created his own show: Buffalo Bill's Wild West. The circus-like extravaganza "dramatized some of the most picturesque elements of frontier life." Half history, half fantasy, it included "a buffalo hunt with real buffalos, an Indian attack on the Deadwood stage with real Indians, a Pony Express ride, and at the climax, a tableau presentation of Custer's Last Stand in which some Lakota who had actually fought in the battle played a part." One season even included "the slayer of General Custer," Chief Sitting Bull. Cody later played to international audiences and included a "Congress of Rough Riders of the World," with cossacks, lancers, and other Old World cavalrymen, along with the vaqueros, cowboys, and

Buffalo Bill and Sitting Bull. (Library of Congress Prints and Photographs Division.)

Indians of the American West. The show drew enormous crowds in the United States and in Europe over its thirty-year run.

Cody again combined his theatrical work with real life when, in 1890, the army called him back during the Indian uprisings associated with the Ghost Dance. Indians from his troupe accompanied him and "proved effective peacemakers, and even traveled to Wounded Knee after the massacre to help restore order." The juxtaposition of Cody's show with his real life, the involvement of Native Americans actually involved in the previous battles, and his recurring ventures into the West demonstrate the blurred line between western fantasy and western reality.

What drew the thousands who went to each show? While Frederick Jackson Turner described the role of the frontier in creating Americans at the World's Columbian Exposition in 1893, the "real" story played out in the show across the street from the exposition. The Buffalo Bill show romanticized a frontier past that "pitted civilization and savagery under their respective racial standards of white and red." It provided the justification for "Americans' Darwinian superiority" and authorized an "imperial future in which the United States would lead civilized nations in a worldwide struggle with savage races." This vision paralleled that of the political and cultural leadership of the country just prior to the wave of "new" immigration. The message underlying the show fit nicely alongside Josiah Strong's *Our Country* and his teaching that God prepared "in our Anglo-Saxon civilization the die with which to stamp the peoples of the earth."[7]

A study of the show's presentation reveals "the stories that Americans told themselves about themselves" within the confines of the Wild West arena. The ritualized acts—when Buffalo Bill saved a stagecoach from marauding Indians at the last moment, when Annie Oakley proved her sharpshooting skill, or a mock re-creation of the "Battle of San Juan Hill"—affirmed the myth of "American-ness." The performances filled the audience with notions of American exceptionalism, a ruggedness and individuality capable of greatness and destined to fulfill it.[8]

The act attracted all classes and age groups. It created cohesion in an increasingly heterogeneous nation by identifying the Indian as the non-American "other" and provided "the shared lexicon and sign-language of the Wild West symbolic universe." Moreover, Americans eagerly absorbed the overt connection between manhood and racial dominance. Nobody embodied it better than Buffalo Bill, young and sturdy, "a remarkable specimen of manly beauty, with the brain to conceive and the nerve to execute." The program proclaimed "Buffalo Bill par excellence is the exemplar of the strong and unique traits that characterize a true American frontiersman." Eastern viewers experienced vicariously the wild frontier; and with the rifle as an "aid to civilization," the savage was tamed and Americans were positioned to function hegemonically in the twentieth century.[9]

By the end of the run of the Buffalo Bill show, nearly fifty rivals performed imitations throughout the United States and Europe. Historian David Murdoch claims that "Buffalo Bill Cody's contribution to preparing the ground for the myth of the West is difficult to overestimate. He did more than any other individual to re-create the image of the Wild West in the minds of the American public." These stories helped nationalize the West; they sewed together what regional differences had separated.[10]

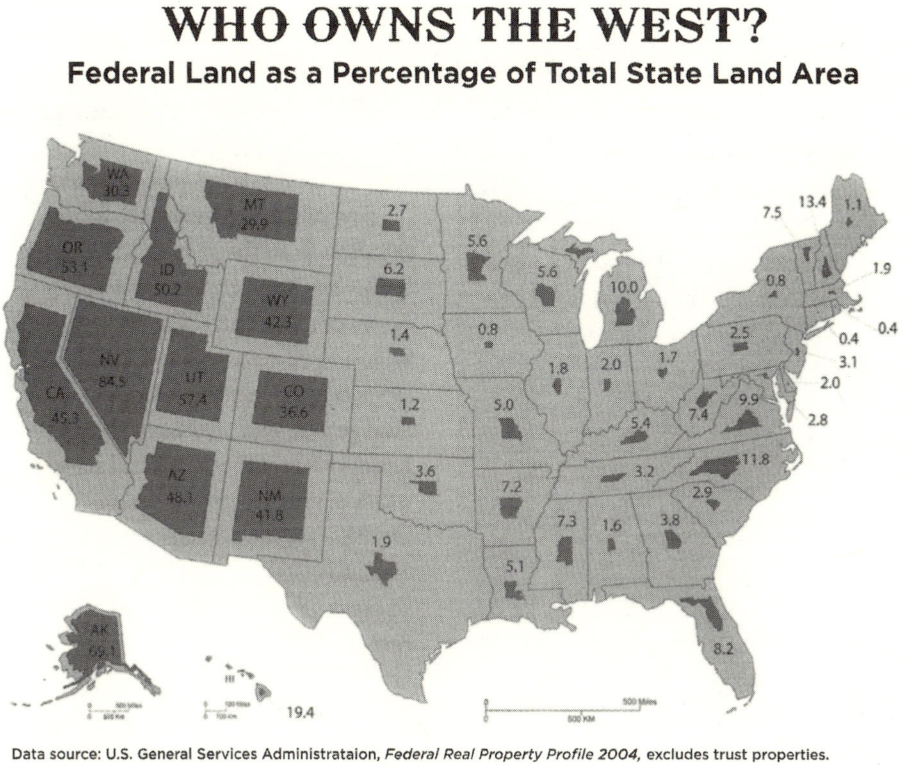

Map of federal land as a percentage of total state land area. (US General Services Administration, *Federal Real Property Profile, 2004*.)

The Federal Government and Popular Culture

While so many of Buffalo Bill's characters epitomized the rugged individual, the reality remained far different. In fact, the federal government impacts the lives of westerners more than those in any other region in America. Its influence pervades the American West. In land ownership alone, the federal government controls properties that vary in size from roadside picnic tables to the Hoover Dam. Although many in the West hate to admit reliance upon government, its actions transformed the region from a bit player in national and international economies at the end of the nineteenth century to a central participant by the twenty-first.

Throughout most of the nineteenth century, the western states and territories operated as isolated regions organized around provincial trading centers—what historian Robert Wiebe described as "an archipelago of island communities." Comparable to the colonies prior to the Revolutionary War, most subregions in the West maintained stronger ties to the East than to each other. However, by the end of nineteenth century the role of the federal government began to change, as did regional identity.[11]

After the drought and depression of the 1890s, federal agencies increasingly initiated development on their own. Some historians dubbed the first two decades of the twentieth century the era of "the federally sustained frontier." Actions taken by the federal government allowed farmers, ranchers, and lumbermen to exploit areas previously unused or unsettled by Americans. Government involvement in water plans, national parks, and a canal through the Isthmus of Panama demonstrated that its role had moved beyond facilitator and mediator, and it projected this role at the world's fairs in Portland in 1905, Seattle in 1909, and San Francisco in 1915.[12]

The government's involvement in water projects is a good example of this active participation. In 1902, Nevada's appropriately named representative Francis Newlands helped pass legislation that established the Reclamation Service, a bureau that initiated construction of irrigation projects throughout the West. Prior to this effort, communities or for-profit corporations sponsored most of the canals and water developments themselves. However, with the Newlands Reclamation Act government sold property in sixteen western states and deposited the proceeds in an "arid land reclamation fund" to pay for major irrigation projects. The resources available to the Reclamation Service allowed it to take on projects such as the Theodore Roosevelt Dam on the Salt River of Arizona and Arrowrock Dam on the Boise River in Idaho, the world's tallest when completed in 1915, and later the Owyhee Dam. These projects opened land previously deemed worthless and allowed towns to rise up out of sagebrush.[13]

During this same era, the federal government also aggressively gave land away—"like a store keeper trying to move backed-up inventory." For example, the Enlarged Homestead Act of 1909 increased the farmstead grant from 160 to 320 acres while reducing the title transfer period from five years to three. Additionally, the Stock-Raising Homestead Act of 1916 increased the grant of rangeland to 640 acres. The federal government published flyers that listed available homestead acreage in each western

Frederic Remington's sculpture ***Bronco Buster,*** created in 1909. (National Archives and Records Administration.)

county, explained the simple procedures for homestead entry, and settlers moved in droves onto marginal lands. The results: in the first two decades of the twentieth century, farmers homesteaded more acreage than in the entire nineteenth century.[14]

The three-century frontier expansion climaxed with World War I. The insatiable demand for food, lumber, and minerals linked the warring world with the resource-rich West. For example, the western share of lumber production increased from 10 to 35 percent, while petroleum jumped from 29 to 68 percent. The wealth drew more people, and as the West grew, so did the legends and stories, with new genres with which to portray these themes.[15]

David Murdoch argues that Theodore Roosevelt, the painter Frederic Remington, and the writer Owen Wister served as the most important easterners to spread the image of the West. All three traveled west to deal with personal problems; Murdoch identifies in their journey a nostalgia that turned them into deliberate and self-conscious mythmakers. "If I had not

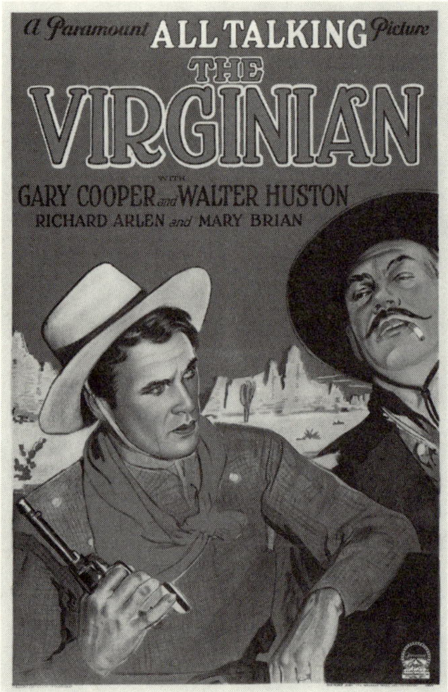

Movie poster for *The Virginian,* 1929.

spent my year in North Dakota, I never would have become President of the United States," Roosevelt claimed. He believed that the time transformed him from "an aristocrat to a democrat," and provided him with the aura of a man of the people. Remington artistically represented what Roosevelt projected about the West, and when Roosevelt lamented its degradation as a national tragedy, Remington showed them what had been lost.[16]

Although Remington was most often identified with the West, the painter, sculptor, author, and illustrator spent most of his life in the East. "It was Remington's connection with the eastern fantasy of the West, and not a true knowledge of its history and people, that his admirers responded to." Certainly his technical skill at depicting the beauty of western landscapes drew appreciation, but his "insight into the heroic nature of American settlers . . . made him great." In his representations of "cowboys and cavalrymen, bronco busters and braves," Remington portrayed "the life and death struggles of the individual against overwhelming odds" and in the process inspired millions. He charged his subjects with such "detail, movement, and energy they seemed ready to leap to life." His depictions of "independence, individualism, and stoic heroism" helped "immortalize the western experience."[17]

While Roosevelt spoke and Remington painted, Owen Wister wrote within the thematic legacy of James Fenimore Cooper to portray western myths and themes. In 1902, Wister penned *The Virginian,* which became one of the classic literary westerns. The novel portrayed cowboys imbued with "wild and manly" traits. "In their flesh our natural passions ran tumultuous; but often in their spirit sat hidden a true nobility, and often beneath its unexpected shining their figures took a heroic stature." Westerners got drunk, frequented prostitutes, gambled, slept with other men's wives, and killed each other, but their life and violence was, nonetheless, somehow "pure." The impact of Wister's book might best be seen from the comment of one cowboy: "Well maybe we didn't talk that way before Mr. Wister wrote his book, but we sure all talked that way after the book was published."[18]

Other writers capitalized on this style. Between 1912 and 1939, Zane Grey authored seventy-eight novels that sold twenty million copies. By the 1950s the western novel constituted about 11 percent of all works of fiction published in the United States. While Grey and later Max Brand achieved overwhelming success in this genre, their numbers pale in comparison to those of Louis L'Amour, one of the world's most popular authors, whose books sold more than one hundred million copies.[19]

However, the stories in these books differed significantly from the reality in the West. By the 1930s the life of the cowboy had become more popularly ritualized in the rodeo setting than in real life, and both Boston Garden and Madison Square Garden hosted rodeos that lasted for nearly three weeks. In New York crowds approached a quarter of a million, as families and sponsors flocked to the arenas to experience western American values. The 1930s and 1940s also marked the peak of popularity for "dude ranches," where urban dwellers vacationed in the West, riding the range and trailing cattle.[20]

Perhaps no historical event changed the role of the federal government in this region more than the Depression of the 1930s. While many western politicians continued to hail their rugged individualism born of the frontier, they also accepted the federal assistance that came with the AAA, CCC, WPA, and a host of other federal programs. Statistics compiled by historian Leonard Arrington reveal that support from New Deal programs had a greater relative impact in the West than in any other part of the United States. The CCC, the Civilian Conservation Corps, enrolled seventy-five thousand on Arizona Indian reservations and another five thousand in

Movie poster for *The Vanishing American,* 1925.

twenty-nine Indian conservation camps in Idaho. The rural electrification programs, which began in 1935 and continued after the 1940s, increased the number of Idaho farms with power from 30 to 54 percent. These programs set precedents for increased government involvement and regional planning.[21]

The Taylor Grazing Act exemplified changed governmental policy. It marked the end of the era of land distribution; within two years the act removed 142 million acres of western lands from potential sale and reserved them for grazing under federal control. Although administered at the district level and benefiting local power interests, the act nonetheless placed the land into federal government management rather than private use and increased government's prominence in the process.[22]

Besides establishing this land policy, the government sponsored projects on a scale no other party could attempt. A series of dams in the 1930s, which included the Boulder/Hoover on the Colorado, the Fort Peck Dam on the Missouri, and the Grand Coulee Dam on the Columbia, permanently changed the role of the government in the West and removed any lingering thoughts of a hands-off policy. The federal government owned 99 percent of Alaska in 1944, 87 percent of Nevada, 66 percent of Idaho, and over 50 percent of Arizona, Utah, Wyoming, and Oregon. It also employed the greatest number of people. For example, in California in 1930, 5 percent of residents drew their personal income from the federal government; a decade later it was 10 percent; and by 1945 it was 45 percent. Subsequent battles in the Pacific during World War II "made the federal budget the essential drive wheel of western growth."[23]

The reality of government involvement in the West differed greatly from the West portrayed in the media, particularly as presented in the new medium of film. The western remains the single most popular Hollywood film genre. Perhaps a total of seven thousand westerns have been made since the first true western film narrative, the *Great Train Robbery* in 1903. As with western novels, these films affirmed the values of individualism, self-reliance, and living off the land. But rather than portraying it as a three-centuries-long conquest of the wilderness, these movies focused on the thirty peak years of the cowboy era. The audience for these films reached far beyond the US territorial boundaries and helps explain later perspectives of America. In 1954, American films accounted for 40 percent of those viewed by western European nations. In fact, the proportion of screen time devoted to American films reached 65 percent in Italy, 70 percent in Britain, and 85 percent in Ireland—and 22 percent of those films were Westerns. By 1958, Hollywood was turning out a western a week, and familiar characters appeared many times: ten films had Daniel Boone as the central character; Davy Crockett appeared in eleven; General Custer in thirty-four; Billy the Kid in forty-four; and Buffalo Bill Cody in forty-seven. No one embodied the traits of the American West more popularly than John Wayne, who made eighty-nine films with a western motif. "No conventionally religious mission society . . . has ever come close to matching the achievements of the Hollywood western in global proselytizing and conversion."[24]

Besides providing content for the silver screen, the romanticism and emotion of the western myths made them irresistible to politicians. Teddy Roosevelt consistently presented an image of the robust and active westerner in his presidency. John F. Kennedy used the term the "New Frontier" to represent his view of America's future. Lyndon Johnson was photographed in the saddle on his ranch and constantly used western metaphors in his speeches. Yet perhaps no one played the role of the westerner any better than Ronald Reagan. An actor in westerns himself and a ranch owner in California, the line between his acting roles and his life roles became so blurred as to be indistinguishable.[25]

These politicians sought an audience that marketers had targeted for decades. John Charles Fremont worked as one of the earliest great publicists of the West. His fictionalized inventions of Kit Carson, Jesse James, and Billy the Kid enjoyed immense success and served as precursors of efforts to capitalize on the western image. From the 1870s to the present day, western icons have helped sell beef, whiskey, tobacco, automobiles, and countless other products throughout the world. American music shifted from the South toward the West in the 1930s, as singers such as Tex Ritter, Gene Autry, and Roy Rogers added a cowboy hat and sang of western themes. In 1954, advertiser Leo Burnett invented one of the most recognized commercial western images—the Marlboro Man. Most recently, Ralph Lauren bought a portion of land on the western range and rebuilt it to match his imagined West. Lauren then offered to make over a nearby twentieth-century town in a fictionalized western style: giving an entirely new meaning to the notion of cleaning up your town.[26]

One of the greatest marketing schemes since the Buffalo Bill show came with Walt Disney's Frontierland in California. If the Buffalo Bill show stood as an exceptional metaphor for the power of the myth and its marketing at the turn of the century, Frontierland did so at the mid-twentieth century. Disney's writings suggest a Turnerian view of the frontier; he felt that both his own life and that of the nation had been affected, even forged, by the frontier experience. For him the East could not escape its European roots tainted by Old World values, while the West offered a tabula rasa, ready for new beginnings and opportunities. His romanticizing of the "Old West" helped lay the groundwork for the "New West" of amenity tourism and chic residence. This vision of the region made it ripe for both exploitation and preservation of its beauty.[27]

This effort to conserve and preserve paralleled a revision by mythmakers of traditional stories of the West. Mythic formulations are "at every moment implicitly subject to tests of validity or truth." Consequently, as societal attitudes changed in the 1960s and 1970s, western films did, too. "Savagery" symbolized by outlaws or Indians became good, and "civilization" represented by the town or farmers or the US Cavalry became either evil or weak. The defeat of the Indians and the conquest of Billy the Kid represented oppression over freedom—the meanings had been reversed. Films such as *The Searchers, Shane, High Noon, The Left Handed Gun, Pat Garrett and Billy the Kid, One-Eyed Jacks, Little Big Man*, and *Dances with Wolves* exemplified the reaction against conformity and the desire to review the West in this light.[28]

In the 1990s the movie *City Slickers* portrayed one of the hundreds of dude ranches that offered easterners the "real" experience of the West. The movie reinforced the hope that the West would continue to provide therapeutic, medicinal, and restorative forces. Perhaps the attitudes and actions of Ted Turner rather than Frederick Jackson Turner best portray the viewpoint at this time. Ted Turner bought a large ranch where the manager, Bud Griffith, had spent three decades building corrals, fences, and cattle pens. In an attempt to return the land to open terrain, Turner hired Griffith to undo all his work. "If I want to save the West, I am going to have to buy it," Turner said.[29]

While individuals such as Ted Turner took action, the government also created opportunities for larger numbers of the public to recreate and connect to the land—through national parks. In 1920, almost one million visitors traveled to western national parks; in 2010, 3.6 million visited Yellowstone National Park alone. With the advent of interstate highways and cheaper motels, the wilderness moved beyond the domain of the wealthy. As the twentieth century came to a close, "less and less of the West fit the description of the true wilderness, but more and more Americans believed they needed a pilgrimage to that special environment. Parks allowed people to step back in time."[30]

However, as larger numbers visited and many argued for more recreational opportunities, others questioned the impact on farming and ranching communities. In a movement of the late 1970s known as the Sagebrush Rebellion, ranchers, farmers, and mining and timber interests expressed fear of the ever-increasing role of the federal government and its perceived push to preserve and conserve natural resources at the expense of local investment and employment opportunities. Environmentalists, on the other hand, looked toward the federal government the way early settlers had: they hoped to find in federal agencies the necessary support and protection of nature.

Although within the United States westerners traditionally affiliated the least with institutional religion, at times belief in the mythic Old West resembled more conventional religious doctrines. In the western legend the hero mediates between civilization and savagery—culture and nature, order and chaos. He employs the gunfighting skill of the frontier West to establish the peaceable society of civilized values that will succeed the frontier. Hollywood and dozens of novelists made millions as they reworked this formula through countless versions in their storytelling. "Myth uses the past as an idealized example in which heroic achievement in the past is linked to another in the future of which the reader is the potential hero." Claude Dallas, the focus of the next chapter, loved these stories. It was within these formative forces that this midwesterner moved west and became the center of one of the most spectacular cases in Idaho history.[31]

CHAPTER SIX

Claude Dallas: The Myth Comes to Life

Growing up, Claude Dallas loved to read and imagine the stories of the West. He soaked in the characters of Louis L'Amour's books, ventured west with E. H. Staffelbach in *Toward Oregon,* and met with Indians in *The Horsemen of the Plains* by Joseph Altsheler and *The White Feather* by Merritt Allen. He could not get enough. With time he added Zane Grey and Jack London novels and repeatedly checked out every book on the West he came across, including two western classics—Owen Wister's *The Virginian* and Andy Adam's *The Log of a Cowboy.* Someday he hoped to live in the West as these characters did.[1]

Claude Lafayette Dallas was born on March 11, 1950, in Winchester, Virginia. Named after his father, Claude was one of nine children of a Catholic family that moved often. Claude Sr. worked as an engineer for Firestone in Ohio, later operated a dairy farm in the Upper Peninsula of northern Michigan, and in 1962 returned to Ohio at Mount Gilead, where he worked for the state on bridge design and construction. From Claude's youth, Claude Sr. exposed his son to guns, being outdoors, and hunting and trapping. By age nine he had killed his first deer. "He shot a 30.06. I was proud of him, and he was awfully proud of hisself," remembered Claude Sr. "He lived on the creek and the river—strictly outdoors." The first time he heard the song

"North to Alaska," he told his father, "That's where I am going." In high school, his friends thought he dressed like some character from a western novel—flannel shirt, jeans, and work boots, occasionally dress pants. They remembered him as shy, "the most silent guy in the class." While sports or cars interested others, Dallas meticulously worked his trap lines, catching fox, raccoons, muskrats, and occasionally a mink. For his graduation picture, Claude wore an old-fashioned string bow tie. "He had that dream from the start," said classmate David Hartpence. "He wanted to get established as a mountain man."[2]

Playin' Cowboy

While the rest of his classmates worried about being sent to Vietnam, Claude fulfilled his lifelong dream and traveled west. He hitchhiked most of the way to California, where he eventually found work as a cowboy on the Alvord Ranch. "He had been searching for the Alvord all his life," wrote author Jeff Long. Although Claude had no experience working on a ranch, he toiled relentlessly to prove himself and learn the lifestyle. When machinery broke down and others stopped working, Claude plowed ahead and labored by hand. Through sheer determination he completed in two days a week's assigned work. He willingly took on the least desirable jobs. Hoyt Wilson, the owner of the Alvord, testified: "Every morning before daylight he'd be packing seventy and eighty pounds of steel posts and barbwire on foot to a section five miles and a thousand vertical feet up the mountainside, then descending at dark. We knew a good thing when we saw it." Hoyt's wife, Coco Wilson, concurred: "He's the hardest worker I'd ever known." She described Dallas as well mannered, levelheaded, intelligent, and a pleasure to talk with. After two years she treated him practically like a son.[3]

Those who worked alongside of him noticed something different; they felt like he was playing a part, was working hard to be someone else. Earlier, Dallas had traveled to town and purchased an outfit "that looked like a lift from a Frederic Remington portrait." "He's playing cowboy," one ranch hand commented, "and he plays it hard." He used outdated cowboy vernacular and with money from his first paychecks bought a centennial Winchester Model 94 rifle, commonly known as "the gun that won the West." He always packed the rifle with him, even when he was performing simple chores. Once he hitchhiked three hundred miles to Reno to have a silversmith construct a silver-mounted spade bit, which had not been used since the turn of the century. Before long fellow workers also noticed that he wore a pistol strapped to his hip in the old western style. One local commented that Dallas "was the only man in decades who wore a gun just to pick up his mail."[4]

While Dallas played the western role, the US government wanted him to play another—the role of soldier. When Dallas failed to report for induction to the military on September 17, 1970, the government issued a warrant for his arrest. His boss, Hoyt Wilson, later argued that Dallas simply lived the way he wanted and failed to feel any responsibility toward the government. "He was doing what he was doing. If they caught him, they caught him," Wilson stated. After nearly two years of working for the Wilsons, Dallas finally confided to them about his draft situation and informed them of his plans to go to Canada. He purchased two horses from the family and loaded one with supplies. For two months he traveled the country and lived off what he carried and caught. It was during this time that Dallas first familiarized himself with the Idaho–Oregon–Nevada (ION) region, traveling the open high desert country as far as Paradise Valley in northeastern Nevada.[5]

Eventually the draft board tracked him down, and on October 15, 1973, three police officers dressed as cowboys arrested him. Dallas argued that the officers treated him poorly and failed to allow him time to care for his animals. Nevertheless, the government transported Dallas back to Ohio and released him into his parents' custody. While preparing for the trial, Dallas's attorney discovered a loophole in the draft board's notification and successfully had the case excused. Although he never was incarcerated, his supporters believed that this experience critically impacted Dallas and furthered his contemptuous attitude toward governmental authority.[6]

After the trial, Dallas returned to the Alvord Ranch, but he informed the Wilsons that he wanted to work for a larger outfit that still "fed their hands out of chuck wagons." He said, "I like sleeping on the ground. I like riding horses that're so wild that you don't dare get off even to take a leak 'cause you might have to walk home." Dallas assured them, "That's the life for me," and he successfully landed a job that met these criteria. With his army surplus overcoat, handmade tapaderas that covered his Levi pants, and a set of silver spurs that decorated the backs of his boots, Dallas looked like he had walked off a movie set.[7]

The first year he apprenticed and learned how to shoe a horse, braid rawhide, reload cartridges, and make his riding gear. In the evenings Dallas devoured Louis L'Amour novels, often reading them three and four times. While others played cards or drank beer, Dallas oiled, polished, and repaired his gear. At a time when many cowboys wore Levi's and tractor-sponsored baseball caps, Dallas looked like something "from the Buffalo Bill show catalogue." Sometimes when he rode near the interstate, motorists stopped and took pictures of him—an opportunity for them to capture the "authentic cowboy." Sipping beer with other buckaroos, he even posed for a picture that appeared in a *National Geographic* study: "The American Cowboy in Life and Legend." When others went to town for their days off, he traveled to Montana to see the Charles Russell western art museum—"a seminarian going to Lourdes." His favorite painting remained "A Bronc to Breakfast," in which a stubborn mount bucks up in front of an early-morning crew similar to the outfit he worked for.[8]

While some thought he overplayed the western motif, his fellow workers always complimented his work ethic and integrity. "Claude's about as good a bunkie as you'll ever meet. Sharp, on time, always there," commented one worker. "I'd trust him with my daughter, my sister, my wife. . . . When we work together he always does the lion's share." Another noted Dallas's polite manner—how he removed his hat upon entering a home and consistently responded, "Yes, ma'am" and "No, sir," when spoken to. A fellow worker stated, "I'm already a Christian, but talking to Claude brings out the depth of my own religious feeling, because he's such a good listener. He never uses foul language. He could have dinner with the governor tonight."[9]

Yet they also noticed that Dallas remained alone. He seemed distant and cold, and never built close relationships with the other workers. Around Christmastime, the hands all went to other places for the holiday, but Dallas stayed at the ranch, noted camp cook Irene Fischer. "I felt so sorry for him because he just seemed so lonesome. I told Walt [her husband], 'There's something really deep in that guy. He's gonna be famous one of these days.' But I meant in the way of something good."[10]

Others noticed that he often treated animals harshly and regularly poached in the wild. One working mate recalled that he never walked around an annoying dog; rather, he would crack it with a stick. One time he knocked out a Labrador, and on another occasion he attacked a stallion with a shoeing hammer and had to be restrained. Dallas also regularly poached and saw nothing wrong with the practice. He maintained that while growing up his family poached, and that even the game warden allowed their practices. Dallas argued that game laws did not apply to subsistence hunters; consequently, he regularly killed deer out of season and employed a seamstress to sew a deerskin outfit. Although the hands enjoyed a surplus of prime beef, Dallas consistently killed wild game and left it at the chuck wagon, which placed the crew in an awkward situation when wardens visited the camp. Dallas believed that since he asked nothing of his fellow countrymen, he remained exempt from tax payment, military service, and hunting laws. Many shook their heads in bewilderment, but no one challenged Dallas on these positions; mostly, they left him alone.[11]

Dallas continued to immerse himself in western ways, especially in firearms. He loved to discuss guns and used shorthand for weapons—the 94, the Python, the 20. He upgraded the .22 trap pistol that he usually wore for a more powerful .357 and filed down the grip to match his hand. "Claude is true Old West," a fellow hand said. "A lot of guys try it, but the first time they have to shave with cold water they change their mind. Claude keeps going after it and after it." While he continued to work hard and earn the respect of his peers, some wondered if he had gone too far. He referred to living in his trailer as being "in camp," and read for hours, engrossed in western works such as Mark Twain's *Roughing It.* One worker commented that when Dallas stared at one of the Charlie Russell prints, "he thinks he is in the painting." They also noticed that his attitude began to change, to harden. His readings started to focus more on works about guns, self-defense, quick-draw, military tactics, and police techniques; he slept with a gun. Dallas grew increasingly bitter toward the government to the point of near paranoia. He claimed, "I just don't want anybody to mess with me. That's why I came west in the first place."[12]

Dallas embodied what Richard Slotkin described when heroic achievement of the past is linked to another in the future, where the reader is the potential hero.[13] His formative years coupled with his move to the West set up these conditions. Dallas's practices later engendered a battle over their suitability in the late twentieth century, with essentially two opposing perspectives of his life—one sympathetic and one quite critical.

From Cowboy to Mountain Man

The West that Dallas sought was not the West he found. Increasingly, the federal government regulated land use, and ranch work practices were modernized. For example, the Bureau of Land Management progressively tightened ranging laws, while ranchers frequently transported cattle by truck rather than employing traditional cattle drives. These changes unsettled Dallas and left him with little alternative but to go to town for work. By the summer of 1970, he was in a small, desolate, sagebrush-filled town in northeastern Nevada, just over the border of Owyhee County, by the name of Paradise Valley. Situated eighteen miles south of Paradise Hill, the town had changed little since its founding in 1863 and the later period when Shoshone Mike and his band sought refuge there. The few buildings that supported the population of eighty residents continued in use from the original days. An old rusted gas pump sat in front of the mercantile—it had pumped gas for Model Ts. The local slogan read, "It ain't heaven, but it's paradise." Others disagreed. Washington Irving once declared this barren, treeless, high desert country "the ruins of the world." Another author added, "Everything here seems to declare that, here man shall not dwell."[14]

The attitudes of the locals tended to match the tough terrain. Traditionally, they blamed their hard times on the sheep industry, but more recently they held corporations and the Bureau of Land Management responsible. Local bar owner and California transplant George Nielsen often mentioned how Mark Twain spent time there when Paradise Hill operated as a stage stop in the mid-1800s. While he loved to reminisce about the past, he also regularly criticized the federal government—specifically the BLM—for its current land practices, which he argued had devastated the area. George Nielsen and Claude Dallas became close friends. Their favorite topics of conversation included guns, horses, game wardens, and the West's demise due to liberalism and government bureaucracy. One local commented: "George is a great guy, but he loves to stir shit, to get something going and then slide out of it himself. And he hates cops, hates authority." Dallas felt the same.[15]

Within this small community and these attitudes, Claude Dallas again established himself. He lived in a small trailer, worked at a variety of jobs, and continued to toy with guns, practicing his shooting "the way others hit a bucket of golf balls." He became an excellent marksman, able to "throw a can out, turn his back to it, then turn around and keep it rolling." Dallas began to shoot with speedloaders, guns with the capacity to fire rounds very quickly. Townspeople overheard him say, "People with the right equipment will be able to go into the mountains and protect themselves."[16]

Before long Dallas and Nielsen shared poaching stories and traded hides. Since moving to the area, Dallas had regularly set traps. Mostly he killed bobcats and sold them at fur auctions for two hundred dollars apiece. Initially he purchased a license to trap in Nevada and generally operated there until he gradually migrated into Idaho to take advantage of opportunities. Government trapper Santy Mendieta approved of Dallas's hunting practices. "We trap the same areas, and he never bothers any of my traps and never picks up any of my coyotes. If he's not an honest man he has plenty of chances to clean me out." However, the Fish and Game Department headquarters in Boise heard rumors to the contrary. Reportedly, Dallas shot a mountain lion near Riddle, Idaho, on the road to the Duck Valley Indian Reservation. One lead officer warned, "That guy Dallas has killed everything from lions to trophy rams to kit fox. Tell your men to be very careful." Meanwhile, from the bar, Nielsen bragged about owning mountain lion pelts. Dallas trapped five of them and sent two east to his father while Fish and Game tried to locate and confiscate the others.[17]

An old-timer critiqued Dallas's trapping practices. "He saturates the mountain with traps, and when you do that, you're gonna catch what's there, period, and trapping's gonna be over in that area for a long time," he warned. "It's like he's more interested in killing than he is in trapping." Once, the old-timer spotted "a rabbit hanging over it [Dallas's trap]. Well, that's illegal," he declared. Dallas even shot wild mustangs and used them for trap bait. To his friends he praised the taste of the meat, but none of them wanted to risk the possible fine or jail time. Some thought it a ridiculous practice—to kill a beautiful wild mustang "for a couple of ratty coyote pelts." Yet Dallas continued the practice.[18]

In March 1976, Dallas finally got caught. A Nevada Fish and Game warden named Dale Elliot found a line of traps baited with wild mustang hair, jackrabbit fur, bones, and other illegal lures. Elliot cited Dallas and required him to pay a one-hundred-dollar fine to retrieve his equipment. But he also praised Dallas's demeanor throughout the ordeal and said he wished others would behave as reasonably. However, months later, Dallas supposedly commented that he allowed Elliot to cite him in order to protect the landowner where he trapped. "Otherwise, I'd have shot him," Dallas allegedly boasted. If Elliot and the other warden had found lion pelts on their second visit, Dallas claimed, "I'd have killed them both." Dallas's rhetoric grew increasingly violent. In Nielsen's bar he purportedly stated, "You can always go out and shoot a BLM man."[19]

Dallas transformed from a cowboy to a mountain man. He trained to walk for hours without tiring, appeared impervious to the heat and cold, and treated public lands and wildlife like personal property. He made comments to his friends about hiding and surviving on his own in the mountains. He declared that a solitary mountain life "[would] be perfect, no government, nobody to bother me, nobody snooping around my camps." He pointed out locations "that would be a good place to hide. You could hide in there for a long time." Or he imagined pursuits: "It'd be fun to be on the run, going from one cache of weapons to the next and fighting it out." One friend acknowledged, "He gave the impression that his caches were already prepared." In the fall of 1980 Dallas confided that if an enemy ever occupied the United States, he planned to hide in the nearby mountains. Just in case, he stockpiled five thousand rounds of ammunition and survival tools.[20]

In the meantime, Dallas continued to poach, practice his shooting, and devour books on handguns. Two of his favorites—*No Second Place Winner* and *Kill or Get Killed*—included tips on how to draw quicker, with the tenet, "Be first or be dead—there is no second place in a gun fight."[21] In town Dallas presented a friend with five new deerskins and asked her to tan them and fashion a buckskin outfit. He even bragged to his friends about reaching the pinnacle of poaching—the grand slam, which required record-class heads from four different kinds of sheep. While complaints from the ION region continued, Dallas failed to stop. In fact, he pledged never to be caught again.[22]

In spring 1980, Dallas canoed along the South Fork of the Owyhee River and identified it as an ideal location to trap. The next winter he returned and bivouacked at Bull Basin in Owyhee County. Dallas believed the area to be "maybe the most remote place in the United States, as far away as you can get." He professed to love the seclusion. To prepare himself for the hard ground, he slept on the floor. In December 1980, three friends—George Nielsen, Craig Carver, and Jim Stevens—assisted Dallas in setting up his camp. Jim Stevens commented to Dallas that he enjoyed the outing and pledged to return for another visit.[23]

The Showdown

No doubt Bull Basin was isolated, but it was also a portion of a federal grazing allotment for Don and Eddy Carlin, who recently had purchased the rights from the Bureau of Land Management. Their ranch, the 45, ran 220 head of cattle on nearly two hundred square miles of public range. Out of this land the Owyhee River had worn away a mile-long canyon, and the Carlins relied on it to provide sheltered winter range and reliable year-round water. To buffer against difficult times, the Carlins also set a few bobcat traps in the basin, which proved profitable, with pelt prices surpassing $250 [$642 in 2014]. The Carlins noticed other trappers had worked the area and identified a number of illegal traps. Since Don Carlin had been cited previously for setting unlawful traps, he wanted to ensure his innocence. Consequently, the Carlins called Bill Pogue, a Fish and Game warden, to appraise the situation.[24]

Idaho Fish and Game warden Bill Pogue. (*Idaho Statesman* Collection, Boise State University Special Collections and Archives. Used by permission of the *Idaho Statesman*.)

Bill Pogue loved this land. Although he had been transferred to another county, he eagerly responded to the call and drove all night to the Carlin ranch. Those who knew Pogue testified that this was typical. The fifty-year-old senior conservation officer passionately protected the Owyhee country from any illegal activity. His friends and coworkers described him as the "last of the real game wardens." He had rejected desk promotions in order to continue the job he loved. Like Claude Dallas he loved reading about the West; Vardis Fisher's elegiac *Mountain Man,* which became the basis for the famous movie *Jeremiah Johnson,* remained one of his favorites. "My brother was born a hundred years too late," his brother Eddie said.[25]

He also loved western art in the Charles Russell style and painted and sold numerous western scenes. Many believed that his art reflected his personality; Pogue drew rough, hardened, western scenes but always with an element that softened the picture. One of his favorites graced the cover of *Idaho Wildlife* magazine, the official publication of the Idaho Department of Fish and Game. It depicted a mountain man standing with a clenched fist around a barbed-wire post. The character looked weathered and hardened, but a teardrop in his eye revealed another side of the man. Since Pogue had sight in only one eye and used dots and lines to ink the paintings, the process took a considerable amount of time.[26]

Similar to Dallas in so many ways, Pogue nevertheless reached many contrary conclusions. Rather than exploiting the land or wild game, Pogue preached protection. He identified poachers as prime examples of those who abused the environment and thought nothing about the future or sustainability, but rather killed for short-term gain. Pogue was not naïve. He fully recognized the $100 million [$257 million in 2014] netted annually from poaching and illicit trade in wildlife parts and wanted to do his part to stop it. Pogue rigorously enforced the law and worked tirelessly to protect these lands and animals.[27]

When Pogue received the call from the Carlins, he gathered his gear and went out the door. He nearly forgot his gun since on principle he had stopped hunting, but as a game warden he remained aware of the extremist "Wild West mentality" of many hunters and the large amount of drinking that often went on in their camps. Because of these dangers, regulations required that wardens carry a gun and never travel solo. Pogue had lobbied for these stipulations. So he put in a late-night call to a colleague named

Idaho Fish and Game warden Conley Elms. (*Idaho Statesman* Collection, Boise State University Special Collections and Archives. Used by permission of the *Idaho Statesman*.)

Conley Elms, who agreed to accompany him, and together they drove to the Carlin ranch.[28]

Like Pogue, Elms loved the outdoors and from birth lived on an old-fashioned ranch without indoor plumbing in the Cascade Mountains of Oregon. Growing up, he spent most of his time outdoors—working, fishing, and hiking in the area. After getting married he took a job in a lumber mill so his wife, Sheryl, could earn her teaching certificate. When she completed her degree and he earned his in wildlife management, the two decided to move to Boise. Above all, Conley wanted to work for the Idaho Department of Fish and Game, and after three years of working part-time and taking other odd jobs he reached his goal. He loved his work. Although not scheduled to be on duty, when other officers failed to respond to Pogue's call, Conley left with him despite his wife wanting him to stay.[29]

Five hours and 175 miles later, Elms and Pogue arrived outside the Carlin ranch house at three in the morning, slept a few hours in bedrolls in the back of their truck, and awoke at dawn to meet with them. The rancher informed them of his conversation with Claude Dallas and their agreement about trapping territory, despite Carlin's initial reservations about the competition for pelts that Dallas's presence posed. However, other things concerned Carlin about his conversation with Dallas. At one point, Carlin claimed, Dallas turned toward a bobcat pelt and said, "That cat thinks it's January 9," the opening of the 1981 bobcat hunting season. "When the cat's prime, you take him," Dallas said. Dallas also informed Carlin that he rejected man-made laws and vowed to take matters personally if challenged. Dallas notified Carlin of his intent to trap this one final year; by the next he would be in Canada. Carlin felt uneasy with Dallas, as he had when they first met two years earlier. He warned Dallas that "the Fish and Game came every year to check us out," to which Dallas responded that "he would be ready." Carlin again warned Pogue, who replied, "All right, we'll keep each other covered." The wardens left to investigate.[30]

Claude Dallas had set up his camp about fifty yards from the river. He stationed his white ten-by-twelve-foot wall tent and settled in with the other items that he and his friends had hauled down from the canyon rim. One of them, Jim Stevens, made the five-hour, bumpy dirt road drive from Paradise Valley. He looked forward to visiting with Dallas again. Early on the morning of January 5, Stevens first stopped at George Nielsen's, picked up groceries and mail for Dallas, and continued on to the camp. Stevens signaled as he and Dallas had agreed—two shots, wait ten minutes, and fire twice more—then ate a sandwich and drank coffee while he waited. He fired twice more but after a half hour decided to hike down. Halfway down he ran into Dallas, who wanted to know if Stevens had brought fruit. Stevens responded that not only did he have fruit, but baked goods and homemade pistachio pudding as well. "We're going to have a real good time," he told Dallas. Stevens continued down the trail and unloaded the supplies into Dallas's tent. Then as he waited for Dallas to return with the rest of the groceries, Stevens meandered down the river with the metal detector he had brought to search for Indian artifacts and arrowheads. As he returned to the camp he heard voices and saw Dallas speaking with Elms and Pogue. At six feet, 280 pounds, Conley Elms made quite a presence. Pogue introduced himself and asked Stevens for his firearm. Pogue returned the gun and put the unspent shells in Stevens's shirt pocket.[31]

Jim Stevens sensed the anxiety in the air and attempted to converse with the wardens. Dallas seemed familiar with one of them and said to Stevens, "Mr. Pogue here, he was chief of police in Winnemucca a few years back." Stevens had been an officer there as well, but their times had not overlapped. Then the tone of the conversation shifted as Pogue sternly questioned Dallas about the reported trapping violations. Pogue also noticed a bobcat pelt in the tent and the deer quarters hanging from the tent poles—both obviously killed out of season. "I have some meat hung up. I have to eat," Dallas admitted to the officers and reminded them of the distance from town. "Not anyone else I know . . . lives like I do or under the conditions I do." Pogue countered that the law did not differentiate. "It's unreasonable to give me a citation living this remote and under these conditions," Dallas reportedly answered.[32]

The questioning continued; Pogue interrogated Dallas while Stevens and Elms sat by silently and watched. After a while Dallas opened his wallet and produced his Idaho trapping license. Pogue argued that since he had Idaho papers, he certainly must have known that the bobcat season did not open until January 9. Pogue stated his intent to search the tent. Dallas asked for his search warrant. "That tent is my home. If you can't produce a search warrant you can't enter my tent." "You can go easy or you can go hard, Dallas. It doesn't make any difference to me," Pogue allegedly responded.[33]

Then Pogue motioned to Elms to check the tent and heard him respond from inside, "There's a raccoon hide in here also." Elms emerged with a fur stretcher in each hand and laid the pelts on the ground.

"We're going to confiscate those cats, Dallas," Pogue said.

Dallas stated, "I guess you know I'm gonna tell the judge I got those hides in Nevada."

"You're still being cited for possession of illegal cats," Pogue answered. The confrontation continued, with Dallas facing the tent and Pogue off to one side. In the midst of the conversation Jim Stevens turned his back and looked toward the river. He felt awkward being there and withdrew, although he remained within earshot. He heard Dallas ask, "Are you going to take me in?" Then Stevens heard a shot and Pogue gasp, "Oh, no!" He wheeled around just in time to see Dallas fire a second round at Pogue and saw smoke puff out of his chest. Dallas pivoted toward Elms and emptied two rounds into the other warden. He continued to shoot, the noise deafening and the action stunningly quick. Pogue fell face first, while Elms lay on his back, twitching. Dallas entered the tent and returned with a .22 rifle. He placed the gun to the back of the head of each warden and shot—what trappers call "finishing shots."[34]

Instinctively, Stevens retreated about eight to ten feet. He was stunned. His ears rang and he shook his head and asked himself, what happened? What just happened? He looked at Dallas and asked, "Why, Claude, why?" Dallas declared, "I swore I'd never be arrested again. They were gonna handcuff me." Then he apologized: "I'm sorry I got you involved in this. I've gotta get rid of these bodies and you've gotta help me."[35]

Stevens tried to think if the wardens had threatened Dallas's life in any way. No, he thought. Then Dallas said, "I know that what you think is right and what I think is right aren't the same. But nobody has the right to come into my camp and violate my rights. In my mind it's justifiable homicide." Dallas told Stevens that he "would have taken them on the rim [where Pogue, Elms, and Dallas first met], but they would have killed me up there." Then he shifted his focus to removing the bodies. "Maybe we should hide them up on the rim. No," he said, "they radioed in when they came here. They'll send planes, dogs, find the bodies sure. We'll have to haul them out. I'll get the mules. You cover the bodies with brush." Stevens wanted to run away but nervously realized that he had no choice but to stay with Dallas. He deferred to Dallas for all of the decisions, offered his car, and hoped for the best. Dallas apologized: "I'm really sorry about doing this to you. I mess up everybody's life. Everybody's always doing stuff for me and all I do is cause people trouble." However, he remained resolute in his actions. "They had no business in my camp."[36]

The pair successfully packed Pogue's body out of the canyon, but Elms's 280 pounds overwhelmed the mules and they buckled under the weight. Dallas surmised, "The only way a guy could get this body out of here is to quarter him." But neither he nor Stevens could do it, so he reversed directions and used the mule to drag the body to the river, where he dumped it. The body floated along the surface. Dallas then instructed Stevens to cover his tracks, and they destroyed as much evidence as possible. They used kerosene on blood spots and burned the warden's bloody clothing. The two then climbed out of the canyon and loaded Pogue's body into the Fish and Game truck. Dallas told Stevens, "This is murder one for me. I didn't weight

[Elms's] body and they'll find it in the morning." Jim Stevens realized that he was the lone witness to the events.[37]

Together they drove to Paradise Valley and devised a story to free Jim Stevens from any culpability. They pulled up behind George Nielsen's bar around midnight and rousted him. Nielsen, suddenly awakened from a sound sleep and likely a little drunk from a two-day binge, foggily responded to the scene. Wild-eyed and nervous, Dallas told Nielsen that he had "dusted two guys off." He told Nielsen to keep the lights off while they talked and explained the story. Then he said, "Gimme your pickup—gas it up." Nielsen also heard one of them say, "We've got a body to cache."[38]

Nielsen, like Stevens, admitted, "I don't want to have anything to do with it either." But Dallas convinced him to loan him his pickup so he could dispose of the body. Dallas told Stevens to burn his clothes and shower; then he filled the pickup with three tanks of gas and put the body in the back along with a shovel and pick. About two hours later Dallas returned and asked Nielsen for some provisions, camping gear, and money. Dallas kissed Nielsen's wife, Elizabeth, and told her that he loved her. Nielsen then drove Dallas thirteen miles south of their home to a dirt road. Dallas hopped out of the truck, turned to Nielsen, and said, "Don't try to contact me, I'll contact you."[39]

Manhunt and Myth

Jim Stevens's mind raced as he returned to Winnemucca, Nevada, and told his wife the concocted story. But she saw through the lies and Stevens confessed the truth and agreed to report to the authorities. The two drove to George Nielsen's place and informed him of their decision. Nielsen agreed to cooperate as well, and, along with his wife, the four recounted their story to an attorney and the county prosecutor in Winnemucca. Darkness prohibited any immediate action, but authorities laid plans for the following morning. Owyhee County sheriff Tim Nettleton flew his chartered plane over the crime scene, identified the location, spotted the Fish and Game truck, and directed the search parties. About a quarter of a mile from the camp, authorities found Elms's body floating in the water. Conley's older brother Michael arrived on the scene soon after and confirmed identification. However, officials failed to locate Pogue's body. The trail from where Dallas parked Nielsen's truck continued out into the desert, then circled back toward the road. Besides that, no clear signs remained. Since hunting season had opened in Nevada, the tracks from hunters made it increasingly difficult to pick up Dallas's trail.[40]

While statistics show that game wardens are killed in the line of duty more frequently than any other officers, this was the first time that anyone had been killed in Idaho. Dallas's description crossed law enforcement desks nationwide. He was described as a five foot ten inch, 175-pound, brown-eyed, thirty-year-old male with glasses, a cinnamon-colored beard, and brown hair in a short ponytail. Officials believed he wore a down jacket and portrayed him as a "very capable man in the backwoods." Humboldt County sheriff Frank Weston described Dallas as "extremely dangerous." "He loves guns and I suppose we will have to take him the hard way." Weston also cautioned that the manhunt could be prolonged since Dallas "knows the area like his own living room." Dallas's reputed ability to cover as much as forty miles a day through this rugged terrain heightened the importance of capturing him as soon as possible.[41]

The crime had occurred in Idaho—two and a half miles north of the Nevada border and thirteen miles east of Oregon—but Dallas had crossed state lines, which meant involvement from law enforcement officials at all levels of government. County sheriffs, state police, the Idaho National Guard, and a dozen FBI agents, including a four-member SWAT team from Reno, along with numerous volunteers and friends and family of the victims united in the effort. The party on foot searched in old shacks, mine shafts, caves, fissures, and ledges, while others drove in patrol cars. Pilots surveyed from the air in two fixed-wing aircraft, while others patrolled with helicopters, including a blue and white "Huey" military-type helicopter. While one search party concentrated on finding Dallas, the other focused on the search for Bill Pogue's body. They looked everywhere—along dirt roads, in draws, and even in an old gravel pit; scuba divers dove in area reservoirs for the body. They continued around the clock, shooting infrared photographs at night. National news media drawn to the area had no idea that such a large expanse of open space still existed in the United States.[42]

While the search continued for Dallas and Pogue's body, many of the residents of the Paradise Hill region seemed surprised at the news and readily defended Dallas. "Claude is as fine a man as you'll ever meet," claimed Paradise Hill resident Dean Taylor. "He doesn't have an enemy in this whole valley." Taylor lamented the entire episode, "It started over a little poaching violation. What does that amount to—a $300 [$771 in 2014] fine? There's not a soul here that wouldn't have helped him pay it."[43]

However, the officers investigating the murders—especially the other eight game wardens that worked in this area—offered a different perspective. They referred to Dallas as "the creep" or a "renegade," and since two of their fellow officers had been killed, they quickly rallied to the effort. "They are really a close-knit group, and now two of them are dead," Owyhee sheriff deputy Gary Olsen explained. "It's different when somebody kills a cop. That's the reason why you see so many officers down here—we want that man [Dallas]." This division of perspective reflected the polarized positions toward government in the West. Many viewed Dallas as a throwback to old times, a true cowboy; others viewed him as a criminal who broke laws and abused the common good.[44]

Within six days, 110 searchers had worked 4,890 man-hours, ridden horseback over 128 miles, walked 1,666 miles, and driven 5,000. But they had failed to apprehend Claude Dallas. They employed every conceivable tool in the effort—including a psychic—but eventually called off the manhunt. The search for Pogue's body continued, and focused within a forty-mile radius of Paradise Hill. Dallas's disappearance spawned countless theories about his location, and with time the number of theories multiplied.[45]

Sheriff Tim Nettleton of Owyhee County warned of a search lasting a year or more. Nettleton noted Dallas's mountain skills and warned that "Dallas will probably hide out in a big, wild area and he'll be tough to find." Survival specialist Larry Olsen argued that with the available plant and wildlife Dallas could live indefinitely in the desert. "If he's as good in the outdoors as I've read, he's got it made," Olsen argued. Nettleton feared the worst. "I just hope he doesn't gun down someone. I'm afraid that's how we might end up getting on to his trail." As time continued, the legend grew larger.[46]

When officers searched Dallas's converted school bus, they found evidence of a survivalist mentality: seven rifles—including an M16—ten handguns, a bulletproof vest, a gas mask, an Israeli tanker's helmet, cartridge reloaders, speedloaders for his hand guns, knives, and gun clips. There was also a small library on firearms, homemade machine guns and silencers, police and military techniques, combat shooting, and quick draw—all stored in excellent condition. They also found a new sealed case of two to three thousand .30 caliber bullets, which did not match any of the other guns. This supported the rumors of Dallas's desert caches.[47]

The search shifted to waiting for clues and tips. Investigators learned as much about Dallas as possible—his religion, reading interests, likes and dislikes, his quirks, anything they could use to create a profile that might predict his movements. In the meantime, efforts continued to find Bill Pogue's body. His brother, Ed, fueled by revenge, joined the search. "Bill and I were awfully close—as close as brothers can be. He was my only brother, and you can imagine how I looked up to him. Even after we grew up, we still made it a point to hunt together in Owyhee County."[48]

Bill Pogue's son, Steve, also assisted. "I know my mom would feel a lot better if my dad's body was found," he said. "I wouldn't mind it if I was the one who found him." Steve Pogue described his father as a dedicated officer who "followed the letter of the law." "He was going to arrest me once for shooting doves off a power line," the younger Pogue recalled. He also described the difficulty of the search, "The thing people don't understand—and I didn't at first—is how big this country is. It's like a needle in a haystack. I don't think they'll find him until they get more information." If the body was recovered, the family planned to have the corpse cremated and the remains sprinkled over one of Bill Pogue's favorite spots in the Owyhees.[49]

With a county population base of barely eight thousand and a tiny budget, Sheriff Nettleton had few resources to use. Within three months he had already overdrawn on his annual budget, so he devised a different tactic. Nettleton decided to exploit the mythical image that the media pumped out in stories. He said, "Let me play the dumb bumpkin sheriff, let me just play it to the hilt. I'll sit right here and they can write whatever they want about me. I'll just keep things flowing out to keep this thing going." With all of this attention added to the resources of the FBI and other agencies involved, he hoped to be successful.[50]

The media loved the story—the old-time, rough-and-tough, law-and-order sheriff versus the independent, self-sufficient, mountain man outlaw. The command post out of Murphy played well as a backdrop. Writers described the scene of the isolated county seat: forty miles from the nearest community, with "no mayor, no council, no firemen or policemen, no markets, theaters, churches, schools, or newspapers." Virtually every article mentioned the one parking meter: "in front of the squat courthouse, but a slug from someone's .38 had reduced its earning power." Harkening back to the Old West, "wanted posters" hung throughout the country, and police agencies, outdoorsmen, and family and friends of the deceased raised a reward of $20,000 [$51,000 in 2014]. Articles appeared in the *New York Times* and *Los Angeles Times,* and features popped up in *Rolling Stone,* the *American Rifleman, Startling Detective, Time, Newsweek, Outdoor Life,* and *People Weekly.* Nettleton estimated that perhaps two hundred thousand pictures of Claude Dallas circulated at the height of the media frenzy.[51]

As the case drew greater attention, the number of sightings rose as well. In August the *New York Times* reported that Sheriff Nettleton had received over five hundred tips from around the country. They included sightings of Dallas in every western state, including Alaska, as well as in many midwestern and eastern locations. People spotted him walking, riding a bike, driving a car, flying on a plane, exercising in a gym, getting his hair cut in a barbershop, and eating at a McDonald's and a Kentucky Fried Chicken. There were even sightings in Guadalajara and Toronto. Once, officials swooped down and prepared to arrest a Claude Dallas look-alike in Fairbanks, Alaska. The man matched all of the information, identified himself as a trapper, and knew the Owyhee desert well. But it turned out his name was Charlie Fannon, a retired Army survival instructor.[52]

In mid-July a foreboding tip came from a note left in a restaurant in Auburn, Maine. The message read, "My name is the capital of Texas. I killed two wardens January 3 / Bobcat trap—out of season / Only one person in this state can catch me / Vermont a family / but here I am / you'll never get me." Even though the capital of Texas is Austin, officials believed the note referred to Dallas. The waitress who attended to the man who left the note matched his description with a picture of Dallas. She described the man to officials as polite but rushed and said he had quickly left in a white van. But nothing more definitive connected Dallas to this sighting, and Sheriff Nettleton went on to the next tip.[53]

Officials contacted Dallas's parents, and their home remained under surveillance. But nothing appeared, and the parents commented, "We're all tore up but we're standing close by him." Those who interviewed his father gained insight into Claude Jr.'s mindset. Police had cited Claude Sr. numerous times in Upper Michigan for dairy-code violations. In Ohio the family had had trouble over a small oil well they had built on their property, and there were problems in South Carolina as well. Claude Dallas, Sr., stated, "I never in all my life had a good experience with a cop or a lawyer, and I'll be 67 this year. I've never known an honest cop." He further commented that "whenever I want to buy my boys something nice, I buy 'em a gun. Give a boy a gun and you're makin' a man."[54]

As the search continued and the media hyped the story, it became clear that the Claude Dallas saga exposed a larger division within society. The Dallas case pitted the Old West against the New, antigovernment radical individualists against pro-government collective protection. For many, Claude Dallas embodied the western mystique, and they wanted to see him and that image win. The media exposure helped with the hunt of Dallas; but their embellished stories contained exaggerated and false statements, ones that further enlarged the myth.

For example, instead of hitchhiking or driving to the West, "[Dallas] reportedly showed up in Nevada about 10 years ago, riding a horse and leading two packmules. Acquaintances say he rode west on horseback from the East." Stories claimed he traveled "sixty miles in a night—Two hundred!" claimed another. Another story claimed, "Claude's in his backyard and he is not going to leave." "He can live days without anything other than just a little place to lie down," added another. "Claude knows every damn gopher hole and cave in the Northwest," opined one writer. Features depicted Dallas as "a first rate outdoorsman, a crack shot, a white-water canoeist, a survival expert, Dallas, he was the renaissance man of the West." The stories crested with, "Change the color of his eyes and hair and he was Jeremiah Johnson, a fictional broth of real mountain men."[55]

Writers loved to point to the pages of the 1972 *National Geographic* where Dallas appeared as the authentic cowboy—the genuine Marlboro man. Many lived vicariously through Dallas. George Nielsen's brother Cortland described it this way: "Claude's lived the kind of life most of us only wish we could live. He knows the cowboy life. He knows about open country and taking care of himself." One writer claimed, "No cowboy mounted his air-conditioned pickup who didn't reckon his ancestors had had it better, clearer, purer." They saw in Dallas a return to those times.[56]

Moreover, for many in the area, Dallas's problems with government matched their own. They identified in the federal government the meddling, bureaucratic presence that took away their livelihood and ruined the West. *The Idaho Statesman* reported that many of Dallas's acquaintances were "openly rooting for him to escape." His friends framed Dallas's actions as self-defense. They hid possible evidence, tore down wanted posters, refused to give information, or distorted what they knew. A McDermitt, Oregon, rancher stated that if Dallas appeared at his house he would supply him with "a big meal and my best horse." Other sympathetic residents confirmed that they left their pickup trucks out every night, "keys in the ignition, gas tanks topped, sandwiches and beer in coolers."[57]

The manner of those involved in the search aggravated many Dallas supporters. The officers' abrupt, prying, brusque, impersonal manner sharply contrasted with the defensive, slow, rural rhythm. The investigators epitomized so much that supporters disdained in modern life. George Nielsen's place became one of the local hubs of Dallas supporters and curiosity seekers. He printed and sold T-shirts inscribed "GO CLAUDE GO!" The bar filled constantly with supporters, reporters, and those who waited for the latest news.[58]

However, a few of the locals remained critical of Dallas and the inflamed story. One woman stated that "some folks are trying to blame the wardens. That's how people make a hero out of the wrong man." She believed that they protected Dallas to defend themselves and their way of life. "They want to be able to say, I met him, I seen him. I'm a friend of his. Then their loyalty lays in sticking up for him. They do it for their own ego. And pretty soon a man has an image that's not true." "It's the nature and location of their work," explained another man from Winnemucca. "In country like this, folks get pretty coyote. They're estranged from the law because they're so much without it. It's almost a tradition that a wanted man isn't gonna be turned in. We're still the Wild West in that respect." Another bluntly declared, "I think the son of a bitch just wants to be chased. Claude's acting out something he read in a book."[59]

Expecting Daniel Boone

A year after the crime Dallas had still not been captured. By the spring, however, there were signs that Dallas had returned to one of the least expected places—Paradise Valley. The number of sightings drastically increased, and in mid-April the FBI received a tip that Dallas had returned to a friend's house only three miles down the road from where he previously lived. Law enforcement officers summoned assistance from all agencies and devised a plan. FBI officials came from Boise, San Francisco, and other locations with aircraft, while SWAT teams came from Butte and Las Vegas. Together they quickly formulated a plan to encircle Dallas and keep him from climbing up into the mountains. Late in the afternoon on Sunday, April 18, 1982, a helicopter dropped off five FBI agents about six hundred yards east of Dallas's suspected hideout in a trailer, while others arrived by car and an FBI surveillance plane patrolled overhead.[60]

With all the teams positioned, the helicopter swooped down on the trailer, hit the siren, and announced, "This is the FBI. Claude Dallas, come out with your hands up!" When Dallas heard the warning, he jumped through the trailer window, breaking the glass and the screen, and ran for the pickup. He hopped in and sped off. He broke through a barbed-wire fence and zigzagged through the desert traveling about thirty-five to forty miles an hour and bouncing as high as five feet over the rough terrain. The helicopter followed him as officers jumped in vehicles and chased him. It was almost dark. As the officers closed in on the pickup, Dallas shot at the helicopter and other vehicles. The police returned fire. Dallas grabbed a rifle and broke out of the pickup on the run, but a bullet pierced his Achilles tendon, and he could only crawl into the sagebrush. With dust from the helicopter and cars swirling, and the last traces of light quickly diminishing, the SWAT team members closed ranks on the chaotic scene. As they leapfrogged their way into position, they feared walking into a trap. "He could have wiped out six FBI agents because they had walked right past him," an officer later described. But from the brush, the officers heard, "Here I am. Don't shoot me." A veteran FBI agent pointed his M-16 at Dallas and told him not to move. Dallas responded, "I'm not going to do anything."[61]

Officials arrested Dallas and placed him in a Winnebago with four flak-jacketed deputies and an escort car to ensure no further problems. They kept the siren on past the Paradise Bar. Medical staff treated Dallas in hospitals in Winnemucca and Reno, and then the sheriff transported him to Sparks, Nevada, and extradited him to Idaho and the Owyhee County Jail. The trip took place under extremely tight security, with deputies armed

Claude Dallas under arrest, March 12, 1987. (*Idaho Statesman* Collection, Boise State University Special Collections and Archives. Used by permission of the *Idaho Statesman*.)

with automatic rifles stationed on the roof and in a broad semicircle as the convoy arrived. For security purposes, officials later transferred Dallas to the Canyon County Jail in Caldwell, Idaho.[62]

Stories from the capture threw water on the inflamed legend—at least for those who wanted to hear. One FBI agent commented, "I'm sure he could do what people said he could. But I was sort of expecting Daniel Boone or someone." Sheriff Nettleton stated, "I thought he'd be tougher than that." "If you watch John Wayne often enough," warden Gene Weller observed, "you get to thinking you're indestructible. But when the bullets start flying, the hands go up in the air." As Humboldt County undersheriff Steve Bishop summarized, "We knew what his potentials were. Some of it was potential and the rest of it you might call a myth." He also pointed toward the danger of myths. "You can get anything out of myth. You can make a myth as big as you want."[63]

However, the reality differed significantly from the myth. Dallas had lived much softer and closer than many imagined: he slept on a foam pad, and had people bring him food rather than living off the land. "He was too clean, too neat. I started to feel that maybe he wasn't that much of a mountain man," claimed Bishop. After ditching Nielsen's pickup, he had hiked to a friend's home in the area. He had stayed there until the story began to fade from the news broadcasts and then headed north and eventually east.[64]

Officials learned that Dallas had worked briefly under the alias "Jack James Chappel" at a South Dakota factory in early 1981. He left the factory not long after an altercation with another employee. "I had hit him accidentally with a steel gate and apologized," explained Randall Curry, "but he [Dallas] said it was too late for that and made an obscene remark." About two months later, an employee reading a magazine article recognized Dallas and contacted authorities. This last tip proved to be the final lead before his capture. Nettleton estimated that he checked out one thousand tips during the fifteen-month manhunt.[65]

Dallas's capture again brought to the surface a difference in attitudes about his actions. "Whoever turned Claude in should be hanged" became the mantra of his followers. They consistently argued self-defense and painted Pogue as a relentless law-and-order officer who had pushed Dallas into a corner and provoked him to shoot. Bill Pogue's brother countered that perspective. "Let's knock off the mountain music. He's a goddamn murderer as far as I'm concerned." Many supported this position. They viewed Dallas as a killer, someone trying to live a nineteenth-century life at the end of the twentieth. The incongruity resulted in the deaths of Pogue and Elms, victims of this anachronistic fantasy.[66]

Eventually Dallas was released on bail and headed back to his first employer in the West, the Wilsons' ranch. Hoyt Wilson was astonished at Dallas's next act given his current situation. Dallas got together some gear and began setting traps for bobcats. According to Wilson, Dallas hiked up to where a "band of prize big horn sheep were hanging around, maybe a hundred of them, planted about twenty years ago." The state had been slowly building up the band and consequently offered a drawing for only six to eight hunting tags for the entire mountain. "He shoots a mountain sheep!" exclaimed Hoyt Wilson. "Then he puts it in our cold room and says we are going to eat this thing, you know? Well, we could not have eaten it if we wanted to. It was a typical winter sheep, no fat, no nothing, tough as could be." It dismayed the Wilsons, and they both recognized Dallas's changed behavior since they first met him ten years earlier. "He was so tickled," Hoyt said, "and that was more appalling than anything—at a time when you'd think he'd be on his best behavior. But all he could think about was now he's got this trophy ram."[67]

On September 15, 1982, Dallas's trial on first-degree murder charges began at the Canyon County Courthouse in Caldwell. The national media gathered for the trial represented the largest collection for a court proceeding in Idaho since Governor Frank Steunenberg's assassination in 1904. Each day a diverse collection of people—from those aligned with one side or the other to simply curious attendees—waited in line for a chance to observe the proceedings. Writers from all of the major wire services, and reporters from many magazines and journals, crowded into the small courtroom and inflated the legend. "He was unlike anything most of us had ever seen," commented AP reporter John Kennedy. "He was almost a clinical specimen of a lifestyle none of us have ever experienced. He seemed to be the real thing."[68]

In the trial, Dallas took the stand. He recalled the first time he encountered Bill Pogue at a Star Valley campsite in 1979. According to Dallas, Pogue left a card with a handwritten note that read, "I'll check on you later." Dallas said, "I thought it was a hell of a way to introduce yourself." He stated that when informed by Carlin of warden visits to the area, he had answered, "I'll be ready," but did not mean it as a threat. Rather Dallas testified that he made no attempt to cover up and held steadfast to the legitimacy of his practices. "You can't bring in cut meat and frozen meat. Meat has to be hung in carcass form to keep." He maintained to the jury of ten women and two men that Pogue "seemed like he was primed to fight. He read me the riot act." Dallas said, "I've got a lot of friends in law enforcement and I've never been approached like that." After further discussion Dallas claimed that Pogue said, "You can go easy or hard, Dallas, it doesn't make any difference to me." Dallas understood "that meant dead" and testified that he responded, "You're out of line, Pogue, you're crazy. You can't shoot a man over a game violation." According to Dallas, Pogue responded, "I'll carry you out." He claimed that Pogue drew his gun first after consistently making gestures that way beforehand. Dallas then went for his gun, and "I just, I did the only thing I felt I could've done to save my life."[69]

In the aftermath Dallas admitted he feared "a lynch-mob attitude." "It would have been suicide if I had been picked up then," he claimed. Dallas then described burying Pogue's body and pinpointed the location on a map. Authorities found Pogue's body later that day. However, they never found Pogue's gun, which Dallas claimed he buried in another location he could not remember. The defense portrayed Pogue as a relentless official who consistently badgered and belittled hunters. They illustrated this with other confrontations and connected them to the present case. To a certain extent they successfully turned the table and placed the Department of Fish and Game on trial. They presented Pogue and the organization as bureaucratic controllers that acted as if the land was theirs, not the public's.[70]

The prosecution called nineteen character witnesses to counter this testimony. One witness believed that while Pogue would "cite his own mother" for game violations, he treated everyone fairly. Numerous other witnesses confirmed Pogue's stringent interpretation but strongly contested the characterization of Pogue as violent or belligerent. The prosecution also demonstrated Dallas's habit of dismissing authority and violating the law. "You are welcome in my camp," Dallas had once told a Nevada game warden, "but leave your badge outside." When the warden refused, Dallas responded, "Don't come into my camp then." Another prosecution witness, Gene Weller, a Nevada Fish and Game warden who had been dealing with Dallas's violations for three years, testified that hauling Pogue's body out of the canyon "didn't compute." Weller claimed that Dallas "brought it back to show George Nielsen, the same way he used to bring back poached deer and lions."[71]

The trial continued for a month—one of the longest trials in Idaho history—at an estimated cost of $100,000 [$206,094 in 2014]. The makeup of the trial audience represented the two sides battling it out—the ten-gallon-cowboy-hat-wearing Old West versus the game warden, city-living, government-supported New West. Both sides wanted to see their perspective vindicated. Dallas's side also sported a group of female supporters who called themselves the "Dallas Cheerleaders." They claimed, "He emits a charisma. He's the type of man that most women would admire . . . a survivalist, a man's man."[72]

To the surprise of many, the jury deliberated for a full week—one of the longest in Idaho judiciary history. Instead of the verdict of first- or second-degree murder that the prosecution anticipated, jurors returned with the verdict of voluntary manslaughter. Jurors later admitted that "if he hadn't put in those finishing shots, we probably would have let him off on self-defense." Jury member and rancher W. H. "Bill" Lewis stated, "We just thought the wardens were overbearing." Fellow juror Milo Moore added, "It doesn't take very long to release six shells, six bullets from a pistol. . . . [Dallas] was in fear of his life, and if you are in fear of your life, it's very hard to calm down and rationalize." Bill Lewis further added, "We just figured Pogue drew his gun and Dallas was a better marksman, that he was put in a position of self-defense. Dallas was a faster draw."[73]

Dallas declared that he "was not satisfied with the verdict," and defense attorneys predicted a possible appeal. The prosecution was bewildered. Owyhee County prosecutor Clayton Andersen called the verdict "a tremendous injustice." "I think he [Dallas] lied on the witness stand. . . . The Claude Dallas who was in the courtroom and the Claude Dallas [at the shooting scene] are two different individuals. I think the jurors believed who they saw and heard on the witness stand." Anticipating a verdict of first-degree murder, family members of the deceased were disappointed as well. "I feel really, really let down," said Carol Elms, Conley's sister-in-law. "This man just killed two of the greatest guys. It's just appalling." Her husband, Michael, Conley's older brother, worked as a game warden himself. "You know, my husband has been threatened so many times," said Carol. "And now these women [ten of the twelve jurors were women] let the man off. It's not enough. It's just not enough." Bill Pogue's wife, Dee, called the verdict "unbelievable," and added, "It's ironic that a man who had so much respect for the law should in turn have the court system fail him." Idaho Fish and Game director Jerry Conley worried that the verdict jeopardized officers, "The jury has told us . . . enforcement of game laws is meaningless and that the lives of our fish and game officers . . . are expendable." He added, "We've received comments today like, 'Well, if this guy gets off, I'm going to dust one off myself.'" Owyhee County sheriff Tim Nettleton concurred: "When we go up to someone to arrest them, and they say, 'Go to hell,' are we supposed to say we're sorry and walk off?"[74]

Judge Edward Lodge sentenced Dallas to thirty years in jail and in his stern, hour-long speech depicted the shootings as "premeditated . . . totally unjustified and morally reprehensible." Prior to receiving the sentence Dallas told Lodge: "I do regret what happened in Bull Camp, but I feel I reacted the only way I could under the circumstances." The judge viewed Dallas as generally without remorse, although the sentence would allow Dallas "to prove to society that you are the type of person that you have told us you are." He would be eligible for parole in ten years. On January 5, 1983, two years to the day after killing the game wardens, Claude Dallas began his prison sentence.[75]

His father reacted predictably. "Hell, if a man gets thirty years in the penitentiary for protecting himself, there's something wrong in the state of Idaho." Immediately upon hearing the sentence, Dallas's brother Robert stomped out of the courtroom. However, Bill Pogue's wife, Dee, commended Judge Lodge for his "very fair" sentence. Most importantly, she felt that "the judge believed the officers were in the right." Pogue's daughter, Jodi, wished the sentence had been longer but felt "really good about what the judge said. I just wish the jury had felt the same way."[76]

A *Newsweek* article summarized many attitudes about the trial. It stated that the jury's verdict was "uncertain," because many were sympathetic to both sides. The article quoted a local who explained: "People in this part of the country live in their own world and by their own rules. Here you have a perfect example of a world of the past colliding with the world of the present one time too many." The article concluded: "Dallas' real crime was that he was born 150 years too late for the Wild West life he wanted."[77]

After the trial, state officials transported Dallas to the Idaho State Penitentiary to begin his jail sentence. Many state officials expressed relief that the episode had finally concluded. However, Dallas's story rekindled the western myth. In the following years, singers wrote and recorded two songs about Dallas, authors penned two books about him, ABC's *20/20* program devoted an episode to him, and a TV movie was made about him. In June 1983, the *Idaho Statesman* interviewed two authors writing books about this saga—Jack Olsen and Jeff Long. In the article the writer attempted to reconcile the dilemma that Dallas's actions presented. Both Olsen's *Give a Boy a Gun* and Long's *Outlaw: The True Story of Claude Dallas* tended to fall into one of the two camps that had formed in response to this case. Long insisted, "I'm not trying to romanticize Claude Dallas. I am trying to explain the romance that surrounds Claude Dallas." However, clearly he interpreted the evidence in favor of Dallas. His work became the basis for the movie script.[78]

Cover of Jack Olsen's *Give a Boy a Gun*. (Image used by permission of Penguin Random House.)

Cover of Jeff Long's *Outlaw: The True Story of Claude Dallas*. (Image used by permission of HarperCollins Publishers.)

Olsen's research focused on the folkloric attitude that surrounded Dallas and how it contrasted with perceptions of other killers. What he discovered disturbed him. Like many he emphasized that Dallas's mentality "came from the 19th century." But he also pointed to Dallas's decision to root himself in that mind frame. "He not only was mired psychologically in the 19th century, he was mired in the 19th century by choice." The extensive support that Dallas enjoyed after the killings surprised Olsen the most. "People automatically assumed that if this hard-working man killed two game wardens, somehow the game wardens had to be at fault. . . . They jumped to that conclusion immediately." That supporters would leave food and trucks available to Dallas surprised him. "To them, this man is the most wanted man in the United States. But at the same time, 10, 15, 20 people have jumped to the conclusion that this is a man deserving of help. And hundreds of others felt drawn to his side, without taking an active role."[79] Little did the authors or the general public realize that some of the most interesting chapters remained to be written.

"Claude Dallas Had Risen"

On Easter Sunday evening, March 30, 1986, convicted killer Claude Dallas escaped from the Idaho State Penitentiary just outside of Boise. He cut a triangular hole through two chain-link fences that enclosed the visitors' facility. Hours later officials found his prison-issued eyeglasses next to tire marks in the visitors' parking lot. Prison guards pointed to Geneva Holman, a Reno woman who had raised $28,000 [$59,700 in 2014] for Dallas's court

Reward poster for Claude Dallas. (Courtesy of Owyhee County Historical Society Museum and Library.)

defense, as an accomplice. She last visited Dallas just prior to his escape. They also questioned the involvement of Margaret Lundy, an avid Dallas supporter who quit her job as a secretary in Palo Alto, California, two days before Dallas escaped.[80]

On May 16, the FBI placed Dallas on its list of ten most-wanted fugitives. Federal officials also established a toll-free phone number and quickly gathered rewards of $10,000 and $25,000 [$20,609 and $51,524 in 2014] for the capture of Dallas. When news of the escape broke, authorities in Paradise Valley noted the déjà vu. "This is the same damn thing that happened in 1981," said Humboldt County sheriff James Bagwell. Articles extolled Dallas's calculations for the escape. "The timing of his breakout was perfect: The snow line on the surrounding mountains had lifted enough to make travel possible in the high country." Many supporters also connected the event and the religious observation of the day: "It was Easter Sunday, and Claude Dallas had risen."[81]

Those who had earlier predicted Dallas's escape seemed not the least surprised. In the midst of his trial one of his friends commented, "If he ever gets a clear shot at the wall, he's gone, there's no doubt in my mind." Another friend predicted, "He'll see a low wall or an open door. One slight chance they say and Claude will do the rest." Earlier, guards had uncovered wire cutters in Dallas's cell and he was transferred to maximum security, but with time he was returned to the medium-security cellblock. One observer predicted that "if he escapes he'll either get away or he'll be killed, because he'll never be captured again."[82]

With the escape and search came another round of media stories, which further substantiated the Dallas legend. Once again sightings poured in from all over the United States and as far away as Australia. Notorious bounty hunter Ralph "Papa" Thorson, who claimed to have tracked down twelve thousand fugitives, agreed to take on the case, which drew even more attention. Thorson, whose life was depicted in the 1980 film *The Hunter,* felt confident that he and his assistants would capture Dallas. Thorson's assistant Dale Rogers argued, "We have a more sophisticated network of information than they [the FBI] do, because they listen to anybody." Ada County sheriff Vaughan Killeen countered, "I don't care if the Girl Scouts caught him. We just want him back."[83]

Time magazine reported, "The myths of the romanticized West die hard, a fact that was making a tough job even tougher last week for a 100-man posse in three states." The search party "engaged in an all too familiar chore: hunting down Claude Dallas, 36, a self-styled 'mountain man' who cold-bloodedly killed two game wardens in January 1981." The article recounted Dallas's abilities in eluding law officials for sixteen months earlier in the high desert and predicted difficulties in recapturing him. In the meantime, officials discovered a baseball cap near the prison, and bloodhounds trailed the scent back to the Paradise Hill Bar and the mobile home where Dallas originally had been captured. The article concluded with a statement from Sheriff Nettleton: "the only difference between Dallas and other escapees is that he rides a horse and the others drive a car." He again cautioned that Dallas had lots of support in the area, which was evident from the number of phony tips called in to protect Dallas.[84]

A variety of stories and theories surfaced. One woman, who had earlier initiated a legal defense fund for Dallas, argued that government officials aided Dallas's prison escape in order to get more money for the poorly funded Idaho prison system. "I don't know who gave him the bolt cutters," Laura Miller said, "but there has been some speculation he was helped out by someone on the inside, and I don't mean by one of the inmates." "Maybe someone said, Hey, let's get some headlines. Who's the most famous person who's not going to hurt anyone?" Idaho corrections director Al Murphy responded, "That's asinine."[85]

Margarette Eckstein, from her coffee shop at the intersection in Burns Junction, Oregon, argued, "They're trackin' a mountain man, they're not just chasin' a city slicker." Eckstein admitted Dallas's wrongdoing in the wardens' deaths but refused to help in the capture. "I haven't seen him," she said. And then whispered, "If I had, I wouldn't tell anybody." In Boise, T-Shirt Plus owner Sue Davis sold "Claude Dallas Easter Basket" shirts showing a nest with a pair of bolt cutters. She believed that the enthusiastic response demonstrated the support for the escaped convict.[86]

For the families and friends of Bill Pogue and Conley Elms, news of Dallas's escape ripped open a wound that had only recently begun to heal. Yet again, in interviews and questioning, they were forced to defend the actions of their friends and loved ones. They returned to fund-raising for reward money. Pogue's daughter, Jodi Rupe, a secretary for the Boise regional office of the Department of Fish and Game, sold prints of her father's painting *Mountain Man.* "It makes me feel sad he is out there when I don't feel he has come close to paying for what he's done," she said. The committee set a fund-raising goal of $50,000 [$103,047 in 2014], double their last effort. "Despite what people think, we know about the quality of the guys Dallas hangs out with. A sizeable reward will lead one to turn Dallas in," Sheriff Nettleton predicted. "People are going to get tired of Claude Dallas. Hiding him will take more effort than most of his acquaintances will want to invest. I look for a short hunt, maybe a year." Nettleton added, "He had a lot of friends but he can't trust them."[87]

Again the media played a role. Previously, CBS producers had decided to make a movie of the Claude Dallas story based on Jeff Long's work. Dallas escaped during the filming, creating a truth stranger than fiction. Matt Salinger, son of the famous writer J. D. Salinger, played the lead in *Manhunt: The Search for Claude Dallas.* Officials briefed the actors about Dallas's escape and the possibility that he was hiding in the hills surrounding the filming location. The producers' choice to use Long's book certainly elicited a response from fellow Dallas author Jack Olsen: "*Outlaw* is essentially mythology, and for the movie people, mythology sells better than the truth."[88]

FBI agents admitted that the movie brought forth a large number of false leads. People phoned in thinking they had seen Dallas when it was actually the actor, Salinger. Nevertheless, law officials remained confident that they would eventually apprehend Dallas as long as they remained patient. FBI special agent George Calley stated, "We're all creatures of habit, and Claude Dallas is no exception. . . . We do what we feel comfortable doing . . . and for Claude Dallas, that was getting help from his friends." In contrast to the image of Dallas as an individualist, Calley claimed that he relied on friends who remained susceptible to the temptation of the reward. Dallas supporters laughed at the idea.[89]

Articles continued to appear. Although some portrayed the realities of Sheriff Nettleton's job—"We have the same criminal problems everybody else has, ranging from drugs to sexual abuse of children"—most continued to emphasize the Wild West angle. On January 26, 1987, *Time* magazine published a piece titled "In Idaho: A Killer Becomes a Mythic Hero." The article portrayed Nettleton as a quaint country sheriff. "As cold winds whistled across the jackrabbit badlands and swirled outside his cramped office, Nettleton kindled another cigarette, propped his scuffed cowboy boots on the desk and pondered the renegade Dallas." Then, "abruptly he blew out the match and turned, a flinty glare transforming his hound-dog eyes. The sheriff wanted Dallas dead or alive." Cue western background music. Then the writer quoted the lean and lanky lawman: "If they'd bring one of his hands back from Mexico, I'd be happy, I guess, I just wanta know something's been done." The article concluded by stating that the sheriff would eagerly "wager a pint of whiskey that Dallas will return, inevitably to the badlands that begot the legend."[90]

But Claude Dallas did not get caught in the "badlands" of Owyhee County; he was arrested outside of a Shop N Go convenience store in Riverside, California, fifty miles east of Los Angeles. The mountain man who supposedly lived off the land got caught with two bags of groceries containing peanut butter, orange juice, bread, and cheese. Several blocks away he had checked into the $25-a-night Skylark Motel. Although Dallas had pledged never to be taken alive, officers arrested the unarmed Dallas without incident. It turned out that, contrary to the legend builders, Dallas left Idaho almost immediately after his escape and traveled to the San Francisco area, where he stayed for two and a half months. He then traveled to the small town of Eureka, Nevada, where two dozen FBI agents stormed the town of 350 following the July 4 holiday. But Dallas had already left.[91]

Acting on a tip, the FBI agents broke down the back door of Dallas's suspected location at about five in the morning and threw in a percussion grenade. Although no sign of Dallas remained, agents wrecked the living room of Richard and Anna McKay and broke their china. "If they had done that to my house, I would have gone to Reno and bombed the FBI's office," said Al Hammond, a local magistrate. "Those guys were acting crazy. I'm going to start wearing my gun here, it was just like the wild, wild West." Later the agents tracked down the McKays, and their son, Richard Jr., in their pickup and after encircling them ordered them out of the car at gunpoint. "They made my brother Richard lie face-down on the ground and kept calling him Claude," said Nancy Minoletti, the McKays' daughter. "Richard is 6 foot 3 and doesn't look anything like Claude. They told my dad they were going to put Mom in jail if he didn't talk." The raid on the McKay home provided further evidence for pro-Dallas advocates that law enforcement operated too aggressively.[92]

For the next eight months officials lost Dallas's trail as tips of sightings came from Oregon to as far south as Mexico and as far east as South Dakota. The FBI then picked up Dallas's trail by following Dan Martinez, a friend. Martinez introduced Dallas to his friend Greg Davis, who agreed to take Dallas to a motel in Riverside. Using the alias Al Schrenk, Dallas had shaved his shaggy beard down to a trim moustache and, perhaps with plastic surgery, had changed his appearance significantly. Nevertheless, the FBI caught up to him. The special agent in charge of the Los Angeles office of the FBI, Richard Bretzing, said, "This is a particularly dangerous man and we are pleased and relieved to have him in custody."[93]

Back in Owyhee County Sheriff Tim Nettleton sighed in relief. "It's been a good day, a great day," he said. "Claude Dallas, in the exception of being a game hog and game officer killer, was a nice guy. . . . A lot of people share his sentiments but they don't kill people." Jack Olsen, the author *of Give a Boy a Gun,* harshly criticized any sympathy for Dallas. "He's as much of a Western hero as Charles Manson. Dallas would kill a lawman with about the same guilt and conscience as he eats his Wheaties in the morning."[94]

When Claude Dallas escaped from prison, Shadow Elordi, one of his supporters, "bet that s.o.b. Tim Nettleton a bottle of Early Times he couldn't catch Dallas in a year." A week before that deadline Dallas was in custody. After he waived his extradition rights, Dallas was flown by a private chartered plane to the Ada County Jail in Boise. As usual he drew attention and controversy—about a half dozen protestors picketed his imprisonment with signs outside the jail, including one that read "A Man's Home Is His Castle." If found guilty of escape charges, Dallas's sentence would be increased by five years.[95]

As Dallas and his defense lawyers prepared for the trial, other supporters planned an unusual fund-raiser. In Reno in mid-September 1989, local businessmen held an auction of many of Dallas's possessions connected to the killings. Although other cities had refused to allow the auction, Reno authorities permitted it. Items included seventeen guns, dozens of knives, thousands of rounds of ammunition, snowshoes, clothes, and his library, including the book *Kill or Be Killed.* Perhaps the most unusual items for auction were four "petrified" biscuits found in Dallas's oven when he was originally captured by the FBI. Bids for the biscuits topped out at $25. In signed certificates given to each successful bidder, Dallas described the various items. For example, "This is the gun I had when I was captured by the FBI." "This rifle helped me through the winter when I was hiding out." More than 150 people came out for the auction, which raised over $10,000 [$18,235 in 2014]. Dallas's attorney said, "We're overjoyed with the results." He felt that "this money is going to go a long way to achieve justice in our struggle to get his freedom."[96]

However, many felt otherwise. Outside of the auction, over forty law enforcement officers from a variety of government agencies picketed the event. They carried signs that read, "What Next, Charlie Manson's Property?" "Blood Money," "If You Bid, Contribute Equally to the Victims'

Family," and "Claude Dallas Is a Murderer. He's No Hero." One three-year-old son of a game warden officer carried a sign that read, "Daddy, It's Really Not OK To Kill Game Wardens, Is It?" Nevada game warden Fred Messman commented, "I can't believe what is going on. It's really bizarre. Those people are glorifying a murderer." Another FBI agent stated, "Those people are in there making a hero out of a man who shot two policemen. That's why we're here. It just isn't right, and we want the public to know how we feel." A Reno detective and a president of the Reno Police Officers Protective Association summarized many people's feelings: "We want to put a stop to this myth. That's why we came out to protest the auction, to let people know what kind of a human being Claude Dallas really is."[97]

However, those on the inside felt differently. "I'm a hunter," said Walt Weaver of Sparks, Nevada. "I've been stopped by game wardens. They treat you like criminals. In my mind I think Dallas acted properly." Al Marshall of Reno added, "Those officers have no right picketing a private business. I'm against the law of bullying. That's what those two game wardens who were killed were doing to Claude Dallas. They were bullying him."[98]

The familiar scenario played out again. Fund-raisers for the defense gathered cash as the state collected information for its case. In the trial Dallas again testified. His attorney, Bill Mauk, called him "the best natural witness I've ever seen. It's very unusual to get a client like Claude Dallas who can articulate his own defense better than anyone else can." "Charisma," "great eye contact," and "speaks very well" were words others used to describe him.[99] A newspaper article claimed, "Dallas' Defense Puts Idaho Pen on Defensive." Defense witnesses included fellow inmates who testified overhearing a prison guard comment, "I wish the prisoners would riot so I could kill Dallas." One inmate stated that "as a cop-killer Dallas was probably at the top of the echelon of the prison population and at the bottom as far as the prison administration goes." According to the testimony of another prisoner, a guard confirmed that if he had the chance, "he'd be more than happy to take out Claude Dallas." Another allegedly admitted that "if the place would just go off, they could get rid of some scum in the yard, and Dallas would be his first target."[100]

Dallas repeated what the others had said. He also claimed that earlier officers had planted bolt cutters and lock picks in his locker to incriminate him. He feared making any kind of formal protest, though he knew of guards' plans to kill him and that they even used his picture for target practice. "By the end of December 1983," Dallas claimed, "I was convinced that, if they had the opportunity to rid themselves of me, they'd jump on it." A twelve-member jury deliberated for five and half hours before reaching their verdict. Three female jurors wiped tears from their eyes while two others sobbed as they read the statement. To the surprise of many, the jurors acquitted Dallas of the charges. Reactions to the case were predictable.[101]

Dallas Continues to Disrupt

A year after his escape Claude Dallas spent a very quiet Easter in maximum security without any visitors. His story occasionally still appeared in the news accompanied by the divided reaction. On September 19, 1987, for greater security purposes, officials transferred him to the New Mexico state prison near Santa Fe and later sent him to the Kansas state prison at Lansing to complete his sentence. In December 1988, Dallas won another court case that required officials to return his guns, bedrolls, duffel bags, and a mountain of bullets, boots, traps, a saddle, spurs, and other items. The legal battle ended after six years when Third District Court Judge Jim Doolittle rejected Owyhee County's argument that Dallas's items were contraband, maintaining that none of the items were in Dallas's possession at the time of his arrest. Yet even this had its controversial wrinkle, for in September the *Idaho Statesman* reported that Sheriff Nettleton gave one of the seized guns, a .44 caliber pistol, to Judge Lodge as a memento. However, Lodge denied that the gun was a gift and quietly returned the weapon and a trap to the sheriff. In March of 1992, ABC's *FBI: The Untold Stories* dramatized a version of the manhunt for Dallas. Producers acknowledged the fictionalized nature of the filming, although they maintained their intention to be accurate. Legally, Dallas had exhausted his appeal possibilities. On November 21, 1985, the Idaho Supreme Court upheld Dallas's sentence, and on January 22, 1993, the Ninth Circuit Court rejected his appeal. The story had ended.[102]

Yet, as in a B movie in which the character seemingly returns from the dead, twenty years after Claude Dallas killed Bill Pogue and Conley Elms, he was eligible for parole. As evidence of the power of his story, the *Idaho Statesman* featured front-page coverage and a lengthy feature article that once again recounted the events and asked viewers their opinion about

Dallas's potential parole. Titled "Claude Dallas: Stone-Cold Killer or Western Hero?" the article captured well the division in perception and the ongoing debate over Dallas and the West in general.[103]

Not much had changed in Paradise Valley since Dallas's capture. Signs in town read "Eat More Beef; the West Wasn't Won on Salad," and Dallas's defenders continued to support him. Dallas's friend Danny Martinez said, "Those game wardens had in mind to kill Claude Dallas. . . . It was self-defense. Claude Dallas is a gentleman." Paradise Hill mail carrier Dick Henningsen said, "I hope he gets it [parole], by God. Anybody that's met him loved him. I never heard a negative word about him around here." As one of the songs written in tribute to Dallas played in the background, Paradise Valley resident Charlie Whiton said, "You hear lots of stories about what kind of guy he was. One of the stories is that if he knew somebody didn't have much, he'd buy a couple of sacks of groceries and leave them on the porch." In Paradise Valley the Dallas story has become a tourist attraction. A local bartender, Kelley Bell, claims, "A lot of people come here in the summer and ask about him. They want to see the Owyhee Desert, the Bloody Run Hills, the place where they pumped the hot springs looking for the body."[104]

However, other locals remained against him. "He had a lot of supporters in the valley, which I never understood," stated Marie Stewart of the reputable 96 Ranch. "My husband and I never supported him. He's a cold-blooded murderer. It would have been so much easier for everyone if he'd admitted he'd poached those animals and taken his punishment." Another patron of the Paradise Hill bar identified the hypocrisy in Dallas's statements of independence from society, his dodging of the draft, and refusal to pay taxes. He pointed out that Dallas "went to public schools, was protected by a public military, took public animals on public land and was therefore the most public son of a bitch around."[105]

Dallas defense attorney Bill Mauk claimed Dallas "appealed to the Western mythology. It's still a part of the country where people carry a lot of those anti-authoritarian, anti-government sentiments, and they're not all Nazis and right-wing kooks. It's just a part of the culture that exists in this part of the world." But while the attitude remained, the lifestyle continued to shift from the mythical West that Dallas sought. Changing economic and societal forces altered the cowboy and ranching life; they became increasingly mechanized, and the markets for fur trapping made it mostly worthless to pursue. One local claimed: "It's not possible to live now the way he did then. The mystique of the Old West is big in Europe and Asia now, but the reality is that it's pretty much of an illusion. The ambience for the mountain-man style is gone." Nevertheless, many still held fast to the romantic notions that the myths provide. One of Dallas's guns served as a top prize for a fund-raiser for the Lady Elks in Burns, Oregon.[106]

A review of Dallas's records with the Kansas Department of Corrections indicated that since 1997 Dallas had been cited with eighteen disciplinary violations, all for refusing to take random drug tests. "A person's ability to follow rules in prison is considered an indication of whether he'll follow the rules outside prison," stated Olivia Craven, executive director of the Idaho Commission for Pardons and Paroles. Dee Pogue argued that Dallas's sentence wasn't nearly long enough. "He got a short sentence, but the families are spending a lifetime without Bill and Conley. My grandchildren didn't ever get to know their grandfather."[107]

"Slayer of Game Wardens Is Denied Parole" read the headline in the *Los Angeles Times*. Describing him as "unrepentant" and "defiant," on April 21, 1988, the Idaho Commission of Pardons and Parole denied parole for Claude Dallas. During the phone hearing from the El Dorado Correctional Facility in Wichita, Kansas, Dallas claimed that he would not be a threat to law officers if released early. "I don't see that as being a problem. As long as I'm approached in a reasonable manner, I respond in a reasonable fashion." However, when asked if he would submit to random drug testing or electronic monitoring as part of his parole stipulations, Dallas exclaimed, "By God, I will not submit. I've set my mind on this. I see more threat from the damn government than from all the drug lords on the face of the Earth." When questioned about his remorse for the killing of the officers, Dallas declared, "My thoughts and my feelings are my own. They don't belong to the state of Idaho." Olivia Craven, the parole board's executive director, claimed that she received more correspondence from throughout the country regarding the Dallas case than she had received in seventeen years of work. When informed of the denial, Dallas said, "I can leave prison with you people having some control over me or I can leave in four years with no strings attached."[108]

Claude Dallas was released from prison on February 7, 2005.[109]

CHAPTER SEVEN

Saylor Creek Bombing Range: Modern Range War

US Air Force Colonel Victor C. Andrews and local rancher Bert Brackett see things quite differently as they look out over the land in Owyhee County. Colonel Andrews envisions more than a million acres containing a state-of-the-art electronic battlefield and bombing range. He imagines warplanes conducting exercises that require them to maneuver through "enemy" antiaircraft positions and to attack targets with bombs, rockets, and cannon fire. According to Andrews, young pilots need these exercises for their training; it is a matter of life and death. However, Bert Brackett sees something entirely different. For over a century, four generations of his family have made a living off this high desert country. Brackett claims it to be "some of the finest, most productive ranch land in the West." He "sees his birthright."[1]

For the decade from 1989 to 1999 these visions clashed. As in the preceding chapters about contention over land use in the Owyhees, coalitions formed. However, instead of settlers against Native Americans, or sheepmen versus cattle ranchers, in this episode these normally competing interests fought together. This strange alliance of ranchers, Native Americans, and environmentalists battled the very institution that established reservations and encouraged settlement. In the nineteenth century the federal government gave land away; in the twentieth it wanted it back. However, unlike the largely overt and violent nature of earlier battles, this time bureaucratic, behind-the-scenes battles characterized this modern range war. And the government bureaucracy made western myths that much more attractive.

Modern Range War

Starting in the mid-1980s the Pentagon began a policy of securing more land for training exercises. Officials claimed they had outgrown the twenty-five million acres of public property currently under military control and argued for an additional four and a half million. "The nature of warfare is constantly changing," reported a contingent of generals and deputy secretaries of defense. The Pentagon hoped to gain new land for bombing ranges, supersonic air-combat training areas, tank ranges, ammunition bunkers, and gunnery space. However, with fifty-seven national forests already hosting 163 Pentagon training activities, further militarization of public lands met stiff opposition.[2]

Nevertheless, the air force maintained that it needed more space. According to one deputy assistant secretary, "a mechanized Army battalion needs more than 80,000 acres to practice standard maneuvers, compared to 4,000 acres during World War II." In addition to this twenty-fold increase, an eight-fold increase in nautical miles was desired for aerial maneuvers—from five miles during World War II to forty, with the latest tactical fighters expected to need between eighty and one hundred nautical miles.[3]

The air force sought land throughout the United States, although the West attracted the greatest attention. In Nevada, officials pursued 610,000 acres for maneuvers, and in Montana they proposed nearly one million acres for training. In total, the military wanted approximately five million more acres in sixteen states—the largest land procurement since World War II. Among the projected land acquisitions, 1.4 million acres in southwestern Idaho was the largest. The air force previously occupied 109,000 acres known as the Saylor Creek Bombing Range; however, their proposal increased that amount by nearly fifteen times and included simulated bombs and live munitions.[4]

Air force officials had been thinking about the expansion since the mid-1980s. Deputy Assistant Secretary Gary Vest urged the committee in charge of land acquisitions to think big enough to accommodate future needs and wishes. Moreover, since Vest had been a classmate and fraternity brother of Idaho Republican senators Larry Craig and Steve Symms, he was politically well connected in Idaho. Over the next four years, officials developed ambitious plans to expand the training facilities. They scheduled hearings for October 1989, and planned for the range to be ready for use by 1994.[5]

Unlike Hollywood versions of range wars in which combatants used rifles, participants in these contests utilized words, images, and political alliances to gain ground. One general claimed, "Our management of land has secured and even enhanced habitat for endangered species and other wildlife." Many organizations challenged this media spin. They abhorred the Pentagon's ability to control twenty-five million acres of public lands and argued that few contested the military's management "because much of it has been ruined beyond redemption." Coalitions formed to fight the military on these takeovers.[6]

Robert Fulkerson, director of Citizens Alert in Nevada, where the military controlled four million acres, vigorously opposed any further acquisitions. Similar battles were taking place in other parts of the country. In central Pennsylvania, residents opposed a plan by the Air National Guard to create a new military operations area over the Susquehanna River Valley, while in Wisconsin and Iowa local residents fought National Guard proposals to expand a bombing range and add two low-level training routes. In one of the most contentious disputes, residents fought for over seven years against the Air National Guard's plan to expand its airspace and operations over two wilderness areas in southern Colorado.[7]

In August 1987 the press gained access to a "Description of Proposed Action and Alternatives." Although disavowed by the air force, the document proved especially revealing. It disclosed a plan for sixty-four thousand acres in Idaho to be used for live bombing and outlined a tactical range designed to represent anticipated battlefields of Europe, Russia, or the Middle East. The range included front lines and defensive installations with strategic and support targets, such as railroads, airports, and factories. Thirty or more simulated antiaircraft units dotted the desert and allowed for an electronic combat range capable of scoring aerial dogfights.[8]

Pilots training for these missions flew from the nearby Mountain Home base, where the air force appointed Lieutenant Colonel James Cooper to maneuver through the process of expansion. He knew the history there. When the military first established Mountain Home Air Force Base in 1943, they acquired 420,000 acres south of the Snake River for the Saylor Creek

F-15Es of the 366th Operations Group on a low-level training mission out of Mountain Home Air Force Base. (Courtesy of Mountain Home Air Force Base.)

Bombing Range. But after the Korean War, the air force relinquished control of 300,000 acres. When they argued that they needed the land back and another one million acres, many refused to believe it. "He [Cooper] would look at us incredulously when we said we didn't think the Air Force needed more land," Kerry Cooke of a local environmentalist group explained. "Colonel Cooper personifies the Air Force mentality that if they just told the simple folk, we would see the wisdom of their plan. But the opposite happened," he maintained. "The more they told us, the more the plan didn't make sense. It looked more like just greed."[9]

As the press exposed the plans for expansion in Idaho, the outcry grew louder. Roger Hayes, a Boise carpenter, testified at one of the hearings. "The Air Force would like us to believe that the desert lands within the proposed Saylor Creek expansion are a barren wasteland of little resource value. This is far from the truth." Instead, he declared: "The canyon and river systems which lie embedded in the proposed range are as scenic and outstanding as any in the West."[10]

In the midst of this battle, an unimaginable coalition formed. Groups that normally fought against each other—environmentalists, cattle ranchers, wildlife protectors, Native Americans—formed an alliance to fight the "land grab" by the US government. They noted the irony of working together, but agreed to put aside differences and rallied under the slogan, "Idaho is too great to bomb." The government's inability to articulate a clear need for an expanded range remained central to their opposition. "We cattlemen support a strong national defense," said Bert Brackett, president of the Idaho Cattle Association. "If there's definitely a national security need, then we'll sacrifice and do our part. But at this point, we're not convinced."[11]

As the details of the plan became known, other groups joined—outfitters and guides, private pilots, and peace groups. They hoped to protect the rivers and rich wildlife, ensure adequate private airspace, and honor sacred sites of the Native Americans. At their meetings, ranchers in their "go-to-town outfits" sat alongside "Eddie Bauer backpackers" and naturalists and archaeologists in their "beards and tweeds," along with Indians and hunters and fishermen. "We're pretty nervous working with each other," said one member, "but we are working with each other."[12]

However, the other side had its own coalition of powerful supporters. Besides the air force, most of the citizens of Mountain Home near the base enthusiastically supported the venture. The expanded range meant more dollars spent in their community. They applauded this statement from Colonel Andrews: "Idaho presents an ideal opportunity for the Air Force to get what we need." With good flying weather, few civilian aircraft, low population, and no endangered species, "a large, modern range here would supplement the 7.8 million acres of ranges operated by the Air Force in 11 other states," Andrews claimed.[13]

The federal government's acquisition of these large tracts of land represented their continued involvement in the region. Additionally, the size and scope of government forces in the West increasingly allowed it to determine appropriate uses of land. The diverse coalition in opposition to the expanded military range continued to focus on a critical question: Is there a need?

Is There a Need?

In 1988, the Defense Department decided to close George Air Force Base in California and relocate ninety-four F-4 fighter-bombers to Mountain Home. In their report, the commissioners concluded that the "recent expansion of the electronic-combat and weapons ranges in Mountain Home area provides the capability to relocate operational and training assets, which will increase efficiency and enhance mission effectiveness." Furthermore, they maintained that the "military value of George AFB is lower than other tactical-fighter installations due to its distance to specialized training ranges and the increasing air-traffic congestion in the vicinity of the base." Consequently, officials chose to move the F-4s to Mountain Home and accelerated the timeline for the expanded range to be operational.[14]

However, the Pentagon task force that recommended closing the California base mistakenly assumed that Saylor Creek had previously been expanded. But no changes were made, and current conditions failed to accommodate the F-4s' training requirements. Furthermore, the air force rated the range as marginal and too close for any direct approach. Due to the bureaucratic blunder, officials admitted that "significant modification to both range and airspace will be essential to realignment."[15]

In the age of base closures, this stipulation could make or break Mountain Home's future. "If Saylor Creek is not significantly expanded," Colonel Andrews stated, "the training of the crews to man the ninety-four F-4s will be extremely difficult. The level of their combat readiness will be low . . . and eventually Mountain Home will not be very attractive as an Air Force base." However, Herb Meyr, a retired air force pilot living in Mountain Home, described this assessment as "economic blackmail." "You've got everybody in town completely terrified that the base will eventually close if the range isn't built." Having one of their former pilots criticize the plan embarrassed the air force and boosted the hopes of the opposing coalition. Local businesses attempted to discredit Meyr's remarks; suspiciously, his wife lost her job working for the contractor that maintained the targets and ran the scoring equipment at the Saylor Creek range.[16]

Mostly, the enormous size of the expanded range alarmed Idahoans. "It was our impression that they were maybe thinking about doubling the size of the current [109,000] acre range," said a BLM spokesman in Boise. But "they were talking about a 1.4 million acre withdraw and five impact areas, including two for live ammo. . . . This hit the press, and we had a controversy in a hurry." Additionally, the mandated environmental impact survey broadened the "study area" to include about 2.6 million acres, virtually the entire southwestern corner of Idaho.[17]

Excluding Mountain Home residents, many opposed the expansion at public hearings. For example, the Brackett homestead, which covered about a thousand acres near the Nevada line, counted on the hundred thousand acres that it leased from the BLM to graze twelve hundred cattle. Brackett noted that others used the area too. "Sportsmen and recreationists use the area, as well as city people who like to come and enjoy the solitude." Added Randall Brewer: "Miles upon miles of fence, pipelines, roads, and power lines populate the area. Ranchers have spent thousands and thousands of dollars on range and water improvements on an intensively managed grazing system." The air force proposal would have placed a live bombing zone atop the pipeline.[18]

The increased number of sonic booms was another concern. The air force estimated an average of forty a day, which far exceeded the occasional boom experienced at the time. Moreover, the new range pilots flew as low as ten thousand feet, which dramatically increased the impact of the boom. Three Creek, Idaho, maintained a one-room schoolhouse for ten children in kindergarten through eighth grade. The proposal lowered the flight ceiling to a hundred feet, although the air force promised that no jets would fly over the schoolhouse. Despite the air force providing a demonstration, the residents remained skeptical.[19]

The coalition also worried about wildfires. With an annual average rainfall of only eleven inches, fire threatened the surroundings. At the smaller range about two dozen fires started in one year, and in 1976 a fire broke the boundaries and scorched a hundred thousand acres. Opponents argued that increased range size and use of live munitions would result in more range fires. However, air force officials guaranteed 120-foot-wide firebreaks, along with other safeguards. The air force also acquiesced on the need for two live bombsites and instead settled for one. Gary Vest stated, "Are there going to be some fires out there? Of course . . . Will they be very big? I think not."[20]

However, opponents were not satisfied. In 1990, American Rivers, a conservation organization, placed two of the region's waterways, the Bruneau and Jarbridge, on their list of most endangered rivers in North America. At a meeting of the Mountain Home Chamber of Commerce, local dentist Randy Morris presented a slide show on the proposal to make the Owyhee Canyonlands into a national park. For nearly a decade he and members of the Committee for Idaho's High Desert had campaigned for this designation. Morris realized that the park proposal directly overlapped with the range expansion and feared the power of their newest adversary.[21]

Native Americans argued that the expanded range merely represented the latest chapter in the unending exploitation of their land by the US government. "We are a living culture," said Ted Howard, on behalf of the Shoshone-Paiute Tribes. "To Native Americans there is no pre-history, only continuous history." The tribes "came up here for the salmon, until the dams stopped the salmon from reaching our area." Howard also held that the tribes still owned the land. In 1866, the Shoshone and Paiutes signed the Bruneau and Boise Valley treaties, which ceded much of southwestern Idaho to the federal government in exchange for hunting and fishing rights along with the move to the Duck Valley Reservation. "But Congress never signed the treaty," Howard said. "There has never been an exchange of title. The land still belongs to the Indian people." Lindsay Manning, a tribal planner at the Duck Valley Indian Reservation, which would be surrounded by the proposed air force range, stated, "We were given a tribal homeland and sanctity and peace, and now we're being crowded in again."[22]

The opposition coalition also worried about accidents and about debris left behind from training. In November of 1989, while on a training mission near the Joshua Tree National Monument in California, two navy bombers accidentally dropped about a dozen 500-pound bombs a few miles outside the training area. They wounded one camper and traumatized many others. That same fall, in the lands surrounding its aircraft bombing targets at Fallon, Nevada, the navy conducted "Project Ugly Baby"—a mission to gather any spent ordnance on public lands. Among their findings: 1,389 live bombs, 2,230 duds, 28,136 live rounds of ammunition, and 123,375 pounds of ordnance scrap metal.[23]

Yet the military maintained that a "multiple use" arrangement could accommodate hunters, ranchers, nature lovers, and fighter pilots. They insisted that "eternal vigilance remains the price of liberty." Officials argued that combat readiness needed improvement and that prohibition of short-range nuclear missile use meant greater reliance on conventional arms like planes and tanks. Moreover, the "peace dividend" meant cuts in active-duty troops, and resulted in increased dependence on National Guard units, which needed more space to train closer to their home bases. "We have to

Live munitions range clearance in Saylor Creek Bombing Range conducted by the 366th Civil Engineer Squadron on June 22, 2012. (Courtesy of Mountain Home Air Force Base.)

be prepared to go anywhere, anyplace, any time," said Lieutenant Colonel James Cooper. "*Reader's Digest* had a map several months ago with the world marked up in red, white and blue. And there's still a lot of red out there."[24]

Two elements continued to rile many—the lack of demonstrated need for the expansion and its seemingly inevitable creation, with the air force merely moving through the formalities to satisfy the law. For environmentalists, the federal government's actions represented the threat of the military-industrial complex. For conservatives, the actions represented the problems of "big government." Both found inspiration in their understanding of what the West had been or should be. Instead of taking place on dusty main streets, the showdowns played out in courtrooms and town meetings.

Town Meetings: The New Battlegrounds

The air force moved ahead and on August 22, 1989, announced public hearings on September 5, with the first draft of the environmental impact

Idaho Governor Cecil Andrus working at his desk, 1975. (Courtesy of Boise State University Special Collections and Archives.)

statement (EIS) due by October or early November. Their actions galvanized the opposition, who challenged the schedule. "There's no way that you folks can adequately prepare an EIS draft or any other kind, in the time frame that we're talking about," Glenns Ferry rancher Lee Presley testified at the hearing. The opposition also provided public involvement workshops and invited speakers such as Grace Bukowski, who had fought similar proposals in her role as military program director of Citizen Alert in Nevada. She struck a responsive chord with, "Why is it OK to do to rural folks what's not OK for city folks?"[25]

The Glenns Ferry town meeting roused Herb Meyr to seek further information. He visited with Lieutenant Colonel John Cooper, one of his former student navigators who was leading the EIS study, along with a representative from the Boise BLM district office and Andy Brunelle of the governor's office. To the surprise of many, Governor Cecil Andrus, a strong Democrat, consistently supported the proposal. Andrus argued that his support hinged on keeping Mountain Home Air Force Base open and assurances that supersonic flights would not be included as part of the expansion package. Meyr demonstrated to Andrus that the proposal called for live bombs and supersonic flight down to one hundred feet. Meyr also learned that the expansion design was based on not merely the needs of the F-4 fighters, but the needs of all current and future air force aircraft. When questioned, Lieutenant Colonel Cooper maintained, "This will all be in the EIS."[26]

At a town hall meeting in Twin Falls, air force officials prepared for 125 attendees, but more than 400 showed up, necessitating a change of venue. At the Glenns Ferry meeting, Randy Morris exhibited a dummy bomb that missed its target at the Saylor Creek range and landed near a popular campsite, which further heightened fears about allowing the use of live bombs and missiles. Also at the meeting, three retired officers testified that the air force lied to the commission about closing George Air Force Base. Captain William McDaniel (Retired) explained: "We slowly came to the conclusion that it was a carefully orchestrated plan by a few folks in DOD (Department of Defense) and the Air Force."[27]

Ranchers testified that the air force proposal separated key grazing pastures and wells. "It would be like cutting one leg off a table," rancher Bill Swan said. "The leg by itself is not worth much, and the table is worthless without the leg." The proposal left miles of pipeline off-limits and some grazing allotments hacked into unconnected, inaccessible pieces. Tom Basabe, foreman for the JR Simplot Livestock Company, one of the wealthiest ranching corporations in the West, suggested the air force study another section of land in the Owyhees, one less critical to grazing. The air force countered with offers of buyouts, but area ranching families—many who had homesteaded in the area—refused to move. The air force even proposed sharing land, where they would use it during the day and most weekends while the ranchers could access it during the other hours. Ranchers laughed at this proposal—cattle do not take days off.[28]

Conservationists claimed that the range directly clashed with the BLM's proposed wilderness designation and that these lands contained critical zones of animal habitat. Surprisingly, in the course of the meetings, Gary Vest acknowledged that the expansion "was not necessary to support the F-4 mission," and opponents gained a symbolic victory in early January 1990 when air force officials erased the map lines of the proposed expansion. Lieutenant Cooper stated that they would study the entire county for suitable sites.[29]

Since the meetings had not pacified the parties, Idaho politicians convened a "working group" to define issues and suggest alternatives, but divisions quickly surfaced and resulted in a stalemate. Opponents argued that the panel served as a political front and that the air force failed to supply necessary information. They convinced citizens of the influential Sun Valley resort area to hold their own meeting and gathered support from other organizations: Northwest Pipeline Corporation wondered about conducting its aerial patrols of the natural gas pipeline, and federal Animal Damage

Control officials expressed concern about their ability to respond to predator problems. Even the state BLM questioned the necessity, saying, "If they need it, they need to explain it better." Another BLM representative commented, "I don't think it [the EIS] could have been handled any worse."[30]

However, representatives from the Mountain Home community and range expansion proponents countered with their own claims. "This [working] group failed miserably in its charge and in doing so seriously threatened the long-term existence of this base and this community." They maintained that desert preservation was not the goal of environmentalists; rather, they hoped to create "an elite playground for the wealthy urban backpackers at the expense of local residents attempting to make a living off the public land." At the end of February 1990, the air force released its Tier One of the EIS. It targeted nearly two million acres of training range to provide pilot combat training and suggested 7,500 miles of airspace, with supersonic flights above 5,000 of those miles and the use of live bombs.[31]

Then, just as the battles appeared to peak in Idaho, officials in Washington, DC, made decisions that drastically affected the outcome of the proposal. In early May, Mountain Home wing commander Colonel Andrews told the *Washington Post* that training the F-4s would be difficult without the expanded range. Then, just a few days later, on May 12, 1990, the *Washington Post* disclosed a secret air force memorandum that called for the retirement of all the F-4s. The document was a portion of a "Program Objectives Memorandum" required of each military branch by then defense secretary Dick Cheney in May 1990 in anticipation of the forthcoming budget cuts.[32]

When pressed for clarification from the Idaho congressional delegation, Cheney acknowledged that all the F-4s at George AFB might not relocate to Mountain Home. Then on May 18, he announced that the public comment period on the impact statement would be extended another four months to September 15 and later amended that to January of 1991. Five days later, air force secretary Donald Rice reported to the Idaho delegation that the F-4s would likely be retired. Those opposing the range believed the proposal finally had died.[33]

Yet this relatively inexpensive land remained too tempting for the air force to pass up. Even given the constraints on the military budget, Lieutenant Cooper believed the expansion would go ahead. "The dollars involved in the expansion are very small," Cooper said. "You couldn't even buy a new fighter for that cost." Gary Vest confessed similar motives to Herb Meyr at a meeting in May. "We might not need it now," Vest admitted. "But we might in thirty years, and we won't be able to get it then. People will be down there—more and more people using it, and they won't want to go." While town meetings, press releases, and odd coalitions were the obvious elements of this confrontation, the real battle lines began to form behind the scenes. In these trenches bureaucrats from a variety of governmental levels fought for their turf while the public remained frustratingly isolated. Round one had ended, but too many possibilities for land acquisition existed for officials to give up.[34]

Victory?

As opponents celebrated the proposal's apparent demise, local representatives resurrected it under a new format. Idaho state officials, especially Governor Andrus, grew increasingly concerned over the future of the Mountain Home base and led an initiative to expand the range. In the meantime, much of the public remained skeptical about the necessity, particularly given the announced reassignment of the F-4s. Many acknowledged that the air force might require an upgrade in its Idaho training facilities, but the proposed dimensions were far beyond any reasonable projections.[35]

Much of the public grew more irate when in February 1991 news leaked of Andrus's plan, which called for the federal government to purchase private land, and then trade it to the state, thereby maneuvering around the recently placed federal moratorium on military land withdrawals. The plan called for the state to own the land, the Idaho Air National Guard to operate it, and air force to lease it. Gary Vest liked the significant improvements in training flexibility that it offered; however, the governor's plan drew the ire of ranchers and environmentalists alike.[36]

The governor's decision and stubborn pursuit of a range despite public opinion surprised many. Andrus first ran for governor in 1970 on an environmental platform that included protecting Idaho's White Cloud Mountains from an open-pit molybdenum mine. Andrus teamed up with US senator Frank Church of Idaho to create the Sawtooth National Recreation Area, the largest piece of wilderness in the lower forty-eight states. This action gained him national prominence, and in 1977 he joined President Carter's cabinet as secretary of the interior. In that position he again distinguished himself with his efforts to preserve wilderness while balancing that with economic aims.[37]

Andrus returned to Idaho in 1981, and, despite the state's conservative slant, won election as governor in 1986. While in office, he fought to protect more than one million acres of wilderness and faced down the Department of Energy over nuclear waste when he called out the state police to keep shipments from entering Idaho. Andrus accomplished this environmental agenda while the economy simultaneously grew. Given this record, his position on the range expansion seemed inconsistent. Andrus argued that environmental protection remained critical but keeping the base at Mountain Home was equally so. His actions alienated many, even some of his closest friends; his hunting partner, Fish and Game commissioner Richard Meiers, opposed his proposal. Despite the opposition, Andrus remained resolute.[38]

His plan moved the expansion west of the initially proposed area, where some ranchers were willing to sell. He claimed his proposal scaled back the earlier version, yet allowed for improved tactical training. "The truly sensitive canyonlands of the desert expanse have been carefully excluded from the training range, the use of live munitions is prohibited, and the Air Force still will have an essential training facility near Mountain Home Air Force Base." As he threw his political weight behind the project, world events also changed the calculus. Early in 1991, the United States went to war in the Persian Gulf, reinforcing the air force's argument for increased training.[39]

However, despite appeals to patriotic sentiment and Andrus's support, critics remained unconvinced. They argued that the low-level supersonic operations and live bombs banned from the governor's proposal essentially worked in the air force's favor since they would not be required to own or control the ground beneath the airspace. While Andrus's plan moved the target areas to the west, it actually spread the electronic combat range over three million acres of public land—twice the size of the original proposed Saylor Creek expansion.[40]

On April 12, 1991, the air force further complicated matters. They proposed to the Defense Base Closure and Realignment Commission to establish a new "composite wing" at Mountain Home. These new wings had enjoyed considerable success in the Gulf War, and the air force saw them as an efficient rapid global response unit. Officials assured the commission that range development remained unnecessary for the composite wing's training. However, in the "Description of the Proposed Action and Alternatives" document dated May 24, 1991, officials reported that without the state range, training would be limited "until another, more beneficial training alternative is identified." Mountain Home badly wanted to house this new composite wing, which would surely keep it off the list of base closures.[41]

In early May, Andrus began the state-sponsored series of public hearings. As with the earlier round of meetings, critics viewed them as mere formalities. The air force also announced that a single EIS that encompassed all of their proposals—the expanded range, the new composite wing, and changes at the Idaho National Guard—would be conducted. However, to the surprise of many, on May 31 the Base Closure and Realignment Commission listed Mountain Home on its roll of thirty-six bases to be studied for closure or realignment. Reasons for the potential closing included inadequate housing, excessive distance to an adequate bombing range, and the lack of low-level supersonic airspace. While opponents viewed this as a tactical maneuver, Idaho's leaders quickly expounded on the state's intent to enlarge training facilities. Their efforts paid off; officials removed Mountain Home from the list and approved the composite wing. That same day the air force announced its meetings schedule regarding base and range expansion.[42]

Critics remained resolute in their disapproval, yet an air force memo dated March 1991 stated, "Due to its remote location and stark environment, we are anticipating little opposition from local ranchers, Native Americans, or from environmentalists." The opposite occurred. The collective outcry grew and finally caught the attention of the air force director of Environmental Programs, who acknowledged a "fundamental concern with linking the expanding range proposal with the [composite wing] in the EIS." Air force officials decided to split the two proposals—moving the composite wing and the expanded training range.[43]

On August 20, 1991, BLM state director Delmar Vail further complicated matters when he wrote Gary Vest of his apprehension over the inclusion of wilderness study areas in Andrus's proposal. He emphasized that only Congress could legally allow these areas to be used for other purposes. With congressional action pending, Vail pointed the air force toward two alternative areas southeast of the present Saylor Creek range. The BLM also criticized the legitimacy of the company contracted to write the EIS, since it listed the military as its main account. BLM officials remained particularly apprehensive over noise, wilderness, and the impact on bighorn sheep. Despite these concerns, Andrus proceeded with his proposal.[44]

Reactions to these proceedings fired up the opposing alliance, which had re-formed as the Owyhee Canyonlands Coalition. In November 1991, the group attracted a prominent law firm to work on its cause pro bono, an effort that became known as the Greater Owyhee Legal Defense, or GOLD. The firm argued that the air force had failed to investigate reasonable range alternatives. While the legal team worked, other members of the coalition courted the national media in an attempt to inform the public.[45]

In March 1992, the air force announced its decision to establish the composite wing at Mountain Home and released the final EIS. Their plans for the state's range caught many off guard. Officials wanted the range approachable from all sides, stated the need for at least two impact areas, and proposed to drop an estimated twenty-four thousand bombs annually. The proposal also called for greater use of flares and chaff, which significantly increased fire risk and required larger firebreaks. In addition, the plan laid out over thirty different locations—from 0.5 to 5 acres each—where mobile radar emitters would be stationed to simulate enemy air defenses, and included supersonic flights higher than ten thousand feet over most of southern Owyhee County with potentially three hundred sonic booms a month. "Governor Andrus will wish long after he's left office that he never went to bed with the Air Force," opined the *Idaho Statesman*.[46]

Divisions between governmental entities popped up as the process continued. For example, the Idaho Department of Fish and Game expressed concern and argued for alternative sites. Andrus countered, "I continue to be frustrated by public statements made by Fish and Game Department employees. If those employees think there is a better location for the range, for God's sake, let them tell us where." Despite much opposition, he and the director eventually reached an agreement: splitting the range into two parts—one half on the north side of the Owyhee River's East Fork and another to the south. The air force approved these changes and again prepared for the required public hearings.[47]

Numerous groups opposed this latest plan as well; hunters wondered about the effects on bighorn sheep, while environmentalists outlined the ecosystem devastation and noted the loss of recreation areas. Even the Owyhee Cattlemen's Association, normally a staunch military ally, criticized the secretive process and how the range boundaries had been determined. They also maintained that the decision to bring the composite wing to Idaho was made after the 1990 Defense Department's moratorium on land acquisitions and without assurance of a state range. No one had clearly demonstrated the need for the range, and with a $4.4 trillion national debt, this expensive process seemed absurd.[48]

The coalition decided to shift the battle to the courts, and on May 8, 1992, GOLD filed a lawsuit in Boise. It challenged the decision to establish the composite wing and questioned the operational and environmental suitability of the state's bombing proposal. Two other parties also filed suit—the Shoshone-Paiutes and private ranchers Dick and Marie Owen. The lawsuits challenged the validity of the air force's impact statement and claimed that it violated federal environmental law. Critics dismissed the lawsuits as unpatriotic and antimilitary, but the parties went ahead with their cases.[49]

Opponents prepared for the public meetings, only to learn that the air force had changed the format. Instead of sponsoring a large gathering, the air force set up booths staffed by an officer who took individual testimony. One witness compared the booths to confessionals and criticized the divide-and-conquer tactics. The *Twin Falls Times-News* called the format "Operation Sound Barrier" and pledged to provide an alternative forum. The coalition set up its own booths that contradicted air force information and arguments. A common criticism surfaced: the inordinate number of agencies and transactions involved underscored the inefficiency and contradictions of the immense bureaucracy. For example, while air force officials encouraged range expansion, in October 1991 the US Army Corps of Engineers recommended against construction of the range. This organization appraises real estate for the military, and after completing its analysis, it cited concern about damage to bighorn sheep. Critics charged that despite this recommendation, and a federal moratorium on spending, state and federal officials forged ahead.[50]

In early November 1992 state officials announced their intention to swap nineteen thousand acres of state land for twenty-one thousand acres of federal property to help create the range. Since portions of the land swap contained wilderness study areas, it required congressional approval. The elections of 1992 also changed the political makeup at the national and state level. President Clinton replaced George H. W. Bush, Republican Dirk Kempthorne won the US Senate seat vacated by the archconservative Steve Symms, and Republican Mike Crapo took over from Democrat US Representative Richard Stallings. Opponents held out hope when in 1993 GOLD and former Natural Resources Defense Council lawyer Eric Christensen approached President Clinton's staff with a plan for an executive order to be issued that would place a moratorium on all military expansion until the Department of Defense conducted the much called for national training needs assessment. Despite the hope, President Clinton failed to act on the proposal.[51]

Government versus Government

While the negotiations continued, the sheer size and complexity of government interests overwhelmed the opposition. In particular, the military-industrial complex and its ability to relentlessly pursue its interests shocked many of those involved. The federal government seemed to have an unending amount of resources with which to wear down opponents. However, confrontations between the federal and state governments and among state agencies themselves gave the opposition hope.

In August 1993, BLM national director Jim Baca visited Idaho to see for himself what the proposal entailed. Based on his aggressive stand against mining and grazing practices in his home state of New Mexico, environmentalists remained optimistic. Andrus offered to accompany him, but Baca surveyed the area alone. At a news conference Baca voiced his concern over the impact that low-flying jets would have on bighorn sheep, the potential for wildfires, and steadfastly claimed that science and not politics should drive the decision-making process.[52]

Andrus was incensed. Baca's reference to the area as a bombing range rankled him after all of his efforts for approval of the proposal. Andrus, a supporter of the administration, fired off a letter to Interior Secretary Bruce Babbitt. He declared that Babbitt did not have "enough political allies in the western United States to treat us this shabbily." Andrus criticized Baca for going public without consulting him. Baca disagreed. He maintained that they had spoken before the news conference and that he merely reiterated the comments of BLM employees—that the agency should take a second look. “And Andrus went ballistic,” Baca said.[53]

Conflict also surfaced in Congress in September 1993 when Nevada Democratic senator Harry Reid asked the Senate to halt the “unneeded Idaho Training Range.” Reid argued that the deleterious effect from the noisy military jets would be most harmful on the people living at the Duck Valley Indian Reservation, which straddles the Idaho/Nevada border. He asked, “Why are we going to take more away from the Shoshone-Paiute Tribes? Why are we going to desecrate lands sacred to a people who have already been taken advantage of?” However, Senator Kempthorne intervened on behalf of the air force, and the two senators agreed to a compromise that required a feasibility study on creating a fifteen-thousand-foot ceiling and a fifteen-mile buffer around the reservation.[54]

While Reid may have been temporarily placated, Congressman Peter DiFazio of Oregon questioned the need for the range. He was lobbied to take action in a most unusual way. One afternoon in October 1993, Sierra Club representative Rick Johnson and Idaho Conservation League representative Brian Goller got caught in a Washington, DC, downpour and sought cover in a portico at the back of the Capitol, where DiFazio was also escaping the rain. They relayed their story. Since increased air traffic would extend into eastern Oregon, DiFazio sympathized with their effort and agreed to solicit the entire Oregon delegation to write Secretary Babbitt a letter urging him to reject the proposal.[55]

In November 1993, after a six-month delay and a cost of $3.1 million [$5 million in 2014], the air force finally released the EIS of the state range proposal. Andrus supported it even without many of his promised restrictions. However, problems surfaced. The BLM claimed that the proposal failed to comply with either the Endangered Species Act or the Historic Preservation Act. Leaders of fifteen groups wrote a letter to Secretary Babbitt warning him that “they’re fixing to steal your land” and asked that all withdrawals be brought before Congress for proper review. Members of the Owyhee Canyonlands Coalition compared the proposal to the Sagebrush Rebellion of the late 1970s, when miners and ranchers, among others, sought to transfer federal public lands over to state and private control for their benefit.[56]

Environmentalists continually warned of the effects the expanded range would have on pronghorn antelope, sage grouse, and other migratory birds;

but the bighorn sheep became the symbol of their effort to stop the proposed bombing range. The animals appear on ancient petroglyphs drawn by inhabitants of the Owyhee desert thousands of years ago. The journals of early-nineteenth-century trappers in the Rocky Mountains depict the abundance of the animals. However, avaricious hunting practices and disease from domestic sheep nearly made the bighorn extinct. In 1963, Idaho Fish and Game initiated a reintroduction program and replenished the herds. No one could definitively determine the long-term effects that range activity would have on the bighorn sheep. Nevertheless, critics charged that the risks represented too large a gamble for an animal so vital to the region.[57]

As the issue began to gain more national attention, the Owyhee Canyonlands Coalition collected donations from all over the country. They used the funds for radio and television ads, and sponsored a postcard campaign to leaders in Washington. The Snake River Alliance organized a presentation in Boise on how the range would affect the Shoshone-Paiutes. More than two hundred people attended, and the coalition continued to point to the lack of a demonstrated need for the range. At the first meeting for the EIS, 172 signed up to speak, forcing the air force to schedule a second day for the hearing.[58]

The coalition also hired a former Pentagon economist to conduct a cost-benefit analysis of the proposal. William Weida indicated that while neighboring Elmore and Ada Counties stood to enjoy the economic benefits from an expanded range, Owyhee County, through reduced recreation and increased noise, dust, and chaff, would incur the major costs. He estimated that the increased noise and effects on lifestyle would reduce property values considerably, and that the state-proposed land swap meant less income from grazing permits and a smaller county tax base. He concluded that for Owyhee County, one of the poorest counties in Idaho, with 29 percent of the population living below the poverty level, the range would cost $330,000 [$516,446 in 2014] in taxes per year.[59]

When opponents of the range placed Weida's study into the larger national and international context, they saw no reason for an expansion. The USSR had collapsed, the United States was experiencing large budget deficits, and the air force had closed or withdrawn from twenty-eight overseas and nineteen domestic bases. To expand a range in Idaho and spend $60 million [$97 million in 2014] for the composite wing simply did not add up.

Critics claimed that nearly 80 percent of the wing's training could be done within the current airspace, while facilities on nearby ranges in Utah and Nevada were capable of handling the other 20 percent. Air force officials argued that traveling those distances meant linking up and refueling along the way, an inefficient and wasteful process. But former air force pilot Herb Meyr countered that these long flights provided more accurate training since they more precisely mimicked combat conditions.[60]

As the hearings continued, calls for congressional approval grew louder. Although the range was supposedly state managed, critics argued that it was the air force that primarily stood to gain, which made the Engle Act of 1958 applicable. Passed in the wake of unrestrained military expansion, this act reinforced the clause in the Constitution that granted Congress the power "to dispose of and make all needful rules and regulations respecting the Territory or other property belonging to the U.S." Over time the executive branch assumed withdrawal authority, which was later delegated to the secretary of the interior. This department regularly approved applications, especially when much of the land was identified as desert wasteland. The practice finally grew to an alarming rate when the military sought more than fourteen million acres of public land between 1955 and 1956. Representative Clair Engle of California introduced legislation that returned power to Congress. The act required congressional approval for the Department of Defense to withdraw, reserve, or restrict more than five thousand acres aggregate.[61]

While critics pushed for application of the Engle Act, state officials maintained that the state operated the land, with the Air National Guard as primary owners and the air force merely one of the users. However, a House subcommittee revealed that the Air National Guard had no need for a new range, which left the air force and the new composite wing as the true users. Since the air force stood to gain the most, the subcommittee questioned the apparent circumvention of Congress under the Engle Act and asked for an explanation from the secretary of defense.[62]

Meanwhile, in February of 1994, Idaho Fish and Game commissioners in a five-to-one vote withdrew their support for part of the proposal. They cited their charge to protect the state's wildlife, and pointed to inadequate consideration for protecting "unique biological resources" in this area. While they welcomed alternatives, "the Commission [could] no longer support the inclusion of the north training range as part of the preferred alternative." The announcement bolstered the opposition. Coincidentally, the next day Jim Baca, the BLM director, was fired. While the cause remained unclear, his connection to this issue again brought national attention.[63]

Other issues surfaced that seemed to put range expansion into question. In early April, rumors spread that planes due to be moved to Gowen Field where the Air National Guard trained had been switched to another site; thus the existing range was sufficient. This negated any claim that the range was being built primarily for the Air National Guard. Meanwhile the coalition charged that the final EIS failed to meet the requirements of the National Historic Preservation Act of 1966, or the trust responsibilities of the United States for American Indians. Historically, the "trust relationship" between the US government and Native Americans has been defined as a "legal obligation of the United States to protect Native American lands and resources, as well as Indians' rights to self-government." In practice, the US government has violated the "trust relationship" many times, and Native Americans viewed this as another example. They argued that a rocky butte, which served as a sacred site for Native Americans, sat central to the north portion of the range and any disturbance would result in a trust violation. Duck Valley Indian Reservation residents referred to this area as "Sihwiyo," or Willows Growing All in a Row. Tribal chair Lindsey Manning claimed that the tribe honored their dead ancestors buried there through sacred ceremonies. A group of Native American women asked Andrus's air force liaison, "How would you feel if we went to Mountain Home and bombed all your churches? This is sacred ground to all of us Native Americans. It's the same thing."[64]

Although the tribe has rarely revealed hallowed sites for fear of desecration, in September of 1994 and in early 1995 Shoshone-Paiutes took officials from both camps to the site and performed a reverential ceremony that deeply moved the groups. Since President Clinton outlined the government's trust responsibilities with American Indians, the BLM remained obligated to protect areas with important traditional and religious value. This meant that the BLM could not fulfill this responsibility and simultaneously support the air force's preferred alternative.[65]

The tribes adamantly opposed the range proposal. In the mid-1990s, about twelve hundred lived from farming and ranching on the reservation.

They argued that the dropped bombs would poison the water and destroy the animal habitat. Even the current low-flying planes often scared many of the children in Sally Crutcher's Head Start class. She claimed that the jets flew so low that students felt the engine heat and became frightened by the noise. One tribal member argued that this represented merely the latest chapter in a centuries-old battle. Settlers initially took the choice land and gave leftovers to the Indians. Now they even proposed to appropriate that land with no regard for those who lived there. For example, the bombing range would make it nearly impossible to acquire the buckskins that tribes used to bury their dead. While ranchers enjoyed opportunities to make millions off land sales, Native Americans got shorted again. Tribal members sought restrictions that curbed any supersonic flights over the reservation, a limitation of two thousand feet for all flights, and restricted use of flares. Manning felt that Governor Andrus and the air force were dismissing Native American concerns. "Idaho gets the economic benefit. We get the shaft. We're not getting a red penny."[66]

The more the proposal slogged through the legal and political quagmire, the more opponents grew optimistic and continued their campaign. The coalition convinced the Center for Defense Information, a Pentagon watchdog group, to prepare a documentary on the range issue that drew national attention. In Congress, Representative Bruce Vento of Minnesota charged that the proposal deliberately circumvented the Engle Act and should not be allowed. Senators Harry Reid of Nevada, Daniel Inouye of Hawaii, and Ben Nighthorse Campbell of Colorado criticized the range as ill-advised, and in violation of federal law. Actor Paul Newman questioned the reasoning behind risking this natural area for an unnecessary range. Nearly thirty members of Congress asked Clinton not to take action on the range proposal without congressional approval, and forty members acknowledged their concerns about the range to the chair of the House Appropriations Subcommittee on Defense.[67]

In response to this pressure, on October 4, 1994, air force secretary Sheila Widnall announced that the final EIS would not be released. Instead, she declared that the air force would study other alternatives to alleviate environmental and Native American concerns. She informed Governor Andrus that officials had developed a comprehensive mitigation plan, but due to the substantive changes to the proposal and the need to look at other alternatives, the air force would need to release a supplemental EIS and conduct another round of public hearings.[68]

Critics sensed victory—albeit tentatively. Bob Stevens, a coalition activist, still cautioned: "This thing is gut-shot and both kneecaps have been hit, but it's still wiggling. We're not giving up until it stops wiggling." Even Governor Andrus felt the futility. "The blue-suiters marched us down the primrose path, and now, at the eleventh hour, they have walked off and left us," he said. He, along with GOP senators Larry Craig and Dirk Kempthorne and Representative Mike Crapo, attacked the political maneuvering to kill the proposal. However, Idaho attorney general Larry Echohawk maintained that legitimate concerns by the BLM, the Idaho Department of Fish and Game, and the Shoshone-Paiutes rendered the EIS inadequate.[69]

Three days after Secretary Widnall's announcement, US Magistrate Judge Mikel H. Williams concurred. On October 7, 1994, he ruled in favor of GOLD on their lawsuit. Williams concluded that the composite wing and the proposed range were "inextricably intertwined." He acknowledged that, taken separately, each proposal might have insignificant environmental impact, but taken together they "have a substantial impact." Failure to include the range and the composite wing in the same document resulted in "an abuse of discretion and a violation of federal environmental law." He recommended that the air force conduct the process again with the effects of the state range proposal and composite wing considered together in one EIS.[70]

The coalition celebrated their success. "Victories are hard to come by in this business," Craig Gehrke said. But when he heard that the air force had withdrawn the proposal, Gehrke knew the coalition had won. "Oh God, that was sweet." They further applauded when President Clinton learned of public concerns and comments from environmental groups and tribal leaders and ripped up the air force's impact statement. The coalition had successfully survived round two—at least they thought so.[71]

Compromise, Spin, and a War of Bureaucratic Attrition

The availability of resources to fight the battle and the potential large land gain at low cost remained too enticing. Moreover, air force bureaucrats knew that the longer the battle ensued, the greater their chances: they would simply outlast the opponents. They also strategized that if they could separate the groups of the coalition and work with them individually, they could improve their odds. This is precisely what happened: gradually the air force weakened the opposition and defined the parameters of the discussion. Their ability to do this again revealed their power in the contemporary West.

In 1995, Republican Phil Batt took office as governor, while in Congress Mike Crapo and newly elected archconservative representative Helen Chenoweth of Idaho attempted to resurrect support for the proposal. In late April 1995, they invited two influential California Republicans, Duncan Hunter and Randy "Duke" Cunningham, to tour the proposed range and gained their support. Hunter, the third-ranking member of the House National Security Committee, agreed to call for a hearing before his committee and if necessary to subpoena the stalled EIS. Cunningham, a top naval Vietnam War pilot, vowed to stake his reputation in support of the range. However, critics charged that the two congressmen had not come to Idaho simply on a fact-finding mission. According to Fish and Game records, earlier in April Representative Chenoweth paid for Idaho nonresident hunting licenses and nonresident turkey tags for Cunningham and Hunter with money from her own campaign funds.[72]

On May 9, 1995, district court judge Lodge approved Magistrate Mikel Williams's recommendations of the previous October. Lodge's decision obliged the air force to conduct an EIS that combined the composite wing and the range. Even the Department of Defense seemed to recognize the lack of need. On June 30, 1995, the Office of the Inspector General reported that adequate ranges for the composite wing at Mountain Home already existed; any new range would be redundant.[73]

However, efforts to expand the range never slowed. The same day that Lodge announced his decision, Secretary Widnall assured Governor Batt of the air force's intent to complete the supplemental EIS. The next day, in a meeting with Widnall, the Idaho delegation, Governor Batt, a representative for President Clinton, and other officials shockingly announced "one hundred percent complete support from the White House" for development of the range. Senator Craig, as a member of the Natural Resources Committee, and Senator Kempthorne on the Senate Armed Services Committee, had successfully backdoor lobbied for the support. Also, in mid-1995, air force officials separately began to meet with state leaders, the Department of the Interior, and Duck Valley Indian Reservation representatives. They left environmentalists out.[74]

The sudden change in support by the Clinton administration surprised many. However, few knew of the deal made in late 1994 that drew the support of Secretary of the Interior Babbitt and Environmental Quality director Kathleen McGinty. The Idaho delegation and the BLM, the secretary of the interior, the White House, and air force officials all agreed not to oppose the proposal if the process met legal standards and resolved the critical concerns of local groups.[75]

Later in 1995, the air force announced its plans for a new range to be located in the same part of Owyhee County as the failed Saylor Creek expansion. However, this proposal did narrow its scope and size, with low-level supersonic flights and live ordnance banned. Questions continued about the necessity of the range and the possibility of alternative training flights to Utah and Nevada, but the air force painstakingly worked each group separately. Once isolated, each group began to negotiate for its best interest. The air force first targeted its closest allies, the ranchers, and rapidly gained their endorsement. Next, they convinced the Native Americans to drop their lawsuit and settled with them in August of 1996.[76]

In August of 1997, the chief of Ranges and Airspace at the Pentagon, Colonel Fred Pease, told the *New York Times* that pilots gained approximately twice as much training at a range in southern Idaho than if they had to commute to ranges in Nevada or Utah. Although later he admitted that these statistics only represented the few times a month pilots actually performed this training, the spin worked. The newly proposed range meant that an additional 14 percent of the training could be accomplished there, with the remaining 10 percent that required live ordnance to be completed at an alternative site.[77]

In December 1996, the US District Court set aside a portion of its earlier ruling that required the air force to complete a combined EIS. The court reasoned that any injunction against the composite wing operations would have to be denied until a new, legally sufficient impact statement was completed. It also became evident that since the air force had recently invested more than $20 million [$30 million in 2014] during 1996 and 1997 into facilities at Mountain Home AFB and the Saylor Creek Bombing Range, any base closure appeared highly unlikely.[78]

Another round of public hearings on the latest range proposal took place in 1996 and 1997. Although worn down from the endless meetings, opponents continued to rally against the range. In January 1998 the air force finally released its EIS. Despite the resolute opposition of BLM and Fish and Game officials, the document included expansion of military airspace over the Little Jacks Creek Wilderness Study Area. BLM state director Martha Hahn claimed, "This is the only (wilderness study area) in southwest Idaho that does not experience low-level training flights." The Shoshone-Paiute also objected. Although officials had moved the bombing range away from any sacred sites, low-level flight over proposed electronic targets still would disrupt religious ceremonies.[79]

Senator Kempthorne seethed at the opposition. He was certain that everything had been resolved and pledged that "means could be developed to work around the BLM." In early May of 1998, Kempthorne added an amendment to the 1999 Defense Authorization bill that set aside the land for the range. He remained steadfast that the amendment would not undermine the ongoing negotiations between the air force and the BLM but would serve as a "place holder" until an agreement could be negotiated. However, in actuality it removed any incentive for air force officials to negotiate. All they had to do was stall until the existing legislation passed and they would get the range.[80]

Begrudgingly, the BLM let go of protecting the Little Jacks Creek Wilderness area, but in mid-May BLM director Patrick Shea met with air force officers to try and place some restrictions on the range. Critics also noticed another conflict of interest in Kempthorne's legislation. The amendment mandated that the air force compensate Three Creek rancher Bert Brackett for the public land grazing leases lost to the range. For the first time Congress would order a government agency to pay a rancher to relinquish a lease on land already owned by the government. This precedent worried BLM officials, since a cash payment for grazing leases implied a property right contrary to the long-standing BLM recognition of grazing as a privilege. However, the Senate approved the compensation package that totaled nearly a million dollars for Brackett. Senator Craig sat on the appropriations committee that approved the expenditure, and one of his staffers was Jani Brackett, Bert Brackett's daughter. Although Craig's office consistently denied any connection, critics questioned the link. The potential precedent

Saylor Creek Bombing Range warning sign. (Courtesy of the Center for Land Use Interpretations.)

drew concern from many westerners. One Oregon senator wrote, "Does this now mean that every federal permittee can expect federal purchase of grazing rights where those are reduced for reasons of resource protection or when policy changes are made through the land management planning process or other public decision-making?"[81]

Senator Rob Wyden of Oregon gathered opposition to Kempthorne's amendment. In June 1998, he along with Senators Reid, Inouye, and Richard Bryan from Nevada and others introduced an opposing amendment. Kempthorne rebutted. On the Senate floor he argued, "In an unstable world, I don't want to be on the side that denied them [the pilots] the opportunity for adequate training." He also elicited the support of renowned hawk Senator Strom Thurmond who stated "that land withdrawal is necessary to ensure the very realistic military training of the 366th Wing at Mountain Home Air Force Base." Senator Reid countered with a statement from General Ken Peck, who said, "We are the most combat capable unit anywhere in the world right now." Reid also claimed that Kempthorne buried the 86 percent disapproval rating of the comments taken at the meetings. "The fact is," Reid charged, "Idahoans oppose this expansion six to one."[82]

But even with Reid's statistics, Idaho's senators successfully pushed the amendment through, and on October 17, 1999, President Clinton signed the Defense Authorization bill. This ended the national debate, but opponents still hoped that concerns over the land lease, court proceedings from lawsuits, and the grazing permits that had to be transferred might stall the range proposal from moving ahead. However, in the fall of 1998, Dirk Kempthorne won election as Idaho's governor, which ended their hopes. Since the governor sits on the state land board, members agreed to postpone taking up the matter until the newly elected governor took his place. At issue was 960 acres that the state had to swap. The Owyhee Canyonlands Coalition filed a competing application for the same acreage and even submitted a higher bid. But the land board argued that the air force had demonstrated a longer-term commitment to the public school endowment fund since they had leased the Saylor Creek range since 1962.[83]

Nevertheless, the air force did agree to negotiate some points with the Owyhee Canyonlands Coalition, and, after three days of intense negotiation, on July 9, 1999, finally reached a settlement to the decade-long effort. Although they had lost in the battle for range expansion, opponents felt they had gained some concessions. Low-level flights would be restricted to no lower than five thousand feet and supersonic flights to no lower than fifteen thousand during April, May, and June, except for two one-day exercises each month over the canyons of the East and South Forks of the Owyhee. They also agreed to $220,000 [$309,000 in 2014] to be appropriated to monitor the effect of military operations on bighorn sheep. Air force officials also consented to seek funding for other wildlife protection, to restore native vegetation in areas burned by fires caused by training operations, to fund studies of noise levels created by composite wing exercises, and to move one of the simulated targets to ensure some protection of wildlife habitat.[84]

The coalition pointed to membership on an advisory board as perhaps their greatest victory, since it allowed them to voice their concerns along with the BLM. The air force also agreed to pay GOLD's attorney fees. While some members of the coalition believed they had sold out, others thought they had at least gained some concessions and that the range would be less harmful to wildlife, to recreation, or to ranchers than the original 1989 proposal. In July of 1999, US District Judge B. Lynn Winmill approved the settlement.[85]

Conclusion

Patricia Limerick conceived the idea for her landmark work *The Legacy of Conquest: The Unbroken Past of the American West* while attending a summer 1981 conference in Sun Valley, Idaho, titled "The American West: Colonies in Revolt." In her work she identified the American West as "the arena in which an expanded role of the federal government first took hold."[86] Limerick initially identified the role of government as assisting a "legacy of conquest" against Native Americans; now it seemed to engage in a conquest of its own people.

The writer Wallace Stegner remarked, "There are thousands more federal employees in the West than there are cowboys."[87] This is precisely the problem, argued area ranchers. The style and manner of the air force officials left ranchers alienated and despondent about a supposed democratic system that appeared to grant people a say but then decided the outcome behind the scenes.[88] While they traditionally supported a strong defense, the government's intrusion into their livelihood challenged western ideals of freedom and the essence of the noble character they believed developed in the West. Earlier the government assisted them in their efforts; now it chased them off the land. Ranchers and other local parties realized they had to take matters into their own hands.

However, other interest groups learned from this episode as well and prepared for the next confrontation. Roger Singer, a local representative from the Sierra Club, argued that although opposition groups had helped to scale back the size of the bombing range and negotiated site protection and certain restrictions, "All of this had been based on compromise and the defensive. We turned offensive after that."[89]

Not long after President Clinton signed the Defense Authorization bill, air force Lieutenant Colonel Jim Baker of Mountain Home reported to the Twin Falls Rotary Club on the new training complex the air force would enjoy. Baker wondered how the negotiations and court cases could have continued for nearly a decade. "It's just a patch of dirt," he said. For many, the land was so much more. Craig Gehrke of the Wilderness Society stated, "The Air Force put the Owyhees on the map and forced it to the forefront of the conservation agenda." The next battle was on: an attempt to make the vast open land in the Owyhees into a national monument.[90]

CHAPTER EIGHT

The Owyhee Canyonlands: Showdown to Collaboration

In May of 1998, *Sunset* magazine published an article about potential national parks. "Owyhee, Algodones, Grand Gulch: They are not exactly household names, but they should be as familiar as Yellowstone, Yosemite, and Grand Canyon. After all, these lands are among the West's most spellbinding places." The author, Jeff Phillips, quoted Wallace Stegner's "geography of hope" to identify these as lands for future generations. One visitor to the Owyhees, Marcy St. John, a Southern California attorney on a "self-proclaimed sanity break from civilization," looked up while floating through Bruneau Canyon and asked, "Who would have guessed this kind of place still exists?"[1]

Since the 1980s, environmentalists had been working to have this region designated as a national park or monument. With the Saylor Creek Bombing Range expansion completed in 1999, they quickly focused their attention on the remaining land and a new proposal. Environmentalists wanted President Clinton, through use of the Antiquities Act of 1906, to designate 2.7 million acres of Owyhee County as a national monument. They argued that off-road vehicle use created an unauthorized road system that devastated the scenic canyonlands. With the population steadily increasing, the potential damage seemed inevitable. Defenders claimed that the proposal allowed hunting, fishing, grazing, hiking, camping, boating, air force fly-

Owyhee Canyonlands. (Bureau of Land Management.)

overs, and motorized use on designated roads, while it banned only damaging mining endeavors and off-road use. Sponsoring organizations included the Wilderness Society, the Sierra Club, the Idaho Conservation League, the Committee for Idaho's High Desert, the National Wildlife Federation, Idaho Rivers United, the National Parks and Conservation Association, American Lands, American Rivers, and Friends of the Earth.[2]

However, another set of organizations strongly opposed any such action: the Idaho Cattle Association, the Idaho Farm Bureau, the Blue Ribbon Coalition, Owyhee County officials, and Idaho's congressional delegation. These groups did not trust the federal government with protecting private property rights, public access, and grazing. Moreover, the congressional delegation opposed the use of the Antiquities Act since it circumvented their oversight in this matter. Regardless, government would have to be involved throughout this process, since most of the land remained under the jurisdiction of the Bureau of Land Management, the largest landlord in the West, controlling 264 million acres—more than the National Forest and National Park Services combined.

This battle represented the latest in the ongoing confrontations over land use in the Owyhees. Two competing visions attempted to use local government or the federal government to advance their cause, while the western myth permeated the entire episode. As bureaucrats battled, locals in Owyhee County wondered what would happen to their lives if the proposal passed.[3]

Competing Visions

Bill and Margaret Tindall are the most recent generation of Tindalls who have lived on the same land for over one hundred years. They worried that monument designation would end their family's ranching way of life. "A lot of city people have developed a taste for elbow room, and they want to use those canyons as a playground," Bill Tindall said. "My contention is that we're producing beef, and production is what made this country great. We spend a smaller portion of our income on food than anyplace in the world, and we should stick with it." But Tindall was pessimistic for the future. "We have so many environmental regulations I think we'll probably go out of business anyway. The monument could just mean it will happen sooner."[4]

Mistrust of the federal government underlies much of this argument. "If it's like what happened in Utah, they won't allow cattle," said Don Davis, a rancher and former county commissioner. "It will take about half our tax base." In 1996, President Clinton authorized the establishment of 1.7 million acres in southern Utah as Grand Staircase Escalante National Monument. Critics charged that Clinton acted without warning or local consultation, and the Escalante case became the rallying cry for Owyhee County ranchers. Sheriff Gary Aman warned against "the same massive federal lockdown of access and recreation use as has occurred in southern Utah." Aman claimed that "the number of federal agents has increased from 12 to over 100 at the monument site; federal agents have closed down 1,000 miles of county roads; closed recreation areas, challenged rights of way, refused to allow counties to maintain roadways and seized livestock in violation of state law."[5]

Rancher Gene Davis, who has lived in the county since 1950 and still considers himself a newcomer, reasoned, "[Owyhee County is] the largest beef county in Idaho, and 85 percent of the cattle operations in the county are in the monument. If we try to stay, we'd be forced out, because we

Simplot employees on a trail drive in an area called Yankee Bill near Grasmere in southwestern Idaho, 2007. (Courtesy of J. R. Simplot Company.)

know what they're doing with grazing in Escalante." He feared the regulation. "They'll cut into grazing to the point it won't be an economic operation. Basically, there won't be a livestock business in Owyhee County."

Don Banks, spokesman for the Utah office of the BLM, countered that the Escalante case has been broadly misinterpreted. "Nothing could be further from the truth," he said. "The proclamation establishing the national monument specifically authorizes grazing to continue. And it is continuing under the same laws and regulations that apply to grazing anywhere on public lands."[6]

Despite these assurances ranchers remained skeptical. "We first heard about this canyonlands thing in 1966," said Mike Hanley, who lives in Jordan Valley, Oregon, and ranches in Owyhee County. "They wanted to remove the cattle and create a Canyonlands National Park. It's been a cloud over our heads for a long time, and now it looks like they're going to get it." He claimed that the environmentalists have had cattle removal as part of their agenda all along. "Their purpose is to remove us from that land. . . . Every decision goes against the ranchers." Russ Hoffman, Idaho Cattle Association vice president, warned that even if cattle are legally allowed, they will be removed in practice. "Escalante and the Canyonlands will be just like every other special use designation. Cattle have never been banned from the Frank Church Wilderness, either, but there are none there now." Hoffman concluded, "They just tighten down the regulatory screws to the point that it's impossible to have cattle."[7]

The ranchers feared that the creation of a national monument would close roads, restrict their access, and weaken their water rights. This in turn would lower their property values and ultimately end the economic viability of their operations and their way of life. Everett Thomas argued that the monument "would bring too many people and too much traffic. I'd like to see it stay just the way it is here, but the government and the environmental people want to bring tourists in here and lock us out." Bruneau rancher Bonnie Colyer added, "The environmental colony thinks that since this land is homesteaded and we've had it for free for all these generations that now we should give it back. Boise was homesteaded too. How would they like to give that back?" "This is a poor county," rancher Tony Black stated. "It always has been and always will be. . . . This valley is in trouble, and this monument is the last nail in our coffin."[8]

Katie Fite saw things very differently. A Pennsylvania native, Fite lived in Idaho and worked as an environmental activist with the Committee for Idaho's High Desert (CIHD). University educated, Fite worked for eight years on habitat improvement for the Idaho Department of Fish and Game. She criticized the Tindalls' anachronistic way of life and directly challenged the mythical western cowboy. "One of the images people have of ranching is the Marlboro man riding into the sunset," Fite said. "But there's a slash-and-burn and kill aspect of ranching that casts nature as an enemy. Nature has to be subdued so you can extract cows from it." She argued that "the whole idea of national monuments is breaking out of the old ways and managing the land so it's good for everybody." Fite views the canyonlands—this vast high desert country with diverse terrain, plants, and animals—as a public trust.[9]

She also argued that, with the monument, property values would actually increase rather than decrease. "All you have to do is look at other places where there have been special designations. Suddenly you have people interested in purchasing a place. Once a place is designated as something special, it raises awareness and desirability." She vehemently denied that the care from ranchers keeps the canyonlands from needing protection. "What the cows are doing to the land is really sad," she said. "Everywhere there's a road or a cattle trail, there are exotic, noxious weeds because the cattle carry the seeds in their fur and feces." She warned of poor water quality. "When I see a stream that's been overgrazed and the banks are sluffing away, I look at that as a taking from the whole public."[10]

Pam Marcum, chair of CIHD, concurred. She argued that the canyonlands needed a rest. A third-generation Idahoan who enjoys bird-watching, Marcum believed that monument designation does not affect water rights and provides for continued grazing. "We've written a letter to the cattle association explaining that," she stated. "The only things that would be prohibited are mining and off-road vehicle use, and there needs to be some protection of the archaeological sites." However, she added, "Personally, I think it's time to retire some of these cattle allotments. I've talked to a lot of ranchers who see the future and it's not in grazing." She believed that ranching no longer served as a viable option. Even though ranchers had inherited the land and were subsidized by the federal government, they still could not make it profitable and in the meantime continued to destroy the land. "The area must be cattle free, it just doesn't fit," Marcum stated. "The goal is for restoration, to get it back to what it used to be. The land needs to be healed and that means no off-road vehicles and no cattle."[11]

She also argued that education of the public began to shift the tide toward high desert country preservation. "Everybody wants to save forest—forest is the sexiest thing to save," Marcum stated. "However, people are getting more and more educated about the desert, and a place like the Owyhees is drawing a lot of attention." She also maintained that the "cow is the worst environmental choice the West made. We've changed this area into a monoculture of weeds. This area didn't evolve with a heavy-hoofed animal; there weren't many bison in this area. We don't need cattle now."[12]

Fite, Marcum, and other conservationists envisioned a future in which monument ranchers could sell their land at good prices, stay there and make a living providing services to monument visitors, or even form partnerships with environmental groups. Their view directly confronted the western image developed over generations. "It's a different view of how our public lands should be used," Fite said. "It's a cultural difference and a value difference. People want to go out there and see raptors and native songbirds. They don't want to go out there to look at cow flop." However, Mike Hanley argued that Owyhee County will always have one foot in the Old West, and that the cowboy tradition will remain. "I don't think I'd be very good at flippin' hamburgers for tourists."[13]

The battle lines in this latest dispute pitted the legacy of the cowboy against an environmental movement that hoped to restore the land to its pre-cattle days. Both used history and images of the past to justify their positions, and both recognized the important role of government in the outcome. As with each of the episodes examined in this book, the land lies at the heart of the matter, and so we turn to a brief description of the Owyhee Canyonlands.

The Owyhee Canyonlands

The canyonlands encompass an area larger than Yellowstone Park. From Idaho's Bruneau and Jarbidge Rivers of eastern Owyhee County into eastern Oregon, the area includes the South Fork and East Fork of the Owyhee River, Battle Creek, Deep Creek, the Jacks Creek area to the north, and other smaller tributary streams. Wildlife biologists say they are among the most spectacular in the country. In commemoration of the bicentennial of the Lewis and Clark Expedition, the Sierra Club listed the canyonlands as one of thirty-three sites on the Lewis and Clark route that still retain much of the remote, rugged terrain of two hundred years ago. In fact, Charbonneau, Sacajawea's son, lived his final years in this region and is buried near Jordan Valley.[14]

The unique wildlife and geological features set this land apart. The canyonlands contain Idaho's largest population of California bighorn sheep, prairie falcon, sage grouse, antelope, and river otter. Even the peregrine falcon, nearly extinct, has been spotted. However, unlike with most other high desert rivers, in the Owyhee canyon the plateau spills down to the river in many areas, allowing the antelope, mule deer, and other upland wildlife easy access to the river. In some areas whitewater has carved out the basalt in excess of twelve hundred feet, and flows accommodate a twenty-two-day canoe trip—one of the finest desert wilderness experiences in the country.

Rafting down the Owyhee River. (Courtesy of Momentum River Expeditions.)

"The best way to see this country is from a canoe," said Phil Lansing, a river guide from Boise. "It's like driving around in an Ansel Adams photograph."[15]

Protection advocates such as the CIHD point to a history of recreation and preservation. In 1951, commercial outfitter Prince Helfrich used surplus World War II rubber assault rafts and floated from Three Forks to Rome for what is believed to be the first recreational use of the river. Boating use remained light throughout the 1950s and 1960s. However, it steadily increased, and in the 1970s the BLM began recording recreational use statistics. By 1974 the BLM documented 482 people floating the river. Four years later the number had increased to 1,000 annually, and by 1980 2,000 boaters enjoyed the Owyhee.[16]

In 1970, the state of Oregon designated the Owyhee River from the Idaho/Oregon state line to Three Forks, and from Crooked Creek to the Owyhee Reservoir, as state scenic waterways. Six years later, under the requirements of the Federal Land Policy and Management Act of 1976, ten wilderness study areas had been identified. In 1979, the Owyhee Wild and Scenic River Study recommended that a 192-mile segment of the Owyhee

River be added to the National Wild and Scenic Rivers System, under administration of the BLM and the state of Oregon. The South Fork of the Owyhee River remained outside the boundaries of this study, but the National Park Service included it in its Nationwide Rivers Inventory.[17]

In 1936, wilderness pioneer Bob Marshall inventoried the remaining roadless areas in the United States. He identified the Owyhees as the second-largest desert region, with more than four million acres of uninterrupted roadless land spanning Idaho, Oregon, and Nevada. Four decades later, the CIHD also acknowledged the uniqueness of the canyonlands as "one of America's most scenic and important desert wilderness areas." Begun in 1979, the organization formed as a small group of desert advocates who met occasionally to share notes and ideas about the BLM wilderness review and land-use planning process. Over the years the association grew and became especially active during the Saylor Creek range controversy. In 1997 the CIHD, along with the Idaho Watersheds Project, filed the first federal lawsuit over grazing management. The suit charged the BLM with failure to take action after an agency reported poor conditions caused by livestock grazing. The next year the CIHD hired its first employee, a biologist, to conduct studies of the area. After the Saylor Creek range development process, the CIHD and the other environmental organizations formed the Owyhee Canyonlands Coalition in November of 1999. They focused all of their attention on a proposal to protect 1.2 million acres of the Owyhee Canyonlands roadless area as wilderness.[18]

The Sierra Club also anchored the coalition. Local Sierra Club representative Roger Singer said, "Education was the primary goal. We wanted to get people to connect with the land." Since Treasure Valley in southwestern Idaho is the fourth-fastest-growing location in the nation, Singer recognized the importance of setting aside a common space, before developers got hold of it. The project gained the attention of the national Sierra organization, which helped set up meetings with Secretary of the Interior Bruce Babbitt and provided grant money for outreach and education.[19]

The coalition continually maintained that the monument would "keep the land the way it is now"—it would allow the current grazing to continue, but prevent any major new developments such as mining, small hydro development, and any large-scale herbicide spraying and seeding projects. Coalition members argued that since political pressure could change approved land-use plans and protective designation given by BLM, wilderness designation remained the only reliable protection for the unique resources of the canyonlands. The coalition feared that local ranchers would work to place the land under state control, which would provide the opportunity for it to be privatized. Furthermore, while wild and scenic river status for the Owyhee would protect the canyon bottoms from dams and other development, it would not protect the critical wildlife habitat, or the tributaries of the Owyhee, from small hydroelectric plant development. Therefore, they argued that wilderness designation remained the only alternative to keep it "the way it is." The proposal called for protecting 1.2 million acres of a total roadless acreage of 1.9 million acres. The majority of the area lay in Idaho, with 562,700 acres, then Oregon with 536,634 acres, and the remaining 92,406 acres in Nevada.[20]

The coalition hoped that President Clinton would employ the Antiquities Act. This power authorizes the president "to declare by public proclamation historic landmarks, historic and prehistoric structures, and other objects of historic or scientific interest that are situated upon the lands owned or controlled by the Government of the United States to be National Monuments." President Theodore Roosevelt first used the powers and designated one million acres as national monuments. President Carter exercised this power the most generously of all and stipulated fifty-six million acres, primarily in Alaska, as national monuments. Between 1906 and 2000, fourteen US presidents used the act to proclaim 112 national monuments—presidents Reagan, Nixon, and George H. W. Bush remain the only three to never invoke the act. Congress may also designate areas as national monuments, and has done so in twenty-nine cases. Additionally, Congress has redesignated thirty national monuments as national parks. The tension between government branches remains: Congress attempts to reign in the executive branch, with former Senator Craig from Idaho leading that effort.[21]

The coalition released statistics that showed 80 percent of Idahoans strongly and/or somewhat supported the idea. Numerous papers also published editorials that favored the establishment of the Owyhee Canyonlands. Additionally, Clinton signed a proclamation that expanded the Craters of the Moon National Monument in Idaho to include the entire sixty-five-mile-long Great Rift, a gouge in the earth that spread lava across the Snake River Plain two thousand years ago. Even though all of Idaho's conservative Republican congressional delegation opposed establishment of the Owyhee Canyonlands, the coalition argued that if the Craters of the Moon National Monument had been expanded, surely the canyonlands should have at least equal protection. Bill Meiners, an Idaho conservation pioneer, summarized their argument. "The public lands of the United States represent a heritage," he maintained. As inheritors we have a "sacred trust to pass to future generations."[22]

Nonetheless, those in opposition remained just as adamant about defeating the proposal. "I think this whole monument thing is ridiculous," said Harold Tolmie, Owyhee County Commission chairman. "What we should do is sell the whole county for $2 billion [$2.7 billion in 2014] and all move somewhere else." "My comment is, 'Protect it from what?'" said Ted Hoffman, a Mountain Home veterinarian and rancher. "It's fine the way it is."[23]

Many felt the same way. At a gathering in December 2000, hundreds demonstrated their opposition to creating a national monument. "It's a government land grab, pure and simple," commented one local. "There's nothing out there that needs protection from people that live on that land or who go there just to enjoy it." Owyhee County commissioner Fred Grant argued, "They say it's necessary to preserve this grand, pristine area, but if it's so pristine after more than a hundred years of grazing and other uses, what else is there to preserve it from?"[24]

Candidates for commissioner in Owyhee County successfully campaigned on opposition to the creation of a national monument. They argued that individuals could backpack and float the river or enjoy a variety of activities without the area being given a separate designation. One candidate, Chris Salove, warned, "If they don't think there's not going to be enormous changes with the monument designation they're wrong. Any recreation other than foot traffic will be severely reduced." He added, "I don't see tourism being able to replace what we will lose from our ranching." Another candidate, Chet Sellman, stated, "It takes a pretty robust person to go down into those canyons. They don't need to have a designation because they'll protect themselves."[25]

The board of Owyhee County commissioners also urged the public to support their opposition to the designation. Like "Sagebrush Rebellion" advocates, they fought for local control and claimed that grazing, mining, logging, and all recreational uses such as snowmobiling, fishing, hunting, and off-road vehicle races would "be at the mercy of a federal bureaucrat who can end such uses with a stroke of a pen." They insisted that owners of private property would be denied access, that property values would decline, and that water rights would be jeopardized through this restriction on use. Since delivery of county services remained dependent on widespread transportation, open access of the county roads remained vital. They could not afford to be "dependent upon the whim of a federal bureaucrat." Many feared the bureaucratic mismanagement that the commissioners claimed plagued other sites, and supported the tradition of private management that remained strong in the West. The commissioners maintained that the "uniqueness of the Owyhee Canyonlands has been nurtured by responsible local citizens who have managed multiple uses of the land."[26]

Battle for the Myth

Underlying the arguments are distinct visions of land use and accompanying identities. Much of this gets reinforced through stories told and perceptions emphasized. Two newspaper stories provide contrasting perspectives.

> Tim Lowry grew up on a family ranch in Jordan Valley, Oregon, just over the Idaho border. In 1984, he purchased his own land and joined a cattle business that in Owyhee County accounted for $36 million [$81 million in 2014] and created 205 jobs. He married a Basque immigrant and together they raised a family and built their ranch on their pastures and the federal grazing ground spread out 40 miles from their base. However, beginning in 1988, trouble appeared for the Lowrys. One day while Tim Lowry was out baling hay, a BLM official stopped to inform him that due to drought conditions all of his cattle would have to be removed from the public land. "They told me I had five days to get every cow off the allotment or they would impound them," Lowry said. Thanks to the assistance of neighbors who finished baling and stacking his hay, he rounded up his cattle and by splurging on extra feed made it through the year.
>
> After this episode, the BLM initiated a forum for a grazing management plan to satisfy both environmentalists and ranchers. They made progress, but by 1990 had failed to finalize a deal. To meet their

> rules and yet still allow the local ranchers to continue, the BLM proposed a three-year rotation grazing plan. However, the BLM held firm that the plan's success hinged on ranchers building a 4.5-mile fence near the North Fork of the Owyhee River. Moreover, not only did they have to build the fence, but due to an administrative deadline, they had to complete it in four days. At the time Tim Lowry got this news, he was trailing cattle with his father off their allotment and onto private land. They had to complete this work as well.
>
> Lowry was not sure what to do, but decided first to meet with Mike Sanford, who also ran cattle on the same range, to discuss their options. Sanford said, "We've got no choice, we've got to give it a chance," Lowry remembered. So, Lowry left his cattle to the charge of his 71-year-old father, and he and Stanford began the seemingly impossible task of building a 4.5-mile fence across rugged terrain in four days. Discouraged their first day, the pair made very little progress. Then, word got out to the surrounding community and everything changed. "People were coming from everywhere packing post packers and wire stretchers," Lowry said, his eyes misting up. "Men, women, kids bringing up the tail end." To the disbelief of all, in three days they completed building the fence and installed the cattle guard by the deadline. Lowry stood in disbelief, "Without neighbors, I don't know where I'd be."
>
> Their efforts seemed straight out of a western movie, . . . but the scene kept rolling and their relief was short-lived. Since the BLM did not have the authority to allow them to build the fence, environmentalists successfully challenged it in court. A judge ordered the fence to be removed and BLM firefighters yanked out all of the fence except the cattle guard. This episodes represents what many in the West, and more broadly in the nation, point to as the extremism of the environmental movement and the over-reach of government.[27]

The call to build the fence coupled with the subsequent imperative to remove it serves as a symbol for the ongoing conflict in the West. For decades the fence served as evidence of the settlers' control over the land, their ability to bring order over a range that Native Americans left fenceless for centuries. However, environmentalists worked just as hard to remove these fences and what they represented—a devastation of the land. While

Tim Lowry gets ready for spring branding. (Courtesy of Jake Putnam.)

many remain sympathetic to the ranchers in this article, another newspaper's report on land use and the image of the cowboy in the West offers a different perspective.

According to an expansive investigation conducted in 1999 by the *San Jose Mercury News* in seventeen western states, livestock grazing is allowed on 254 million acres of national forests and BLM land—an area equal to California, Oregon, Washington, and Idaho. On that vast expanse, about 26,300 ranchers graze 3.2 million cattle. Yet, in 1999, taxpayers subsidized more than $100 million [$140 million in 2014] in order for a relatively small number of ranchers to maintain this lifestyle. This subsidy remains little known to most taxpayers, and the largest recipients would surprise those paying the bill. It represents one of the latest examples of large businesses exploiting the western myth to take advantage of government programs designed to help the individual cattleman.[28]

According to this study, the lowly rancher rarely enjoys this money; it regularly benefits the well off. Of the 26,000 federal billing records reviewed, corporations, millionaires, and "Rolex ranchers" dominated grazing on the public's range. The top 10 percent of grazing permit holders on BLM property control 65 percent of all livestock, while the bottom 50 percent manage just 7 percent. Through Freedom of Information Act requests, an analysis revealed hotel mogul Barron Hilton, beer giant Anheuser Busch Inc., and HP heir Mary Hewlett Jaffe enjoyed below-market grazing fees. Those whom the subsidy was designed to benefit rarely enjoyed the assistance. Moreover, the large operations inflict the greatest damage on the public land. In 1999 the BLM classified 46 percent of the parcels rented by its twenty largest permit holders as unsatisfactory—compared with 27 percent of parcels overall.[29]

Perhaps most surprising, given the ranching lore and imagery of the West, comparatively little of the beef that Americans consume is raised in the West—a mere 3 percent, according to the US Department of Agriculture. And western ranchers make up just 2 percent of America's 1.1 million cattle operators. Although Wyoming has a cowboy on its license plates, Florida has more beef cattle. Nevada holds a cowboy poetry festival, but Louisiana has twice as many beef cows. Water is the reason. It is much more difficult to raise cattle in the arid West than in the East. Statistics reveal that a cow can live on two acres in the East whereas it needs up to one hundred acres in the West. Most of America's beef comes from private ranches in the Plains, the South, and Midwest. Given these statistics, environmentalists, taxpayer groups, and the Clinton administration sought reform; however, a few western politicians have successfully preserved the status quo, often by hiding behind the mystique of the western cowboy.[30]

Some say public land livestock grazing remains a marginal occupation that should not be favored by federal law. BLM land, generally in dry areas that homesteaders rejected, produces little. That's one reason why Idaho ranks nineteenth in cattle production nationwide, yet sixth in BLM acreage. Public land grazing—on BLM land, Forest Service land, and other public property—provides only 3.5 percent of the nation's beef, according to Karl Hess, Jr., a senior fellow at the Cato Institute, a libertarian think tank in Washington, DC.[31]

In fact, a desire to maintain the image of a cowboy lifestyle keeps many of the wealthy in the cattle business despite financial losses. Their ranches largely exist as quaint settings to entertain clients and companies, and they often buy ranches for water and mineral rights. Defenders claim that corporate domination of public land makes no difference. "They are still running the same cattle and employing the same number of ranch hands," said Jason Campbell, federal lands director for the National Cattlemen's Beef Association. "They are supporting mainstream businesses in places like rural Wyoming and Colorado and Montana." Defenders also argue that reform will further harm an industry already challenged by low beef prices, environmental lawsuits, and foreign competition.[32]

Nevertheless, subsidies come at a cost. In 1998, the Forest Service and the BLM lost on grazing permits more than twice what they spent to restore endangered species. Under a program called Wildlife Services, the Department of Agriculture spent $14.6 million [$21 million in 2014] to kill coyotes, mountain lions, and other predators for Western ranchers. Additionally, the fee that ranchers pay to graze livestock on federal land is lower than the market average on private land in the eleven westernmost states.[33]

However, historical precedent helps the ranchers' cause. Under an old "use it or lose it" permit system, this small group of ranchers enjoys a monopoly on federal lands as they have for decades. "One very small, politically powerful industry is destroying the land," said John Horning, director of watershed protection for Forest Guardians, a Santa Fe environmental group. "But the salt in the wound is that we're paying them to do it."[34]

Idaho native and billionaire J. R. Simplot was dubbed the "king of public lands grazing." Simplot made his money through potato processing (supplying French fries for McDonald's restaurants nationwide) and more recently in the high-tech industry. Simplot regularly made the Forbes 400 list, with a net worth of $3.6 billion [$5.1 billion in 2014], and he reigned as the largest operator of cattle on BLM lands in the United States. His corporation controlled permits to graze on at least 1.9 million acres of BLM land—mostly in Idaho, Nevada, and Oregon. Simplot Livestock maintained the largest feedlot west of the Mississippi, with over one hundred thousand head, and exported beef around the world.[35]

Operations like Simplot's reflect a national trend where fewer small ranches exist while the number of cattle in general has increased. For example, the number of ranching operations in Idaho has fallen by half since 1965, from 25,000 to 12,500, according to the Department of Agriculture, while the number of cattle has increased. "Small ranchers could not afford to stay in business," said the leader of the Idaho Cattle Association. The trend toward fewer ranches matches trends in the agricultural industry nationwide. The number of farms and ranches has fallen to 1.9 million, the lowest number since the Civil War.[36]

Simplot Livestock Company president Tom Basabe defended their practices and argued that all should be entitled to pay the same amount to graze on the land. He asked, "Are you going to have two prices for a loaf of bread?" Moreover, he reasoned, "We make our living off the land. We would be very foolish and shortsighted if we abused it." Basabe also criticized the federal bureaucracy: "Government already imposes too much paperwork and too many regulations and it's gotten worse with Clinton and Babbitt." Simplot public lands manager Chuck Jones argued that cattle reduce invasive plants and fire danger and maintained that their cowboys patrol the vast open area. "We'll never apologize for being the biggest. We admire Mr. Simplot for being an American success story."[37]

Ranchers like Simplot are able to maintain control over such large tracts because they obtain ten-year permits for large blocks of public land known as allotments; therefore, their only requirement is to keep a private ranch and run livestock such as cattle, sheep, or horses. Once one gains control over a permit, it remains in one's possession. Critics like to point out that it costs more to feed a hamster than the federal government charges to feed a one-thousand-pound cow. They claim that the federal government should more accurately charge what it actually costs. "Clearly taxpayers are not getting their money's worth," said John Berthoud, president of the National Taxpayers Union. Even some cowboys call the fee too low, although most having this opinion live in the Great Plains where nearly all land is private. "We consider it to be an unfair subsidy," said Scott Dewald, executive vice president of the Oklahoma Cattlemen's Association. "The fee should be based on public auctions, high bidder takes it." Furthermore, they argue that half the fee ends up back in the pockets of ranchers as "range betterment funds" to pay for fences, water tanks, and other equipment.[38]

However, defenders of the practice maintain that the fee simply reflects drops in beef prices and that few cowboys get rich. "We are almost in a life-and-death situation out here," said Caren Cowan, executive secretary of the New Mexico Cattle Growers' Association. "It's getting tough to be a cowboy." Moreover, they add that comparing public and private grazing is inaccurate since private grazing often includes veterinarians, fencing, and water tanks. They also claim that if fees are raised to make corporations pay more, small operators will go bankrupt and real estate speculators will carve up the empty private ranches. In some cases, the choice is condos or cows. "What are the alternatives?" asked Mike Dombeck, former US Forest Service chief. "Are we better off with subdivisions? I think it's in everybody's best interests to try to maintain these large unfragmented tracts of land."[39]

Many claim that without access to the public range, ranchers would disappear. Montana economist Thomas Power concluded that only 17,989 jobs in eleven Western states, or 0.06 percent of total employment, originated from federal grazing. "We have cowboy socialism," he stated. "It's a romantically based, phony attempt to protect something from the past that no longer exists." An extensive study by the Department of the Interior concluded that although overgrazing of "upland" pastures, deserts, and meadows had fallen in recent decades, stream areas continued to suffer severe damage from grazing. The study blamed cattle for most of the widespread, destructive influence on the streams and rivers of the West. One biologist frankly stated, "They have just beat places to hell."[40]

Cows require water, and rather than roam they congregate, which can wipe out fish and bird habitat. However, since few Americans travel to these sites, grazing damage remains out of sight. Also, banks use grazing permits as collateral; if the system changes dramatically, thousands of ranches plunge in value. Many bankers quietly lobby against change. With the cowboy image so popular, bipartisan western senators have successfully fought changes. President Clinton pledged reform but initiated very little. Environmentalists point to the buyout program—where groups purchased ranches in order to protect the land—as their sole consistently successful initiative.[41]

These limited successes revealed to conservationists and environmentalists that they were fighting a campaign on two fronts. While they battled western corporations and land holders, they also squared off against one of the most treasured of national symbols—the cowboy. Although cowboys were statistically few in number, the iconic cowboy way of life prevailed, and politicians and marketers exploited that image. Reformers also realized that the battle continued on another front—between the local and federal governments. Local government officials consistently campaigned on the threat of federal control. Both dominant elements in the West are at work—the myth and the role of government—and each side fought to control them.

Owyhee Initiative

On January 17, 2001, using the Antiquities Act of 1906, President Clinton established eight new national monuments. In this announcement, made on one of his last days in office, the president added, "In the years to come, more areas will doubtless require our common protection. I'd like to mention just two, for example. First, the Owyhee Canyonlands in Idaho. This fractured maze of ancient canyons is a rugged paradise of leaping big horn sheep and soaring birds of prey."[42]

In a separate announcement, Secretary Babbitt further clarified intentions. He acknowledged the insufficient time to meet with ranchers and motorized recreationists to assuage their worries. However, he claimed that "the Owyhees are the most important unrecognized and unprotected landscape in the American West." He pledged, "As a very public private citizen, I intend to devote time to work to see they are protected." He reiterated the need to safeguard the area before "big-time road development and speculative land deals" carve up the natural values. Babbitt claimed there was national support for this and predicted that "within the next decade the Owyhee Canyonlands and uplands will be protected by Congress as a national monument." The announcements provoked diverse reactions from Western interests: environmentalists and Native Americans lamented the lost opportunity, while many ranchers, farmers, and developers heaved a sigh of relief.[43]

Most in Owyhee County cheered the news that the canyonlands had failed to gain monument status. But leaders in the county realized that the proposal had come close to passing; that some designation appeared eminent; that many ranchers and organizations faced increasing numbers of lawsuits and grazing reductions; and that they had better get control over the process before the establishment of an irrevocable policy without their input. "The Owyhee Monument was within 24 hours of designation last time," said Fred Grant, attorney for Owyhee County. "The next time it's going to be put at the top of the list."

It was time to change tactics. Grant advised collaboration with environmentalists and negotiation with the federal government in order to design the most favorable agreement. The county sent letters to the Nature Conservancy, the Wilderness Society, and the Idaho Conservation League to join other interests in drafting a bill. They also solicited the assistance of Idaho's congressional delegation, and Senator Mike Crapo responded. He agreed to be involved but cautioned, "I am publicly committed to pursue in Congress only those matters about which there is working-group consensus." On December 27, 2001, county commissioners announced their plan for an "Owyhee Initiative."[44]

The initiative surprised many, since until this time the county had advo-

Shoshone-Paiute Tribes chairman Terry Gibson, second from left, speaks during a 2004 meeting in Murphy, Idaho, regarding the Owyhee Initiative process. Also present were US Senator Mike Crapo, left, and Owyhee County commissioners Harold Tolmie, Dick Reynolds, and Chris Salove. (Courtesy of the *Owyhee Avalanche*.)

cated local rights and challenged federal authority over public lands. "We believe that it is extremely important that Owyhee County now make the effort to attain a level of certainty that will provide stability for our citizens," commissioners Hal Tolmie and Chris Salove said in a letter to US Senator Mike Crapo, asking for his help in the process. Critics charged that they were merely using the local government to gain control of national interests.[45] However, many environmentalists credited the efforts of these groups and supported the initiative. "They're putting their necks on the line to put this together, and we need to recognize this," said Craig Gehrke, Wilderness Society regional director in Boise. "There is likely to be a lot of hard work ahead, but the first step is the hardest one," said John McCarthy, Idaho Conservation League director.[46]

The commissioners invited a diverse group of interests to develop legislation to protect the Owyhee Canyonlands and the local culture and economy: the Shoshone-Paiute Tribes, US Air Force, Nature Conservancy, Wilderness Society, Idaho Conservation League, Owyhee Cattlemen's

Association, Owyhee Soil Conservation District, various hunting organizations, and the Owyhee Borderlands Trust. This last group included ranchers who worked with the Nature Conservancy to develop "grass banks" along the Idaho/Nevada border so that ranchers could protect their rangeland.[47]

One group rejected the invitation: the Shoshone-Paiutes. Based on their position of prior ownership and status as a sovereign nation, they dealt directly with the federal government and saw no need to join. "We have been satisfied with the response of the BLM," said Ted Howard, cultural resources director for the tribes. He also reiterated the sacred nature of the Owyhees. "Everything out there plays a part in the well-being of the whole, the water, the rocks, the plants, the animals, even the smallest insects." "It's all a tightly woven quilt," Howard noted, and cautioned, "Humans are a part of all of this, not above it."[48]

However, some groups remained left out and argued that the commissioners, instead of inviting all comers, limited the process. For example, those viewed as most antagonistic to the position of the Owyhee County commissioners—the Sierra Club, Western Watersheds, and CIHD—were not invited. A few of these, including the Sierra Club, successfully negotiated a seat at the initiative discussions, although they remained nonvoting members. The most notable group not invited was the Western Watershed Project, headed by executive director Jon Marvel, an outspoken proponent of cattle removal from western lands. Active in bringing lawsuits to remove cattle from the range, Marvel threatened, "Wilderness with new pipelines, fences and cattle is a dead duck in Owyhee County, we'll stop it." He asked, "Why are these people [ranchers] treated differently than anybody else? How many other lifestyles are subsidized other than agriculture."[49]

Sandra Mitchell, who represented the motorized recreation community, had fought in Idaho's wilderness wars for decades and held the line here. She argued for protection, but of a different kind: of the motor recreationist's ability to use the Owyhees, "We're going through this process because we love the Owyhees and we believe they need to be protected." However, she warned, "We don't believe wilderness is an essential part of the package."[50]

Nonetheless, those parties involved began the painstaking process of collaboration. It took time. "[We'd been] trading barbs for so many years with Owyhee County. Harsh things were said all the way around," said Craig Gehrke. "It took a long time for everyone to get off their high horse."

They started small. The "mark of a successful meeting at the beginning was if no one threw a chair," Gehrke said. Building trust and understanding one another's perspectives were the keys.[51]

They did that by going out to the land. "It's easier to be frank and honest when you're sitting on a canyon rim," said Gehrke. The group sponsored a series of field trips where experts from various interests spoke on critical issues. They took the time to learn about one another's values, needs, and deal-breaking points. Ranchers explained their concerns about access to quality range, water rights, and vandalism. Environmentalists outlined the threats of noxious weeds, species extinction, and the lasting effect of trail-building. Something surprising occurred in this process: some actually began to enjoy each other. "I think it's incredibly possible that I could be walking into Congress with guys with big belt buckles and big hats," said John McCarthy of the Idaho Conservation League. For his part, Ted Hoffman, president of the Idaho Cattle Association, said, "If you would have told me a year ago I could be working with people like John McCarthy, I would have said you were crazy." Hoffman added, "What's crazy is, I kind of like him."[52]

The initial talks focused on three core areas: a grazing science advisory panel that would review controversial BLM decisions, a stewardship council that would carry forward the agreements reached and oversee long-term restoration efforts, and wilderness and wild scenic river designations for the canyons and other special areas. The initiative also had to deal with area access. Off-road vehicles wore an estimated five miles of new tracks and roads into the land every week during the summer. County Commissioner Jerry Hoagland estimated that forty-three acres of vegetation were lost each year, an alarming amount for such an arid location. "If you ask any land manager in the state or federal [government], 'Is [current motorized use] sustainable and well managed?' No, they're getting run over—literally and figuratively," said John Robison, public lands director at the Idaho Conservation League. "Everyone has a right to use public lands, but no one has the right to abuse it," he said.[53]

The working group pledged to keep open more than ten thousand miles of roads—most of them dirt—to public access, while closing several hundred, most of which had been created in the last decade. This ensured that roughly 90 percent of wilderness area would be within two miles of a road. "What good is this land if you can't get to it?" asked Robison. The initiative hoped to address the commonly told story of hunters who spent several months scouting an area for game and then on opening day found a four-wheeler riding across and scaring off the game. They hoped improved signage would help alleviate the problem.[54]

Grazing practices, water rights, and scientific verification remained at the top of the agenda. Wilderness designation allowed for cattle grazing, which would have been banned under national monument status. In exchange, environmentalists gained the concession that no new grazing allotments could be created or reissued if retired by the current holder. They also hoped to raise private funds to buy out from permittees grazing rights that covered roughly fifty-five thousand acres. Initiative members essentially sidestepped the contentious water rights issue. They guaranteed some rights for future development, recognized the precedence of senior water rights, and left the ongoing confrontations to be dealt with through the Snake River Adjudication Court. They also planned for the creation of a science center to resolve questions about the data from both sides: scientists from the University of Idaho and other independent experts would be contracted to provide information on issues brought to the group. The initiative working group could serve as a review panel for the BLM, the primary implementer of any legislation, but it would not have the power to overrule any decision. Despite the issues that remained, initiative participants realized they had far more in common.[55]

"What it really amounted to is that we're all really on the same page," noted Jerry Hoagland, an Owyhee County commissioner and a lifelong cattle rancher. "We want nearly the same thing. Once that trust and that idea was built, we started working out the details." Working through these issues and getting it through the legislative process took time—eight years to be precise—but the accrued time, possibilities, and shared experiences spurred many on. "We were all on a pretty steep learning curve," noted Chad Gibson of the Owyhee Cattlemen's Association. "I don't know how many would have signed on if they knew what they were in for. But once you have so much invested, you have to keep going." Craig Gehrke concurred: "At times we drove each other nuts, but we kept going. We also had the habit of having lunch together," he stated. "Then we realized that we were dealing with many of the same issues personally: kids, aging parents, this helped the process too." He also acknowledged the groups' desire to prove everyone wrong. "We were going to make it because nobody said we could." He joked, "We had 1,000 cups of bad coffee. Something good better come from that."[56]

It did. On Monday, March 31, 2009, President Obama signed legislation that consolidated more than 150 separate public lands, parks, and water bills into one package. It designated 2.5 million acres of additional wilderness in nine states and one thousand miles of new wild and scenic rivers, and created one new national monument, three national park units, and ten national heritage areas. The Owyhee Initiative was part of this legislation. Specifically, the bill

- Designated 517,000 acres of wilderness, including 55,000 acres of wilderness that will not be grazed by livestock.
- Designated 316 miles of wild and scenic rivers.
- Closed two hundred miles of motorized trails in candidate wilderness areas and initiated a travel-planning process to establish a designated system of motorized routes for all public lands in Owyhee County.
- Instituted better regulation and enforcement of indiscriminate and illegal ORV use in Owyhee County.
- Increased protections for Shoshone-Paiute cultural sites and resources.
- Initiated a county process to abandon all of its RS 2477 road claims in designated wilderness.
- Gained a commitment by those involved to seek support for research and conservation projects in Owyhee County.
- Established scientific review of data and information used in BLM decisions on livestock and other management issues by an independent, balanced panel of experts.
- Opened closed roads across private land to provide better public access to public lands.
- Resolved decades-old public lands conflicts that will allow groups to move forward and address other important issues.[57]

The Owyhee Initiative, as part of the Omnibus Public Lands Management Act, was signed into law by President Barack Obama on March 29, 2009. (Courtesy of Associated Press Services.)

The initiative drew the support of a wide array of interest groups: the Shoshone-Paiute Tribes, Idaho 4x4 State Association, Owyhee Cattlemen's Association, Idaho Steelhead and Salmon United, Idaho Water Users, American Whitewater Association, Mountain Home Air Force Base, Idaho State Land Board, Nature Conservancy, Sierra Club, Idaho Rivers United, Southern Idaho Desert Racing Association, Idaho Cattlemen's Association, and the Wilderness Society. A number of organizations issued statements after the signing:

> "The collaborative process was long, and at times very difficult. But in the end we did good work for the rivers, the landscapes and the people of Owyhee County." (Bill Sedivy, executive director, Idaho Rivers United)
>
> "Thanks to the unwavering support from ICL members, Senator Crapo's office and all of our partners, the pristine high desert land-

> scapes and remote river canyons will remain as they are to inspire future generations of Idahoans." (John Robison, public lands director, Idaho Conservation League)[58]

"It's a grass-roots Idaho approach to resolving long-standing issues," said Grant Simonds, executive director of the Idaho Outfitters and Guides Association. "That's why it has worked. "If you have can-do folks at the table, then collaboration is going to have more of a chance of succeeding." However, not everyone saw it the same way. Sandra Mitchell, now of the Idaho Recreation Council, represented motorized recreation and did not support the final bill. "We felt very strongly that the ranchers had a stake in it, and out of respect for the ranchers, we backed off and didn't oppose it, but we also didn't support it." Mitchell cautioned: "We think they're [the designated wilderness lands] too small to be effectively managed as wilderness, and we believe that in a short amount of time they'll come back and ask for more wilderness for that exact reason; it's too small." She added: "A lot of the land that is now wilderness had been grazed for generations, ranched for generations. There were roads and trails everywhere that were used by motorized recreationists and ranchers, so we didn't believe that land truly qualified for wilderness."[59]

"It was collaborative only among the group of hand-picked people who agreed to go along with what the cowboys wanted," said Katie Fite, who had taken a position as biodiversity director for Western Watersheds. "It was not collaborative," she commented. "[We are the] only group that would say a peep about cows." She also criticized the emphasis on local decision making, "Public lands belong to all [of us]. Someone in New York has as much interest in the Owyhees as someone who lives there," Fite said. "If you elevate the interests of the locals, [it is] a way to undercut the interests of everybody in the land."[60]

However, Aden Seidlitz, Boise district manager for the BLM, the organization centrally charged with implementing the initiative, stated, "I think they did a phenomenal job. You do have to bring a group of people together who are willing to listen to each other and compromise a little and take a holistic view of what's good." One year later, the working group formalized into the Owyhee Initiative Board of Directors and included representatives from those organizations previously engaged in the process. The group reported a successful first year: BLM hired staff to implement the legislation; livestock grazing management facilities were inventoried and improvements were made in the newly created wilderness; conservation groups secured $2 million in private funds to compensate grazing permittees; the Shoshone-Paiute Tribes initiated the Three Sovereigns Consultation/Coordination process to facilitate legislation implementation; official maps were created and signage added; and the group worked to secure future funding for implementation of the legislative provisions.[61]

Chad Gibson, of the Owyhee Cattlemen's Association, recognized the importance of implementation. He maintained that the group had learned from previous efforts regarding land use that had looked at legislation passage as the finish line rather than the setting up of necessary processes for ongoing implementation. "We knew there was still much to be done." Yet he noted the diversity of the group involved throughout, appreciated the effort it took to reach agreement on road access and wilderness boundaries, and acknowledged that ranchers were "pretty satisfied" with the outcome. It was "far better than if the monument would have passed and boundaries and conditions set by outsiders."[62]

Craig Gehrke agreed on the importance of ongoing implementation and acknowledged the impact the Owyhee Initiative had on him and his organization's conservation policy. "It absolutely changed our approach. We became much more cognizant of local buy-in than we were in the eighties and nineties." Currently the Wilderness Society is working on a similar collaborative process regarding the Clearwater River in northern Idaho, and Gehrke backs the bottom-up approach in resolving land issues. "We have to do it here, locally."[63]

Is this a model for other communities throughout the West and United States? Critics such as Katie Fite felt betrayed by the process, "We got to sit around and listen to them wheel and deal and give away wilderness." However, participants disagreed. They thought that while this effort was a unique, place-based agreement applied at a particular time and region, the process could have broad implementation and serve as a model for land management decisions at the local level.[64]

"The county and all other players would have a collaborative process to stake out an Idaho position on the future management of public lands in Owyhee County rather than having something rammed down Idaho's throat," said Grant Simonds. Gehrke admitted, "We are certainly not above criticism. We made the decision that there is an overall gain, and the overall benefits outweigh the detriments." Trust remained paramount. "They know we're going to work to solve everyone's issues, not just ours," said Gehrke, adding, "It couldn't be every dog for themselves or it would have fallen apart pretty quickly, then it just falls back to what had been happening, which was nothing." He called the Owyhee Initiative "one of the most rewarding things I've ever done."[65]

Bruneau Canyon. (Courtesy of Owyhee County Historical Society Museum and Library.)

CONCLUSION

Lesions and Lessons from the West

The collaborative approach of the Owyhee Initiative proved the exception to the rule of conflict over land use in the American West. Why did it work? Was it an aberration or is a new model emerging in the West? Comments from Senator Mike Crapo and Craig Gehrke reveal how land, myth, and government combined to produce a collaborative, nonviolent outcome. A revisiting of Frederick Jackson Turner's thesis and recent work by historian Patricia Limerick places this latest episode within a broader context.

Senator Mike Crapo emphasized that all those at the table were "better off under the Owyhee initiative than they were under the existing law, or under the status quo. That includes everything from private property owners to environmental concerns, to the Tribes, to the Air Force, to the hunters and fishermen, to the off-road vehicle users, and the list goes on." While those not at the table would contest the claim, Crapo argued that "everybody is better off because we worked together, and we developed a comprehensive land management solution that literally boosted everyone's stake in the management of the Owyhee's."[1]

One interviewer commented to Senator Crapo, "It must have been a big surprise to the folks in Washington, D.C. to see this unusual group walk in together, all in agreement." Senator Crapo agreed: "What the Owyhee

Initiative did was to bring those who had been for years engaged in that kind of conflict that our federal laws kind of promote, and it brought them together to collaborate." Something else happened in the process: "they not only developed confidence in each other but, I think, in many cases, friendships." Finally, at the end of this long and difficult process, "when they came to Washington, DC, those who had for decades seen this battle going on between different interest groups and stakeholders, and they saw those stakeholders standing shoulder to shoulder, . . . [it] was a big part of the success that enabled us to get that bill to the President's desk."[2]

Commenting on his own involvement, Senator Crapo claimed, "I don't think that there are words to describe how happy I am at the outcome here." His enthusiasm stemmed from the success of the Owyhee Initiative, but also his belief that "this has become recognized nationally as a model. We still have a conflict mode of approaching land management decisions mostly across the country, but here is a model that showed how we can get past the conflict and actually build consensus."[3]

Senator Crapo emphasized the changed role of government in this instance: "Well, this was different, because this literally put the decision-making in the hands of the people who lived on the land, and who worked on the land around the area from whatever perspective they came from." The more they worked, the more they realized their overlapping common interests and the imperative to move beyond the status quo. It meant denying the temptation to use litigation or administrative delays to halt the process, the dominant mode of operation in the "conflict mode of decision making." Crapo commented: "Pretty much any interest group with any kind of significant backing can stall or even stop something from happening, but it is very hard to build progress and to help create something that moves forward unless you are willing to involve a true collaborative approach." It required a vision beyond the narrow interests of any singular group to address the concerns of all at the table. However, "Once you are committed to working together for a solution rather than trying to figure out how to gum it up or to drive it through against opposition, then you can make progress—and I think that is one of the lasting lessons we get from the Owyhees."[4]

Craig Gehrke, one of the participants in the Owyhee Canyonlands initiative, reiterated that "there would have been no Canyonlands Initiative without the Saylor Creek Bombing Range issue." It moved the parties from the defensive to the offensive, shifted the government's role to one of mediation, and brought the Owyhees to the forefront of the agenda. "If somebody said we would get an agreement in the Owyhees before the Boulder White Clouds [wilderness area in central Idaho long sought for protection], that's laughable. It was the ultimate dark horse."[5]

Gehrke emphasized the importance of the land and meeting there. "We went to their [ranchers'] places, their schools, met them on their land—it made a big difference. Their places mean everything to them." Since Gehrke grew up on a ranch, "I could speak their language." In the day-to-day negotiations, "If you can get them on your side, you've really got something. They would love to perpetuate their way of life." He noted that "they were more than polite [and] they were willing to work with us." He emphasized their common sense. "They were pragmatic, they got it, and if we supplied a solid reason for wanting to protect an area, they generally went along. They realized we needed each other and it meant a lot to them that we went and met them there."[6]

Gehrke explained how the conservationist approach has evolved. "We've changed since the 1970s; we try to be more sensitive to people's place on the land. Earlier we thought almost exclusively about the natural resources; now we are more sensitive to people." In Gehrke's estimation, "Far more people are sympathetic to them [cowboys] than they are to fish, land, or animals." He emphasized the importance of local support. "I'd rather not have a national monument in the Owyhees and have local buy-in—in the long run it will be best." He warned that "we fall quickly and too easily into the Rural/Urban, East/West divide," cautioned that "collaboration doesn't work in very instance," and wondered whether "we can devote that much time?"[7] (The Owyhee Initiative took ten years.)

However, he also emphasized that "success breeds success, [and] we now have collaborative efforts going on the Payette, White Clouds, and Clearwater Basin" (other areas in central and northern Idaho). It speaks to the "power of collaboration—the logging people get it." Gehrke noted the significance of western myths in this region as well. "In northern Idaho, it's not cowboys but loggers. If he has the White boots on, the checkered flannel shirt, people will eat this up. People still respect American loggers and miners, those who go out and work on the land." He believes "they still like to know there are people out there making a living, cutting trees, doing what they have to." Most importantly, "Many Americans are sick of the conflict and want collaboration; they want people to sit down and solve problems."[8]

Throughout the process Gehrke recognized the importance of the cowboy image. Never underestimate "the power of the belt buckle," he said, and continued: "the cowboy image is a powerful one; there's a lot of sympathy for people that still wrest a living from the land, that maintain a way of life that people fantasize about." Gehrke believes that "when we went back to meet with congressional representatives, it made all the difference to walk in with these guys with handlebar mustaches, big belt buckles, boots, and cowboy hats." He could read the senators' and representatives' minds: "You're not from around here. You're a real American and I want to talk to you."[9]

Above all, "We realized that these were human beings and not 'the enemy.'" Gehrke will never forget "the first time we went down there and one of the ranchers' young daughters baked us some cookies in her Easy Bake oven. It made me stop, and see that there was a real courtesy here, that they respected visitors. It made me open my mind up a little bit more."[10]

Craig Gehrke's and Senator Crapo's descriptions of the collaborative Owyhee Initiative depart from the dominant narrative of this work: conflict and conquest. Perhaps surprisingly, their descriptions also parallel rarely quoted passages from Frederick Jackson Turner's address on the "Significance of the Frontier in American History" and the evolving thinking of Patricia Limerick. In the later part of his address, Turner noted the need for government in social construction. He argued that the western settler "began to face the problem of magnitude in the areas he was occupying." He had to "adjust his life to the modern forces of capital and to complex productive processes; as he began to see that, go where he would, the question of credit and currency, of transportation and distribution in general conditioned his success." Therefore, Turner argued, "he sought relief by legislation." The settler "began to lose his primitive attitude of individualism, [and] government began to look less like a necessary evil and more like an instrument for the perpetuation of his democratic ideals. . . . He was coming to regard legislation as an instrument of social construction."[11]

Patricia Limerick has recognized the enduring power of western mythology and its ability to both devastate and heal the land and people. In her 1987 work, *Legacy of Conquest: The Unbroken Past of the American West*, Limerick outlined how diverse groups in the West battled for social and environmental dominance. This seminal study stimulated dozens of scholars who followed this line of thinking. However, in 2009 she published another important work, *Remedies for a New West: Healing Landscapes, Histories, and Cultures.*[12] In the prologue Limerick describes preparing for a lecture where, rather than typing "Lessons of History," she inadvertently typed "the really much more interesting phrase 'Lesions of History.'" Certainly the episodes described in the present work reveal much of the hurt, injury, and damage caused by competing visions of land use in southwestern Idaho. However, Limerick argued that indeed one of the ways to heal these "lesions" of history lies in the "lessons" that we can learn from them. She acknowledged that early in her career she "struggled diligently to replace the romantic clinging to memories of western history with realism." She challenged her audience to truthfully acknowledge the "legacy of conquest" and tried to "persuade Americans to look honestly and openly at the costs, prices, injuries, lesions, and lingering burdens accrued from the historical episode known as westward expansion."[13]

However, Limerick argues that the same stories that devastated also hold the power to heal. Speaking about the tools with which to address the harm, Limerick maintains, "None outranks for persuasive power the mythic image of the West." She recognizes the ways that this image has been used for devastation, but also sees in it "the mechanisms for motivation, incentive, persuasion, and encouragement, as well as the building and maintaining of morale. The Western Myth is one big mechanism supplying all those features." She argues that the challenge is to focus the "extraordinary courage, persistence, ingenuity, and pluck" of the pioneers into legacies of collaboration instead of conquest.[14]

At Turner's address in Chicago in 1893, he competed for his audience with the Buffalo Bill Wild West show. Joseph Campbell, the noted American scholar of mythology, remembered what first launched his lifetime search for meaning in the myths of our lives. He "fell in love with American Indians because Buffalo Bill used to come to Madison Square Garden every year with his marvelous Wild West Show. And I wanted to know more about the Indians."[15]

The cowboy symbol of the American West appears to be intact. Globally, western-themed parks, parties, and products continue to rake in billions. Locally, a recent headline read, "Ranchers gaining in popularity with public."[16] Not everyone took away the same message; it depends on how we tell and understand the stories. The question remains as to whether we will use the power of the western image toward conflict or collaboration.

Notes

Foreword

1. Richard W. Etulain, *Re-Imagining the Modern American West: A Century of Fiction, History, and Art* (Tucson: University of Arizona Press, 1996), 51.
2. Gordon Morris Bakken and Brenda Farrington, *Learning California History* (Wheeling, IL: Harlan Davison, 1999), 2–3.
3. Walter Prescott Webb, *The Great Plains* (Boston: Ginn and Co., 1931).
4. The best source for Malin's writings is James C. Malin, *History and Ecology: Studies of the Grassland,* ed. Robert P. Swierenga (Lincoln: University of Nebraska Press, 1984).
5. Etulain, *Re-Imagining the Modern American West,* 154.
6. John Phillip Reid, *Law for the Elephant: Property and Social Behavior on the Overland Trail* (San Marino, CA: Huntington Library Press, 1980), 361.
7. Ibid.
8. Ibid.
9. John Phillip Reid, "Some Lessons of Western Legal History," *Western Legal History* 1 (Winter–Spring 1988): 3–21. Also see Gordon Morris Bakken, "The Territorial System since 1862," in *Encyclopedia of the American Legislative System,* 3 vols., ed. Joel H. Silbey (New York: Charles Scribner's Sons, 1994): 1:265–280; "Legal System [in the American West]," in *Encyclopedia of the American West,* 4 vols., ed. Charles Phillips and Alan Axelrod (New York: Macmillan Reference USA, 1996): 2:861–862; "Territorial Law and Courts," in *Encyclopedia of the American West,* ed. Philips and Axelrod, 4:1556–1558; "The Courts, the Legal

Profession, and the Development of Law in Early California," in *Taming the Elephant: Politics, Government, and Law in Pioneer California,* ed. John F. Burns and Richard J. Orsi (Berkeley and Los Angeles: University of California Press, 2003): 74–95; "Contract Law in the Rockies, 1850–1912," *American Journal of Legal History* 18 (January 1974): 33–51; "The Growth of Chattel Credit Law in Frontier California, 1850–1890," *Southern California Quarterly* 57 (Summer 1975): 109–127, "The Development of Law in Colorado, 1861–1912," *Colorado Magazine* 53 (Winter 1976): 63–78; "The Development of the Law of Tort in Frontier California, 1850–1890," *Southern California Quarterly* 60 (Winter 1978): 405–419; "Law and Legal Tender in California and the West," *Southern California Quarterly* 62 (Fall 1980): 239–59.

10. Mark R. Ellis, *Law and Order in Buffalo Bill's Country: Legal Culture and Community on the Great Plains, 1867–1910* (Lincoln: University of Nebraska Press, 2007), 181–209. Compare for Montana: Frederick Allen, *A Decent, Orderly Lynching: The Montana Vigilantes* (Norman: University of Oklahoma Press, 2013); Mark C. Dillon, *The Montana Vigilantes, 1863–1870: Gold, Guns, Gallows* (Logan: Utah State University Press, 2013). For California, see John Boessenecker, *Badge and Buckshot: Lawlessness in Old California* (Norman: University of Oklahoma Press, 1988); Roger D. McGrath, *Gunfighters, Highwaymen, and Vigilantes: Violence on the Frontier* (Berkeley: University of California Press, 1984); Clare V. McKanna, *Race and Homicide in Nineteenth-Century California* (Reno: University of Nevada Press, 2002).
11. Ellis, *Law and Order in Buffalo Bill's Country,* 215.

Introduction

1. Frederick Jackson Turner, "The Significance of the Frontier in American History" (paper presented to the American Historical Association at the World's Columbian Exposition, Chicago, Illinois, July 12, 1893). It first appeared in the *Proceedings of the State Historical Society of Wisconsin,* December 14, 1893, with the following note: "The foundation of this paper is my article entitled 'Problems in American History,' which appeared in *The Ægis,* a publication of the students of the University of Wisconsin, November 4, 1892." Also, Clyde A. Milner, "Introduction: America Only More So," in *The Oxford Dictionary of the American West,* ed. Clyde A. Milner II, Carol A. O'Connor, and Martha A. Sandweiss (Oxford: Oxford University Press, 1994), 3.
2. Richard White, "Frederick Jackson Turner and Buffalo Bill," accessed on August 1, 2013, http://www.studythepast.com/his378/turnerandbuffalobill.pdf.
3. "William F. Cody 'Buffalo Bill' (1846–1917)," New Perspectives on the West, accessed on August 1, 2013, http://www.pbs.org/weta/thewest/people/a_c/buffalobill.htm.

4. Stephen Cook, *Realizing Westward: American Character and Cowboy Mythology* (Boston: Pearson Custom Publishing, 2007). This quotation was taken from James Fallows, "Declaring Victory," *Atlantic,* September 2006, 71.
5. John Mack Faragher, *Rereading Frederick Jackson Turner: The Significance of the Frontier in American History and Other Essays* (New York: H. Holt and Co., 1994); Turner, "The Significance of the Frontier in American History."
6. Roland Barthes, *Mythologies* (New York: Hill and Wang, 1972), 11. For the role of violence in mythology, see Richard Slotkin, *The Fatal Environment: The Myth of the Frontier in the Age of Industrialization, 1800–1890* (New York: Atheneum, 1985), 33–47.
7. Turner, "The Significance of the Frontier in American History"; also, Patricia Limerick, *The Legacy of Conquest: The Unbroken Past of the American West* (New York: W. W. Norton, 1987), 28.
8. Andy Hyland, "16 Things: KU History Professor, Environmental Historian Recounts Personal History," accessed January 12, 2013, http://www2.ljworld.com/news/2011/sep/12/16-things-ku-history-professor-environmental-histo/; Richard White, *It's Your Misfortune and None of My Own: A New History of the American* West (Norman: University of Oklahoma Press, 1991), 58.
9. Richard Maxwell Brown, "Violence," in *The Oxford Dictionary of the American West,* ed. Milner, O'Connor, and Sandweiss, 423.
10. Richard Maxwell Brown, preface to *No Duty to Retreat: Violence and Values in American History and Society* (Oxford: Oxford University Press, 1992).
11. Slotkin, *The Fatal Environment,* 13–32.
12. For a current discussion of honor and conscience, see Daniel Justice Herman, *Hell on the Range: A Story of Honor, Conscience, and the American West* (New Haven, CT: Yale University Press, 2010).

Chapter 1

1. *A Historical, Descriptive, and Commercial Directory of Owyhee County, Idaho, January 1898* (Silver City, ID: Owyhee Avalanche, 1898), 10; "Owyhee County Profile & A Bit of History," Owyhee County, Idaho, accessed March 29, 2013, http://www.owyheecounty.net/index1.php?countyprofile.
2. Titles unavailable, *Idaho Statesman,* November 22, 2006; January 12, 2009; and March 25, 2009. Some newspaper article titles are provided where extant.
3. David D. Alt and Donald W. Hyndman, *The Roadside Geology of Idaho* (Missoula, MT: Mountain Press, 1989), 34.
4. Mark Plew, *BSU Archaeology Reports* (Boise, ID: Boise State University, 1986), 6.
5. Brigham D. Madsen, *The Shoshone Frontier and the Bear River Massacre* (Salt Lake City: University of Utah Press, 1985), 3–13.
6. "Owyhee County Profile & A Bit of History"; Mildretta Adams, *Owyhee Cattle-*

men, 1878–1978: 100 Years in the Saddle (Homedale, ID: Owyhee Publishing Co., 1979), 8.

7. "Owyhee County Profile & A Bit of History"; Adams, *Owyhee Cattlemen,* 8; "Owyhee County Idaho Gold Production," Western Mining History: Reliving the Industrial Revolution of the West, accessed December 28, 2012, http://www.westernmininghistory.com/articles/114/page1; "The Owyhee Country," Idaho State Historical Society, Reference Series, no. 200, 1964.
8. "Don Shannon, Historian, Author of 'The Utter Disaster,' 'Massacre Rocks and City of Rocks,' and 'The Boise Massacre on the Oregon Trail,'" "Pathways of Pioneers," Outdoor Idaho, accessed March 28, 2013, http://idahoptv.org/outdoors/shows/pathwaysofpioneers/DonShannon.cfm; "Site of Utter Party Massacre," Idaho State Historical Society, Reference Series, no. 233, June 1993.
9. "Owyhee County Bannock War Sites," Idaho State Historical Society, Reference Series, no. 1090, 1995.
10. *A Historical, Descriptive, and Commercial Directory,* 10. See also "Owyhee County, Idaho," State & County QuickFacts, US Census Bureau, accessed March 27, 2012, http://quickfacts.census.gov/qfd/states/16/16073.html.
11. Merle Wells, "The Context of Gubernatorial Politics in Idaho," in *Idaho's Governors: Historical Essays on Their Administrations,* ed. Robert C. Sims and Hope Benedict (Boise, ID: Center for Research Grants and Contracts, Boise State University, 1978), 2.
12. "Owyhee Horse and Cattle Ranches (Nineteenth Century)," Idaho State Historical Society, Reference Series, no. 1050, rev. July 1995.
13. *A Historical, Descriptive, and Commercial Directory,* 8.
14. Adams, *Owyhee Cattlemen,* 11.
15. "Owyhee County," Idaho State Historical Society, Reference Series, no. 336, 1975.
16. "The Owyhee Country"; Herbert Hoover, "Message on the Dedication of Owyhee Dam," The American Presidency Project, accessed March 28, 2013, http://www.presidency.ucsb.edu/ws/index.php?pid=23169; "Owyhee County Profile & A Bit of History."
17. Randy Stapilus and Marty Peterson, *Idaho 100: The People Who Most Influenced the Gem State* (Carlton, OR: Ridenbaugh Press, 2012), 62–63.
18. Ibid., 225–26.
19. Ibid., 97–98.
20. Ibid., 91–92.
21. Ibid., 133–34.
22. Adams, *Owyhee Cattlemen,* 18, 23, 60.

23. Ibid., 58–59, 95.
24. Ibid., 118–19.
25. Ibid., 30–41.
26. Shoshone Paiute Tribes, The Duck Valley Indian Reservation, "Culture," accessed March 28, 2013, http://www.shopaitribes.org/spt-15/index.php.
27. "A Short History of Silver City, Idaho," Historic Silver City, Idaho, accessed December 28, 2012, http://www.historicsilvercityidaho.com/; "Owyhee County Profile & A Bit of History."
28. "Owyhee County, Idaho," accessed March 28, 2013, http://www.city-data.com/county/Owyhee_County-ID.html; *A Historical, Descriptive, and Commercial Directory*, 8.
29. "Owyhee County Traditions Preserved at Outpost Days," *Idaho Press-Tribune*, accessed March 29, 2013, http://www.idahopress.com/community/article_5c6ae828-8a7f-11e0-9098-001cc4c03286.html.
30. Ibid. Also, Mike Hanley and Ellis Lucia, *Owyhee Trails: The West's Forgotten Corner* (Caldwell, ID: Caxton Printers, 1973), 5.
31. "Owyhee Cattlemen," *Owyhee Avalanche*, July 30, 2004, section B.
32. Tim Woodward, "Cowboys vs. City Slickers: Owyhee Canyonlands Plan Stirs up Old West Emotions," *Idaho Statesman*, December 24, 2000, 1A.
33. Donald Worster, *An Unsettled Country: Changing Landscapes of the American West* (Albuquerque: University of New Mexico Press, 1994), xi–xii.
34. Ibid.
35. "Delamar Professorship in Biological Chemistry," accessed June 24, 2013, http://webapps.jhu.edu/namedprofessorships/professorshipdetail.cfm?professorshipID=128; "Delamar History!" accessed June 24, 2013, http://www.robertwynn.com/DelamarH.htm.
36. Joe Demshar, director of Owyhee County Historical Museum, e-mail to author, January 18, 2013.
37. *A Historical, Descriptive, and Commercial Directory*, 6–7, 9.

Chapter 2

1. Leonard Arrington, *History of Idaho* (Moscow: University of Idaho Press, 1994), 244–245. For an overview of early mining in Idaho, see Merle Wells, *Gold Camps and Silver Cities: Nineteenth Century Mining in Central and Southern Idaho* (Moscow: Idaho Department of Lands, 1983).
2. *A Historical, Descriptive, and Commercial Directory*, 11. This account was published by the local newspaper and provides useful data for the early years of settlement.
3. Wells, *Gold Camps and Silver Cities*, 36.

4. News brief, *Owyhee Avalanche,* September 25, 1866; Arrington, *History of Idaho,* 244–45; also Wells, *Gold Camps and Silver Cities,* 36–37.
5. Wells, *Gold Camps and Silver Cities,* 36–37.
6. Ibid.
7. Richard Maxwell Brown, "Western Violence: Structure, Values, Myth," *Western Historical Quarterly* 24, no. 1 (February 1993): 4–20.
8. "The California Gold Rush," Social Studies for Kids, accessed June 25, 2013, http://www.socialstudiesforkids.com/articles/ushistory/californiagoldrush.htm.
9. Wells, *Gold Camps and Silver Cities,* 1.
10. Ibid., 3.
11. News brief, *Owyhee Avalanche,* August 19, 1865; "From One of the Original '29,'" *Owyhee Avalanche,* September 2, 1865; see also, "Owyhee County Profile & A Bit of History."
12. Hanley and Lucia, *Owyhee Trails,* 45; also, "The War on the Mountain," *Owyhee Avalanche,* March 28, 1868.
13. For a comprehensive and well-written description of this mining war episode in the Owyhees, see Dale M. Gray, "War on the Mountain," *Owyhee Outpost,* no. 22 (May 1991): 49; also, Wells, *Gold Camps and Silver Cities,* 3.
14. Arrington, *History of Idaho,* 187–88; " 'Owyee War' Results in Death of Six Men," *Idaho Daily Statesman,* July 3, 1932, p. 2, c. 1; "More Man of Mystery Personally Popular," *Idaho Daily Statesman,* June 26, 1932; also, Gray, "War on the Mountain," 50.
15. "Cattlemen Out for Bad Indians," *Twin Falls Times,* May 12, 1910.
16. James Lawrence Onderdonk, *Idaho: Facts and Statistics Concerning Its Mining, Farming, Stock Raising, Lumbering, and Other Resources and Industries* (San Francisco: A. L. Bancroft, 1885), 14–15.
17. Hanley and Lucia, *Owyhee Trails,* 54–56.
18. *A Historical, Descriptive, and Commercial Directory,* 109.
19. Clyde P. Ross, *Mining History of South-Central Idaho* (Moscow: Idaho Bureau of Mines and Geology, July 1963), ii.
20. Wells, *Gold Camps and Silver Cities,* 2, 26–27.
21. Ibid., 27; news brief, *Owyhee Avalanche,* August 28, 1864.
22. "The Original 29," *Owyhee Avalanche,* September 2, 1865.
23. Wells, *Gold Camps and Silver Cities,* 26. In the Washoe process the raw ore was wet crushed with stamps, and then separated from the slurry in a settling tank. Next, the crushed ore was charged with mercury and the gold and silver were extracted from this amalgamation with a retort. "Carson River Mercury Site—

Overview," Nevada Division of Environmental Protection, accessed September 29, 2011, http://ndep.nv.gov/BCA/carsonriver/criver_2.htm.

24. Arrington, *History of Idaho,* 243; Wells, *Gold Camps and Silver Cities,* 28–29.
25. News brief, *Owyhee Avalanche,* June 23, 1866; "Dallas Correspondence, From Owyhee," *Walla Walla Statesman,* May 3, 1867; Liping Zhu, *A Chinaman's Chance: The Chinese on the Rocky Mountain Mining Frontier* (Niwot: University Press of Colorado, 1997).
26. "Escapade of Prisoners," *Owyhee Avalanche,* November 19, 1870.
27. "Black Joe," *Owyhee Avalanche,* June 14, 1875; Mildretta Adams, *Historic Silver City: The Story of the Owyhees* (Homedale, ID: Owyhee Chronicle, 1960), 14.
28. Elliott West, "Five Idaho Mining Towns: A Computer Profile," *Pacific Northwest Quarterly* 73 (July 1982): 108–20.
29. Wells, *Gold Camps and Silver Cities,* 32.
30. Ibid., 30, 32.
31. Ibid., 1.
32. *Owyhee Avalanche,* August 5, 1871.
33. Arrington, *History of Idaho,* 244.
34. Adams, *Historic Silver City,* 31.
35. Ibid.
36. Fred Gillard, "Early Theater in the Owyhees," *Idaho Yesterdays* 17 (Summer 1973): 9–15.
37. Adams, *Historic Silver City,* 24.
38. Hanley and Lucia, *Owyhee Trails,* 201; news brief, *Owyhee Avalanche,* August 29, 1865; "Horrible Accident," *Owyhee Avalanche,* April 3, 1869.
39. Brown, "Violence," 393; Brown, *No Duty to Retreat;* White, *"It's Your Misfortune and None of My Own."*
40. Brown, "Violence," 396; Hanley and Lucia, *Owyhee Trails,* 204. Brown borrows from E. J. Hobsbawm's *Primitive Rebels: Studies in Archaic Forms of Social Movement in the 19th and 20th Centuries* and his notion of social banditry, a phenomenon where notable lawbreakers enjoyed wide support from the law-abiding members of society while they addressed common grievances.
41. Gray, "War on the Mountain," 50.
42. Ross, *Mining History of South-Central Idaho,* 1; Gray, "War on the Mountain," 50.
43. Gray, "War on the Mountain," 50.
44. Ibid.
45. Brown, "Violence," 398; news brief, *Owyhee Avalanche,* March 11, 1868.
46. Gray, "War on the Mountain," 55.
47. "Fatal Shooting" and "After the War," *Owyhee Avalanche,* April 4, 1868; Wells, *Gold Camps and Silver Cities,* 37–38; Gray, "War on the Mountain," 51.

48. Gray, "War on the Mountain," 51.
49. "Owyhee Items" and "Correction," *Idaho World,* March 18 and 21, 1868; news brief, *Owyhee Avalanche,* March 19, 1868; Wells, *Gold Camps and Silver Cities,* 43; news brief, *Owyhee Avalanche,* March 25, 1868.
50. "The War on the Mountain," *Owyhee Avalanche,* March 28, 1868.
51. Gray, "War on the Mountain," 52.
52. "Trouble on the Mountain," *Owyhee Avalanche,* March 14, 1868; "Trouble on Oro Fino Mountain Again," *Idaho-Tri-Weekly Statesman,* March 17, 1868.
53. "Trouble on the Mountain," *Owyhee Avalanche,* March 14, 1868; "Trouble on Oro Fino Mountain Again," *Idaho-Tri-Weekly Statesman,* March 17, 1868.
54. News brief, *Owyhee Avalanche,* March 18, 1868.
55. Gray, "War on the Mountain," 54.
56. Ibid., 55.
57. Wells, *Gold Camps and Silver Cities,* 43.
58. Arrington, *History of Idaho,* 247–48; "Territorial Government in Idaho, 1863–1869," Idaho State Historical Society, Reference Series, no. 48 (1963), 31.
59. Gray, "War on the Mountains," 56.
60. "Fatal Shooting," *Owyhee Avalanche,* April 4, 1868; "Arm Amputated," *Owyhee Avalanche,* May 2, 1868; Gray, "War on the Mountain," 56.
61. Gray, "War on the Mountain," 57.
62. Ibid., 56–57.
63. Ibid.
64. Wells, *Gold Camps and Silver Cities,* 43; Pauline Battien, *The Gold Seekers: A 200 Year History of Mining in Washington, Idaho, Montana & Lower British Columbia* (Colville, WA: Statesman-Examiner, 1989), 12; Adams, *Historic Silver City,* 25; Gray, "War on the Mountain," 58, 50, 58–59.
65. "Escapade of Prisoners," *Owyhee Avalanche,* November 19, 1870; Wells, *Gold Camps and Silver Cities,* 43; Battien, *The Gold Seekers,* 12; Gray, "War on the Mountain," 55, 58.
66. "Probably Fatal Shooting," *Owyhee Avalanche,* May 27, 1871.
67. Wells, *Gold Camps and Silver Cities,* 43.
68. Herman, *Hell on the Range,* 213.
69. Patricia Nelson Limerick, *Something in the Soil: Legacies and Reckonings in the New West* (New York: W. W. Norton, 2000), 215–217.
70. Adams, *Historic Silver City,* 21.

Chapter 3

1. Carlos A. Schwantes, *In Mountain Shadows: A History of Idaho* (Lincoln: University of Nebraska Press, 1991). For a travel guide of Idaho, see Cort Conley, *Idaho for the Curious: A Guide* (Cambridge, ID: Backeddy Books, 2003).

2. Whitney McKinney, *A History of the Shoshone-Paiutes of the Duck Valley Indian Reservation* (Salt Lake City: Institute of the American West and Howe Bros., 1983), 18.
3. "Thieving Reds Murder Young White Men," *Idaho Daily Statesman,* May 10, 1910.
4. Title unavailable, *The Humboldt Star,* May 11, 1910.
5. "Cattlemen Out for Bad Indians," *Twin Falls Times,* May 12, 1910.
6. "Thieving Reds Murder Young White Men."
7. Sources for this event are limited; however, they generally either support the settlers or the Native Americans. Hyde's work favors the latter and was published more recently than most of the other works. Dayton O. Hyde, *The Last Free Man: The True Story Behind the Massacre of Shoshone Mike and His Band of Indians in 1911* (New York: New Dial Press, 1973), 109–118.
8. "Thieving Reds Murder Young White Men"; "Cattlemen Out for Bad Indians"; Limerick, *Something in the Soil,* 44–48.
9. Brigham Madsen's work on Native Americans in this region serves as the seminal study. See Madsen, *The Shoshone Frontier and the Bear River Massacre* (Salt Lake City: University of Utah Press, 1985), 13.
10. Arrington, *History of Idaho,* 37; Madsen, *The Shoshone Frontier,* 8–13.
11. Madsen, *The Shoshone Frontier,* 3–13.
12. Ibid., 12, 31.
13. "Shocking Attack: Indian Massacre," *Owyhee Avalanche,* March 14, 1868; "Shocking Massacre," *Owyhee Avalanche,* October 26, 1867; "Another Atrocious Indian Murder," *Owyhee Avalanche,* May 4, 1867.
14. News Brief, *Owyhee Avalanche,* November 25, 1865.
15. News Brief, *Owyhee Avalanche,* February 18, 1866.
16. "Mischief Thou Art Afoot," *Owyhee Avalanche,* October 7, 1865; Limerick, *Something in the Soil,* 44–48; "Indian Fight," *Owyhee Avalanche,* December 21, 1867.
17. "Editorial," *Owyhee Avalanche,* November 28, 1865; "Outrage by Soldiers," *Owyhee Avalanche,* March 31, 1866.
18. "The Original 29," *Owyhee Avalanche,* September 2, 1865.
19. Madsen, *The Shoshone Frontier,* 15–17.
20. Brigham Young Papers, Stalker to Maughan, January 30, 1863; Maughan to Young, February 4, 1863, as quoted in Edward Tullidge, *History of Salt Lake City* (Salt Lake City: Star Printing Co., 1886), 290.
21. Hyde, *The Last Free Man,* 83, 90; Adams, *Historic Silver City,* 52; Julia Conway Welch, "Two Legends," *Owyhee Outpost,* no. 26 (June 1995), 5.
22. Effie Mona Mack, *The Indian Massacre of 1911 at Little High Rock Canyon, Nevada* (Sparks, NV: Western Print. and Pub. Co., 1968), 19. This is another

major work of this episode and reflects a more favorable attitude toward the settlers' perspective.

23. Ibid., 1.
24. "Captured Squaw Discloses a Portion of Her History When Questioned in Bannock," *Nevada State Journal,* March 5, 1911; Hyde, *The Last Free Man,* 76–77; Mack, *The Indian Massacre of 1911,* 113.
25. Hyde, *The Last Free Man,* 67–73.
26. Ibid., 40; also, Madsen, *The Shoshone Frontier,* 31.
27. Madsen, *The Shoshone Frontier,* 31, 62–64.
28. Ibid., 75.
29. Ibid., 17, 30, 97–101.
30. Ibid., 22–24.
31. Ibid.
32. Ibid.
33. Ibid.
34. Ibid., 39–40.
35. Ibid., 65, 67–73.
36. Ibid.
37. Ibid., 50–51.
38. Ibid., 107–8, 115–16.
39. Titles unavailable, *Humboldt Star,* January 9 and 11, 1911.
40. Hyde, *The Last Free Man,* 126–31.
41. Ibid.
42. Ibid., 68–72.
43. Ibid.
44. Ibid., 130, 132, 138–39, 144.
45. Ibid.
46. Mack, *The Indian Massacre of 1911,* 1; Hyde, *The Last Free Man,* 158.
47. Hyde, *The Last Free Man,* 170–71; Mack, *The Indian Massacre of 1911,* 31.
48. Title unavailable, *Humboldt Star,* February 10, 1912.
49. "Four Slain by Cattle Rustlers," *Idaho Statesman,* February 12, 1911; Mack, *The Indian Massacre of 1911,* 27, 31, 35; Hyde, *The Last Free Man,* 174.
50. "Sheriff and State Police Leave for Scene of Crime," *Nevada State Journal,* February 12, 1911; Hyde, *The Last Free Man,* 175–76; interview with Marcelino Ugalde, University of Nevada, Reno, Basque Studies Librarian, July 9, 2002. To this day a certain mystique surrounds this episode; those involved do not wish to talk about it. When I questioned one area librarian who had family connections to the parties, he felt that even those who knew the truth refused to speak.

51. An undated and unsigned letter as part of a report of research of the US Bureau of Indian Affairs, known in 1910–1911 as the Office of Indian Affairs, and quoted in Mack, *The Indian Massacre of 1911,* 139.
52. Hyde, *The Last Free Man,* 177–179.
53. Titles unavailable, *Nevada State Journal,* February 13, 14, 15, 1911.
54. "Indian Band Near Tuscarora," *Nevada State Journal,* February 24, 1911; Mack, *The Indian Massacre of 1911,* 41, 49; also, Hyde, *The Last Free Man,* 193.
55. "No News from Pursuing Posses," *Humboldt Star,* February 22, 1911.
56. Ibid.
57. "Trail of Murderers Leads through Humboldt County," *Silver State,* February 23, 1911.
58. Ibid.; "Indian Murderers Are Hiding in Vastnesses of Jackson Mountain," *Humboldt Star,* February 20, 1911; Mack, *The Indian Massacre of 1911,* 52; Hyde, *The Last Free Man,* 204, 206; "Posses Reach Winnemucca and Continue Chase after Indians," *Humboldt Star,* February 24, 1911.
59. "Trail of Murderers Leads through Humboldt County," *Silver State,* February 23, 1911; "Indian Murderers Are Hiding in Vastnesses of Jackson Mountain," *Humboldt Star,* February 20, 1911; Mack, *The Indian Massacre of 1911,* 52; Hyde, *The Last Free Man,* 204, 206; "Posses Reach Winnemucca and Continue Chase after Indians," *Humboldt Star,* February 24, 1911.
60. "Murderers Hemmed between Posses Moving upon Them from the East and West," *Nevada State Journal,* February 27, 1911; "Desperate Battle in Clover Valley between Posse and Hunted Indians," *Humboldt Star,* February 27, 1911.
61. Mack, *The Indian Massacre of 1911,* 19.
62. Ibid.
63. Ibid., 65.
64. "Posses Kill Indians in Nevada," *Idaho Statesman,* February 28, 1911.
65. Ibid.
66. Ibid.
67. Ibid.
68. Mack, *The Indian Massacre of 1911,* 19–21, 85–87.
69. Ibid., 74.
70. Hyde, *The Last Free Man,* 218–19; Mack, *The Indian Massacre of 1911,* 63.
71. Hyde, *The Last Free Man,* 222.
72. Ibid., 216.
73. Ibid.
74. Ibid., 80; Mack, *The Indian Massacre of 1911,* 1.
75. Ibid.
76. Mack, *The Indian Massacre of 1911,* 88–89; Hyde, *The Last Free Man,* 223.

77. "Desperate Battle in Clover Valley between Posse and Hunted Indians," *Humboldt Star,* February 27, 1911.
78. "Posse Brings in Indian Prisoners, the Body of Comrade and Trophies," *Humboldt Star,* March 1, 1911.
79. Title unavailable, *Humboldt Star,* March 1, 1911; Hyde, *The Last Free Man,* 231; Mack, *The Indian Massacre of 1911,* 96–97, 100.
80. "Eagleville Boys Head from Home," *Humboldt Star,* March 6, 1911; Mack, *The Indian Massacre of 1911,* 118; also, Hyde, *The Last Free Man,* 258.
81. "Jury Accuses the Girl," *Humboldt Star,* March 3, 1911; "Indian Squaw Arrives in Reno This Morning," *Nevada State Journal,* March 2, 1911; "Indians Brought to County Jail" and "Authorities Puzzled as to Disposition of Squaw and Children," *Nevada State Journal,* March 3, 1911; also, Frank Bergon, *Shoshone Mike* (New York: Viking Press, 1987), 287. This is a novel written about this episode, but it includes some research by the author in the epilogue.
82. "Indian Squaw Tells of Seventeen Deaths She Has Witnessed," *Nevada State Journal,* March 12, 1911; also, Mack, *The Indian Massacre of 1911,* 93.
83. Title unavailable, *Nevada State Journal,* August 19, 1911.
84. Ibid.
85. Slotkin, *The Fatal Environment,* 13–32; "Want Indians for Exhibition," *Nevada State Journal,* March 8, 1911.
86. Herman, *Hell on the Range,* xiv, xxii.
87. Anthony Mora, *Border Dilemmas: Racial and National Uncertainties in New Mexico, 1848–1912* (Durham, NC: Duke University Press, 2011), 281.

Chapter 4

1. Supreme Court of the United States, October Term, 1916, no. 379, Secundino Omaechevarria, Plaintiff in Error, vs. State of Idaho, In Error to the Supreme Court of the State of Idaho (Washington DC: Judd & Detweiler, Printers, November 4, 1916), 1–3. This document contains transcripts from all of the court cases at all levels and will be used throughout this chapter.
2. "The Immigration Act of 1924 (The Johnson-Reed Act)," US Department of State, Office of the Historian, accessed March 28, 2012, http://history.state.gov/milestones/1921-1936/ImmigrationAct.
3. "Taylor Grazing Act," U.S. House of Representatives, accessed March 28, 2012, http://uscode.house.gov/download/pls/Title_43.txt.
4. Paul Herndon, *The Taylor Grazing Act, 1934–1984* (Boise: State Director of Public Lands of Idaho, 1990), 1; Adams, *Owyhee Cattlemen,* 21; also, *A Historical, Descriptive, and Commercial Directory,* 10.
5. Hanley and Lucia, *Owyhee Trails,* 20; Adams, *Owyhee Cattlemen,* 8, 12.
6. Hanley and Lucia, *Owyhee Trails,* 2.

7. Title unavailable, *Idaho Statesman,* April 23, 1867.
8. *Report of the Commissioner of Agriculture, 1891* (Washington, DC, 1892), 313; *Thirteenth Census of the United States taken in the Year 1910, Vol. V, Agriculture 1909 and 1910, General Report and Analysis* (Washington, DC: 1909 and 1910), 402; also, "New Cases in Probate Court," *Owyhee Avalanche,* September 26, 1913, 1.
9. Archer B. Gilfillan, *Sheep* (Boston: Little, Brown, 1930), 5.
10. Herman, *Hell on the Range,* 103; also, Paul H. Carlson, "Cowboys and Sheepherders," in *The Cowboy Way: An Exploration of History and Culture,* ed. Paul H. Carlson, 109–118 (Lubbock: Texas Tech University Press, 2006).
11. Edward Norris Wentworth, *America's Sheep Trails: History, Personalities* (Ames: Iowa State College Press, 1948), 290.
12. Garmendia Letters Collection, Basque Museum and Cultural Center Archives, Boise, Idaho, letter number 10; also, "Spanish-born Loyal to U.S.," *Idaho Statesman,* March 30, 1917.
13. Nick Beristain, interview by author, March 20, 1992, recording, Basque Museum and Cultural Center Archives, Boise, Idaho, tape 1; William A. Douglass and Jon Bilbao, *Amerikanuak: Basques in the New World* (Reno: University of Nevada Press, 1975), 229; Gilfillan, *Sheep,* 3; Elmore County Criminal Records, State of Idaho v. Martin Anceneche (1908).
14. Sabino Landa, interview by author, March 18, 1992; also Jose Mari Artiach, interview by author, June 10, 1992. Both recordings, Basque Museum and Cultural Center Archives, Boise, Idaho.
15. Douglass and Bilbao, *Amerikanuak,* 72.
16. Ibid., 139–68.
17. Ibid.
18. Marie Pierre Arrizabalaga, "A Statistical Study of Basque Immigration into California, Nevada, Idaho and Wyoming, 1900–1910" (master's thesis, University of Nevada, Reno, 1986), 88–92.
19. Ibid. See also Richard W. Etulain, "Basque Beginnings in the Pacific Northwest," *Idaho Yesterdays* 18, no. 1 (Spring 1974): 26.
20. Joe Eiguren, interview by author, December 4, 1991; February 18, 1992; March 24, 1993, recording, Basque Museum and Cultural Center Oral History Collection; also Wentworth, *America's Sheep Trails,* 290.
21. Grant E. McCall, "Basque-Americans and a Sequential Theory of Migration and Adaptation" (master's thesis, San Francisco State College, 1968), 83.
22. Louise Shaddock, *Andy Little: Idaho Sheep King* (Caldwell, ID: Caxton Printers, 1990), 129; also, Douglass and Bilbao, *Amerikanuak,* 258–59; also Byrd Wall Sawyer, *Nevada Nomads: A Story of the Sheep Industry* (San José: Harlan-Young, 1971), 165.
23. Douglass and Bilbao, *Amerikanuak,* 258–59.

24. All of the following testimony cited from Supreme Court of the United States, October Term, 1916, no. 379, Secundino Omaechevarria, Plaintiff in Error, vs. State of Idaho.
25. Tom Keelan, "With the Miners Came the Sheep," *Idaho Statesman Centennial Supplement* (1990), 2.
26. Supreme Court of the United States, October Term, 1916, no. 379, Secundino Omaechevarria, Plaintiff in Error, vs. State of Idaho.
27. Ibid. The statute in question provides: "Any person owning or having charge of sheep, who herds, grazes, or pastures the same, or permits or suffers the same to be herded, grazed or pastured, on any cattle range previously occupied by cattle, or upon any range usually occupied by cattle, or upon any range usually occupied by any cattle grower, either as a spring, summer or winter range for his cattle, is guilty of a misdemeanor: but the priority of possessory right between cattle and sheep owners to any range, is determined by the priority in the usual and customary use of such range either as a cattle or sheep range." This statute was enacted by the twelfth session of the territorial legislature in 1883. It was part of an act entitled "An Act for the Protection of Stock Growers in Owyhee, Boise, Oneida, Bear Lake, Lemhi, and Custer Counties." It was reenacted as section 6872 Rev. Stat. of 1887. The statute was continued in force by section 2 of the schedule and ordinance contained in article 21 of the state constitution; and the state constitution, together with the schedule, was approved by the federal government at the time Idaho was admitted as a state. The Idaho State Supreme Court also agreed to hear a companion case along with Omaechevarria v. State of Idaho that also dealt with the question regarding the constitutionality of statute 6872. In this case, State of Idaho vs. S. F. Horn, John Eiler, and John Calvin, the court upheld the constitutionality of the statute.
28. Westlaw, Section 6872 of the Revised Codes of the State of Idaho (1908), US Supreme Court in Bacon v. Walker, 204 U.S. 311, 27 Sup. Ct. 289, 51 L. Ed. 499 (1908).
29. Ibid.
30. Ibid.
31. Supreme Court of the United States, October Term, 1916, no. 379, Secundino Omaechevarria, Plaintiff in Error, vs. State of Idaho.
32. Ibid.
33. Ibid.
34. Titles unavailable, *Californiako Euskal Herria,* May 30, 1896, and August 14, 1897; "Shooting Scrape," *Nevada State Herald,* September 1, 1905.
35. Idaho State Court Records, State of Idaho v. Yturaspe (1911), 31.

36. "Sheepman and Farmer Clash," *Idaho Statesman,* May 29, 1918.
37. Will C. Barnes, *Western Grazing Grounds and Forest Ranges* (Chicago: Breeder's Gazette, 1913), 28–29; William MacLeod Raine and Will C. Barnes, *Cattle, Cowboys, and Rangers* (Garden City: NY: Doubleday, Doran & Co., 1930), 251–52; Will C. Barnes, *Apaches and Longhorns: The Reminiscences of Will C. Barnes,* ed. Frank C. Lockwood (Los Angeles: Ward Ritchie, 1941), 127–29.
38. "Sheepherder Shot through Heart by Unknown Party," *Owyhee Avalanche,* June 4, 1915.
39. Title unavailable, *Idaho Statesman,* May 7, 1910.
40. Adams, *Owyhee Cattlemen,* 8–10; "Grazing Cases Appealed," *Idaho Statesman,* April 1, 1917; also, news brief, *Owyhee Avalanche,* August 29, 1913.
41. "Basque Sheepherders Bound Over to February Grand Jury," *Owyhee Avalanche,* November 7, 1913.
42. News brief, *Owyhee Avalanche,* October 1, 1915; Adams, *Owyhee Cattlemen,* 31.
43. "Range Not Exclusive," *Idaho Statesman,* May 6, 1917.
44. News brief, *Owyhee Avalanche,* June 5, 1914.
45. Roy M. Robbins, *Our Landed Heritage: The Public Domain, 1776–1936* (Lincoln: University of Nebraska Press, 1962), 306.
46. Marion Clawson, *The Western Range Livestock Industry* (New York: Arno Press, 1979), 252; also, Paul W. Gates, ed., *History of the Public Land Law Development* (Washington, DC: Zenger Publishing, 1968), 583.
47. Gates, *History of Public Land Law Development,* 582.
48. Ibid., 580; also Douglass and Bilbao, *Amerikanuak,* 282–85; Richard H. Lane, "The Cultural Ecology of Sheep Nomadism: Northeastern Nevada, 1870–1872" (PhD diss., Yale University, 1974).
49. Supreme Court of the United States, October Term, 1916, no. 379, Secundino Omaechevarria, Plaintiff in Error, vs. State of Idaho.
50. Ibid.
51. Douglass and Bilbao, *Amerikanuak,* 284; "Sheepmen Get Basques Excluded," *Humboldt Star,* March 26, 1909.
52. Earl Templeton, "Annual Grazing G Report, District 6," Humboldt National Forest, Winnemucca, Nevada.
53. Sol Silen, *La Historia de los Vascongados en el Oeste de los Estados Unidos* (New York: Las Novedades, 1917), 69, 261, 397. In 1917, Silen published a book on prominent Basques in the American West. Since individuals paid to have their biographies printed, the book is far from representative, although it does provide insight into this group making its way toward acceptance into American culture. Of the 129 biographies in Silen's book, 56 mention land ownership. Yet this figure is undoubtedly low, since Silen's interviews were uneven both in terms of quality of answers and questions asked.

54. Title unavailable, *Humboldt Star,* December 5, 1913.
55. Title unavailable, *Reno Evening Gazette,* June 18, 1913; "Sheepmen and Biscayans," *Caldwell Tribune,* July 17, 1909.
56. Title unavailable, *Humboldt Star,* March 27, 1915.
57. Douglass and Bilbao, *Amerikanuak,* 379; Ada County Naturalization Records.
58. "U.S. to Fix Wool Prices," *Idaho Statesman,* March 27, 1917; "Wool Offered to Government," *Idaho Statesman,* April 12, 1917.
59. "Urge Peaceful Use of Range," *Idaho Statesman,* May 20, 1917.
60. "Sheepherders Ask More Pay," *Idaho Statesman,* August 26, 1917.
61. Ibid.
62. "Spanish-Born Loyal to U.S.," *Idaho Statesman,* March 30, 1917.
63. "Ada Limit Club Has 82 Members," *Idaho Statesman,* June 30, 1918.
64. "Two Sheepmen Add $20,000 to Loan Pledges," *Idaho Statesman,* October 21, 1917.
65. "Basque Women Guests of Citizenship Club," *Idaho Statesman,* May 2, 1917.
66. Decision taken from Supreme Court of the United States, October Term, 1916, no. 379, Secundino Omaechevarria, Plaintiff in Error, vs. State of Idaho.
67. Ibid.
68. Ibid.
69. Douglass and Bilbao, *Amerikanuak,* 294.
70. Douglas C. Baynton, "Defectives in the Land: Disability and American Immigration Policy, 1882–1924," *Journal of American Ethnic History* 24 (2005): 41; Barbara Young Welke, *Law and the Borders of Belonging in the Long Nineteenth Century United States* (New York: Cambridge University Press, 2010), 130.
71. Mora, *Border Dilemmas,* 287.
72. Kim Cary Warren, *Quest for Citizenship: African American and Native American Education in Kansas, 1880–1935* (Chapel Hill: University of North Carolina Press, 2010), 172.
73. Herman, *Hell on the Range,* 212–13.

Chapter 5

1. David Hamilton Murdoch, *The American West: Invention of a Myth* (Reno: University of Nevada Press, 2001), vii–viii, 20–23; Jenni Calder, *There Must Be a Lone Ranger: The American West in Film and Reality* (London: Hamilton Press, 1974), 50.
2. Richard Slotkin, *Regeneration Through Violence: The Mythology of the American Frontier, 1600–1860* (Middletown, CT: Wesleyan University Press, 1973); Slotkin, *The Fatal Environment;* Calder, *There Must Be a Lone Ranger,* 116–20; Carl Sonnichsen, *From Hopalong to Hud: Thoughts on Western Fiction* (College Station:

Texas A&M University Press, 1984), 31; White, *"It's Your Misfortune and None of My Own,"* 621–31.

3. Murdoch, *The American West,* 1–3.
4. White, *"It's Your Misfortune and None of My Own,"* 613–15.
5. Ibid., 613–20.
6. "William F. Cody 'Buffalo Bill' (1846–1917)."
7. Jonathan D. Martin, " 'The Grandest and Most Cosmopolitan Object Teacher': Buffalo Bill's Wild West and the Politics of American Identity, 1883–1899," *Radical Review* 66 (1996): 96.
8. Ibid., 97.
9. Ibid., 98–102, 119–20.
10. Murdoch, *The American West,* 75.
11. Carl Abbott, "The Federal Presence," in *The Oxford Dictionary of the American West,* ed. Milner, O'Connor, and Sandweiss, 473–74.
12. Ibid., 474–75.
13. Ibid., 475–78.
14. Ibid., 474–75.
15. Ibid.
16. Murdoch, *The American West,* 63–80.
17. "Frederic Remington," *American Masters,* PBS.org (1991), accessed July 1, 2013, http://www.pbs.org/wnet/americanmasters/episodes/frederic-remington/about-frederic-remington/688/.
18. Ibid.
19. White, *"It's Your Misfortune and None of My Own,"* 613–20; Murdoch, *The American West,* 31.
20. Abbott, "The Federal Presence," 481; Paul F. Starrs, *Let the Cowboy Ride: Cattle Ranching in the American West* (Baltimore: Johns Hopkins University Press, 1998), 150.
21. Ibid., 482.
22. Ibid., 483–84.
23. Carl Abbott, *How Cities Won the West: Four Centuries of Urban Change in Western North America* (Albuquerque: University of New Mexico Press, 2008), 171.
24. Ibid., ix–xii; Richard Slotkin, *Gunfighter Nation: The Myth of the Frontier in Twentieth Century America* (1992; repr., Norman: University of Oklahoma Press, 1998), 237; Murdoch, *The American West,* 116–20.
25. Limerick, *Something in the Soil,* 75; Murdoch, *The American West,* 75.
26. White, *"It's Your Misfortune and None of My Own,"* 613–18; Murdoch, *The American West,* 62.
27. Richard Francaviglia, "Walt Disney's Frontierland as an Allegorical Map of the American West," *Western Historical Quarterly* 30, no. 2 (1999): 160.

28. Limerick, *Something in the Soil,* 31.
29. Ibid., 93.
30. Martin, "The Grandest and Most Cosmopolitan Object Teacher," 92–123, 96.
31. Slotkin, *The Fatal Environment,* 19.

Chapter 6

1. State of Idaho v. Claude Lafayette Dallas, Jr., 14935, vol. XIV, 2707 (Supreme Court of the State of Idaho). This document is the transcript of an appeal from the District Court of the Third Judicial District of Idaho. As such, it contains the transcript for the entire legal proceedings. See also Jeff Long, *Outlaw: The True Story of Claude Dallas* (New York: Morrow, 1985), 64.
2. State of Idaho v. Claude Lafayette Dallas, Jr., 14935, vol. XIV, 2707; Long, *Outlaw,* 31.
3. State of Idaho v. Claude Lafayette Dallas, Jr., 14935, vol. VIII, 2707; Jack Olsen, *Give a Boy a Gun: A True Story of Law and Disorder in the American West* (New York: Delacorte Press, 1985), 15–16.
4. Olsen, *Give a Boy a Gun,* 15–16.
5. State of Idaho v. Claude Lafayette Dallas, Jr., 14935, vol. VIII, 2707; Long, *Outlaw,* 84.
6. State of Idaho v. Claude Lafayette Dallas, Jr., 14935, vol. VIII, 2707; Long, *Outlaw,* 89.
7. Olsen, *Give a Boy a Gun,* 30–31; Long, *Outlaw,* 79.
8. State of Idaho v. Claude Lafayette Dallas, Jr., 14935, vol. VIII, 2707; Bart McDowell, *The American Cowboy in Life and Legend* (Washington, DC: National Geographic Society, 1972).
9. Olsen, *Give a Boy a Gun,* 56.
10. Ibid., 27; Long, *Outlaw,* 108.
11. Olsen, *Give a Boy a Gun,* 26.
12. State of Idaho v. Claude Lafayette Dallas, Jr., 14935, vol. VIII, 2707; Olsen, *Give a Boy a Gun,* 30–31.
13. Slotkin, *The Fatal Environment,* 19.
14. William E. Schmidt, "Suspect in Killing of 2 Idahoans Leaves Cold Trail," *New York Times,* August 6, 1981; *Give a Boy a Gun,* 18, 27.
15. State of Idaho v. Claude Lafayette Dallas, Jr., 14935, vol. VIII, 2707; Olsen, *Give a Boy a Gun,* 42.
16. State of Idaho v. Claude Lafayette Dallas, Jr., 14935, vol. VIII, 2707; Olsen, *Give a Boy a Gun,* 40–41.
17. State of Idaho v. Claude Lafayette Dallas, Jr., 14935, vol. VIII, 2707; Olsen, *Give a Boy a Gun,* 54–55.

18. State of Idaho v. Claude Lafayette Dallas, Jr., 14935, vol. VIII, 2707; Olsen, *Give a Boy a Gun,* 51.
19. State of Idaho v. Claude Lafayette Dallas, Jr., 14935, vol. VIII, 2707; Olsen, *Give a Boy a Gun,* 52.
20. State of Idaho v. Claude Lafayette Dallas, Jr., 14935, vol. VIII, 2707; Olsen, *Give a Boy a Gun,* 60–62.
21. Bill Jordan and William Henry Jordan, *No Second Place Winner* (Concord, NH: Police Bookshelf, 1965); Rex Applegate, *Kill or Get Killed: Riot Control Techniques, Manhandling, and Close Combat, for Police and Military* (Harrisburg, PA: Military Service Pub. Co., 1943).
22. State of Idaho v. Claude Lafayette Dallas, Jr., 14935, vol. VIII, 2707; Long, *Outlaw,* 108.
23. State of Idaho v. Claude Lafayette Dallas, Jr., 14935, vol. VIII, 2707; Olsen, *Give a Boy a Gun,* 70–71.
24. State of Idaho v. Claude Lafayette Dallas, Jr., 14935, vol. VIII, 2707.
25. Ibid.; Long, *Outlaw,* 132.
26. State of Idaho v. Claude Lafayette Dallas, Jr., 14935, vol. VIII, 2707; "Searchers Fail to Find Pogue," "Slaying Suspect—'As Fine a Man as You'll Ever Meet,'" and "Last of the Real Game Men Reveals Tender Side in Art," *Idaho Statesman,* January 9, 1981.
27. State of Idaho v. Claude Lafayette Dallas, Jr., 14935, vol. VIII, 2707; "Man Says He Threatened to Shoot Pogue in '67," *Idaho Statesman,* October 9, 1982.
28. State of Idaho v. Claude Lafayette Dallas, Jr., 14935, vol. VIII, 2707; Long, *Outlaw,* 132.
29. State of Idaho v. Claude Lafayette Dallas, Jr., 14935, vol. VIII, 2707; "Search Parties Fail to Locate Dallas, Pogue," *Idaho Statesman,* January 10, 1981.
30. State of Idaho v. Claude Lafayette Dallas, Jr., 14935, vol. VIII, 2707.
31. State of Idaho v. Claude Lafayette Dallas, Jr., 14935, vol. VIII, 1731; "'Everything Happened So Fast,'" *Idaho Statesman*, September 25, 1982.
32. State of Idaho v. Claude Lafayette Dallas, Jr., 14935, vol. VIII, 2707; "'Everything Happened So Fast,'" *Idaho Statesman,* September 25, 1982.
33. State of Idaho v. Claude Lafayette Dallas, Jr., 14935, vol. VIII, 2707; "'Everything Happened So Fast,'" *Idaho Statesman,* September 25, 1982.
34. State of Idaho v. Claude Lafayette Dallas, Jr., 14935, vol. VIII, 2707; "Dallas Trial," *Idaho Statesman,* September 24, 1982.
35. State of Idaho v. Claude Lafayette Dallas, Jr., 14935, vol. VIII, 2707; "Dallas Trial," *Idaho Statesman,* September 24, 1982.
36. State of Idaho v. Claude Lafayette Dallas, Jr., 14935, vol. VIII, 2707; "Dallas Trial," *Idaho Statesman,* September 24, 1982.

37. State of Idaho v. Claude Lafayette Dallas, Jr., 14935, vol. VIII, 2707; "Dallas Trial," *Idaho Statesman,* September 24, 1982.
38. State of Idaho v. Claude Lafayette Dallas, Jr., 14935, vol. VIII, 2707; "Dallas Trial," *Idaho Statesman,* September 24, 1982.
39. State of Idaho v. Claude Lafayette Dallas, Jr., 14935, vol. VIII, 2707; "Dallas Trial," *Idaho Statesman,* September 24, 1982.
40. State of Idaho v. Claude Lafayette Dallas, Jr., 14935, vol. VIII, 2707; title unavailable, *Idaho Statesman,* January 7 and 8, 1981.
41. Title unavailable, *Idaho Statesman,* January 9 and 11, 1981.
42. "Search Shifts for Suspect in Killings of Game Wardens," *New York Times,* January 9, 1981; also, "Search Parties Fail to Locate Dallas, Pogue," *Idaho Statesman,* January 10, 1981.
43. State of Idaho v. Claude Lafayette Dallas, Jr., 14935, vol. VIII, 2707; "Searchers Fail to Find Pogue," "Slaying Suspect—'As Fine a Man as You'll Ever Meet,'" and "Last of the Real Game Men Reveals Tender Side in Art," *Idaho Statesman,* January 9, 1981.
44. "F&G Officer Found Slain," "Discovery of Slain Officer Ends Brother's Search," and "Idaho Lawmen Offer Aid in Hunt for Killer," *Idaho Statesman,* January 8, 1981.
45. State of Idaho v. Claude Lafayette Dallas, Jr., 14935, vol. VIII, 2707; title unavailable, *Idaho Statesman,* January 12, 13, and 17, 1981.
46. State of Idaho v. Claude Lafayette Dallas, Jr., 14935, vol. VIII, 2707; "Fugitive Stays Clear of Manhunt," "Pogue's Brother Joins Search," and "Survival: 'Barren' Desert Offers Plenty to Savvy Suspect," *Idaho Statesman,* January 11, 1981.
47. State of Idaho v. Claude Lafayette Dallas, Jr., 14935, vol. VIII, 2707; "Dallas' Weapons Found in Trailer at Paradise Hill," *Idaho Statesman,* April 21, 1982.
48. State of Idaho v. Claude Lafayette Dallas, Jr., 14935, vol. VIII, 2707; "Fugitive Stays Clear of Manhunt," "Pogue's Brother Joins Search," and "Survival: 'Barren' Desert Offers Plenty to Savvy Suspect."
49. State of Idaho v. Claude Lafayette Dallas, Jr., 14935, vol. VIII, 2707; "Hunt Leaves Pogue's Son Tired but Willing to Go On" and "Searchers for Pogue Increase," *Idaho Statesman,* February 15, 1981.
50. State of Idaho v. Claude Lafayette Dallas, Jr., 14935, vol. VIII, 2707; Long, *Outlaw,* 150.
51. Title unavailable, *Washington Post,* July 19, 1981; "Reward Posters Go Up in Search for Dallas," *Idaho Statesman,* April 2, 1981; Jim Zumbo, "Last Day of the Wardens," *Outdoor Life,* July 1981, 44; Alan Prendergast, "The Law and Claude Dallas," *Rolling Stone,* December 9, 1982, 30; Idaho Game Warden Slain; Body

of 2d Official Sought," *New York Times,* January 8, 1981; "A Wild West Trail in Idaho," *Newsweek,* October 25, 1982.

52. State of Idaho v. Claude Lafayette Dallas, Jr., 14935, vol. VIII, 2707; "Suspect in Killing of 2 Idahoans Leaves Cold Trail," *New York Times,* August 6, 1981.
53. Title unavailable, *Idaho Statesman,* July 21, 1981.
54. State of Idaho v. Claude Lafayette Dallas, Jr., 14935, vol. VIII, 2707; "Father of Claude Dallas Grieves for Slain Officer, Sticks Up for Son," *Idaho Statesman,* January 15, 1981.
55. Long, *Outlaw,* 48–49.
56. McDowell, *The American Cowboy;* Long, *Outlaw,* 51.
57. John Kennedy, "Sympathy for Killer," *Spokesman Chronicle,* April 1, 1982.
58. Ibid.; State of Idaho v. Claude Lafayette Dallas, Jr., 14935, vol. VIII, 2707.
59. Olsen, *Give a Boy a Gun,* 64.
60. State of Idaho v. Claude Lafayette Dallas, Jr., 14935, vol. VIII, 2707; "Tip Finally Paid Off for Law Enforcement Officers," *Idaho Statesman,* April 20, 1982.
61. State of Idaho v. Claude Lafayette Dallas, Jr., 14935, vol. VIII, 2707; "Tip Finally Paid Off for Law Enforcement Officers"; also, "Desert Shoot-out with Dallas Described," *Idaho Statesman,* September 30, 1982; Jim Zumbo, "Fugitive Captured: In Game Wardens' Murders," *Outdoor Life,* July 1982, 82.
62. State of Idaho v. Claude Lafayette Dallas, Jr., 14935, vol. VIII, 2707; title unavailable, *Idaho Statesman,* April 25 and 27, 1982.
63. State of Idaho v. Claude Lafayette Dallas, Jr., 14935, vol. VIII, 2707; "Who Is This Man Named Dallas?" *Idaho Statesman,* May 9, 1982.
64. State of Idaho v. Claude Lafayette Dallas, Jr., 14935, vol. VIII, 2707; Long, *Outlaw,* 148.
65. State of Idaho v. Claude Lafayette Dallas, Jr., 14935, vol. VIII, 2707.
66. Robert F. Jones, "An Angry Rebel's Paradise Lost," *Idaho Statesman,* July 16, 1982.
67. State of Idaho v. Claude Lafayette Dallas, Jr., 14935, vol. VIII, 2707; Olsen, *Give a Boy a Gun,* 312.
68. Title unavailable, *Idaho Statesman,* September 23, 1982.
69. State of Idaho v. Claude Lafayette Dallas, Jr., 14935, vol. VIII, 2707; title unavailable, *Idaho Statesman,* September 24, 1982.
70. State of Idaho v. Claude Lafayette Dallas, Jr., 14935, vol. VIII, 2707; "Body of Game Warden Found" and "Dallas Tells of Fear after Killings," *Idaho Statesman,* October 7, 1982.
71. State of Idaho v. Claude Lafayette Dallas, Jr., 14935, vol. VIII, 2707; "Body of Game Warden Found" and "Dallas Tells of Fear after Killings."
72. Gary Strauss, "Dallas Trial Goes to Jury," *Idaho Statesman,* October 13, 1982.

73. "Juror Booted; Dallas 12 Gets Order to Restart," *Idaho Statesman,* October 20, 1982; "Survey Finds Mixed Reaction to Dallas Verdict," *Idaho Statesman,* October 21, 1982.
74. "Juror Booted; Dallas 12 Gets Order to Restart," *Idaho Statesman,* October 20, 1982; "Survey Finds Mixed Reaction to Dallas Verdict," *Idaho Statesman,* October 21, 1982; John Accola, "Dee Pogue Calls Verdict 'Unbelievable,'" *Idaho Statesman,* October 27, 1982.
75. State of Idaho v. Claude Lafayette Dallas, Jr., 14935, vol. VIII, 2707; title unavailable, *Idaho Statesman,* January 5, 1983; "Why Dallas Got 30 Years," *Idaho Statesman,* January 9, 1983.
76. "Why Dallas Got 30 Years," *Idaho Statesman,* January 9, 1983.
77. Gene Lyons, review of Jack Olsen, *Give a Boy a Gun: A True Story of Law and Disorder in the American West, Newsweek,* December 9, 1985, 91.
78. "Ballad of Claude Dallas Aired on Local Radio," *Owyhee Nugget,* February 16, 1983; "'Outlaw' Author Sought to Uncover Myths," *Idaho Statesman,* January 30, 1985; "The Dallas Story," *Idaho Statesman,* June 27, 1983; "Dallas Items Auctioned for $15,000" and "Nampa Rancher Pens Song for Dallas," *Idaho Statesman,* September 17, 1989; Marty Lieberman, review of Jeff Long, *Outlaw: The True Story of Claude Dallas, Los Angeles Times,* May 12, 1985; "Outlaw: The Saga of Claude Dallas" by Jeff Long, *Publishers Weekly,* September 6, 1987.
79. "Author Calls Claude Dallas Scared Little Kid," *Idaho Statesman,* August 19, 1986.
80. "Teen Dallas Dreamed of West" and "State Sues Dallas over Book Profits," *Idaho Statesman,* March 31, 1986.
81. "Call of the Wild: A Mountain Killer Breaks Loose," *Time,* April 14, 1986, 26; "Dallas Placed on FBI's List of Most Wanted," *Idaho Statesman,* May 17, 1986.
82. "Dallas: How the FBI Captured Escaped Killer," *Los Angeles Times,* July 19, 1986.
83. Hugh Nichols, "Wanted Again: Convicted Killer Claude Dallas Runs from the Law," *America West,* September–October 1986, 22; Robert F. Jones, "An Angry Rebel's Paradise Lost; Western Legend or Paranoid Killer, Claude Dallas Retreats to the Wilderness," *People Weekly,* September 22, 1986, 34; "He's in Canada, Boise—Everywhere but Pen" and "Hounds Lose Dallas' Scent at Highway," *Idaho Statesman,* April 2, 1986.
84. Michael Riley, "In Idaho: A Killer Becomes a Mythic Hero," *Time,* January 26, 1987, 10.
85. "Woman Says Officials May Have Aided Killer's Escape," *Los Angeles Times,* May 6, 1987.
86. "Myth of Idaho Mountain Man Is Dying Hard," *Spokesman Review and Spokane Chronicle,* April 6, 1986.

87. "Reward Fund for Dallas Goes over $3,000 Mark," *Spokesman Review,* April 9, 1986.
88. "Matt Salinger Plays the Waiting Game," *Los Angeles Times,* October 28, 1990; "Cameras May Roll on Dallas Sage," *Idaho Statesman,* April 4, 1986; "Elusive Fugitive Kept Police on the Run," "'Mountain Man' Acted Out of Myth of Western Hero," and "From Ranch Hand to Fugitive," *Idaho Statesman,* March 9, 1987.
89. Title unavailable, *Los Angeles Times,* October 28, 1990.
90. Riley, "In Idaho: A Killer Becomes a Mythic Hero," 10; "Rustic Idaho County, Still the Wild West, Has a Modern Sheriff: Videotape and a Cessna Are among Nettleton's Tools; Tracking a Wanted Man," *Wall Street Journal,* February 25, 1987.
91. "Dallas: How the FBI Captured Escaped Killer," *Los Angeles Times,* March 13, 1987; "Bringing in a Badman," *Time,* March 23, 1987, 29; "Hunt for Idaho Fugitive Ends Near Los Angeles" and "Fugitive Mountain Man Caught; Killer Was Subject of TV Movie," *New York Times,* March 9, 1987.
92. "FBI, Seeking Dallas, Raids Nevada House," *Idaho Statesman,* July 9, 1986; "FBI Search Leaves Nevadan Angry," *Idaho Statesman,* July 10, 1986.
93. Ibid.
94. Title unavailable, *New York Times,* March 9, 1987.
95. "Dallas: How the FBI Captured Escaped Killer," *Los Angeles Times,* March 13, 1987.
96. "Bidding for Freedom Auction Benefits Game Wardens' Killer as Police Protest," *Los Angeles Times,* September 17, 1989.
97. Ibid.
98. Ibid.
99. "Claude Dallas Goes to Trial for Escape," *Oregonian,* August 30, 1987.
100. "Dallas' Defense Puts Idaho Pen on Defensive," *Idaho Statesman,* September 3, 1987.
101. Title unavailable, *Los Angeles Times,* September 4 and 5, 1987; *Idaho Statesman,* September 4, 5, and 6, 1987.
102. "Psychologists: Supporters Romanticize Exploits of Dallas," *Idaho Statesman,* April 20, 1987; State of Idaho v. Claude Lafayette Dallas, Jr., no. 20954 (Court of Appeals of Idaho), August 16, 1994. Petition for review denied October 20, 1994.
103. "Claude Dallas: Stone-cold Killer or Western Hero?" *Idaho Statesman,* March 18, 2001.
104. Ibid.
105. Ibid.

106. Ibid.

107. "No Parole for Dallas," *Idaho Statesman,* April 27, 2001.

108. "Slayer of Game Wardens Is Denied Parole," *Los Angeles Times,* April 27, 2001; "No Parole for Dallas."

109. "Convicted Killer Claude Dallas Released from Prison," *Spokesman Review,* February 7, 2005.

Chapter 7

1. Rick Atkinson, "Range War in Idaho: Air Force's Vast Expansion Plan Is Resisted," *Washington Post,* May 9, 1990.

2. Colman McCarthy, "The Pentagon's Land Sighting," *Washington Post,* January 21, 1990.

3. Ibid.; "Millions of Additional Acres Needed for Combat Training, Pentagon Says," *Los Angeles Times,* January 3, 1990.

4. "Millions of Additional Acres Needed for Combat Training, Pentagon Says," *Los Angeles Times,* January 3, 1990; "Pentagon Requests More US Land," *Christian Science Monitor,* May 16, 1990; *Idaho Press Tribune,* October 29, 1989; "Bomb Range Would Raise Noise Levels," *Idaho Press Tribune,* November 5, 1989; "Report Depicts Noisy Desert Battleground in Saylor Area," *Twin Falls Times-News,* September 23, 1989; "Air Force Unveils Plans to Enlarge Bomb Range," *Idaho Statesman,* June 23, 1989; "Saylor Creek Plan—Just One of a Dozen," *Idaho Statesman,* December 3, 1989; "U.S. Military Plots Vast Land Coup," *High Country News,* February 12, 1990.

5. Niels Sparre Nokkentved, *Desert Wings: Controversy in the Idaho Desert* (Pullman: Washington State University Press, 2001), 11. Nokkentved covered the range expansion for the *Twin Falls Times-News* and in 2000 published this book, the only full-length work to date covering the Saylor Creek Bombing Range expansion.

6. McCarthy, "The Pentagon's Land Sighting."

7. "Environmentalists and Ranchers Fight Pentagon Bid for More Land," *New York Times,* January 4, 1990.

8. Nokkentved, *Desert Wings,* 17.

9. "Bomb-range Expansion Deemed Vital," *Idaho Statesman,* August 9, 1989; "The Range That Bombed," *Boise Magazine,* September/October 1990, 32.

10. "Bomb Range Draws Fire," *Idaho Statesman,* June 30, 1989; "Land Withdrawl Key to Bomb Range Expansion," *Idaho Statesman,* July 1, 1989; "Veterinarian: Bomb Range Plans Should Take Wildlife into Account," *Idaho Statesman,* August 24, 1989.

11. "Bomb Range Raises Storm," *Idaho Statesman,* October 21, 1989; "F&G Raps

Cattleman's Threat against Forest Ranger's Life," *Idaho Statesman,* August 29, 1990.

12. "Groups Act to Protect River System," *Washington Post,* July 8, 1990; "Private Pilots Attack Bombing Range Plan" and "Getting Best of Both at Saylor Creek," *Idaho Statesman,* October 22, 1989; "30 Groups Meld to Hit Bombing Range," *Idaho Statesman,* December 27, 1989.
13. "Desert Wings, 4," *Idaho Statesman,* August 12, 1989.
14. "The Defense Secretary's Commission on Base Realignment and Closure," report (December 29, 1988): 75–76.
15. "Air Force Says False Report Spurred Plan," *Idaho Statesman,* October 5, 1989.
16. "Support Turns Up for Bombing Range," *Idaho Statesman,* April 7, 1990.
17. McCarthy, "The Pentagon's Land Sighting."
18. "Congress Urged to Limit Bomb Range," *Idaho Statesman,* January 4, 1990.
19. "Three Say Lies Led to Saylor Creek Expansion Plan," *Idaho Statesman,* May 7, 1990.
20. Atkinson, "Range War in Idaho," *Washington Post,* May 9, 1990.
21. "Groups Act to Protect River System," *Washington Post,* July 8, 1990; "Two Idaho Rivers Termed Imperiled by Bomb Range," *Idaho Statesman,* March 22, 1990.
22. Rocky Barker, "The Owyhee Canyonlands: Worth the Risk to Compromise," *Idaho Statesman,* December 1, 2002.
23. "Groups Act to Protect River System," *Washington Post,* July 8, 1990.
24. "We Need Bigger Bombing Range" and "Bomb Range Plan Not Justified," *Idaho Statesman,* January 14, 1990.
25. Testimony of Lee Presley, Glenns Ferry rancher, at public hearing on air force range expansion proposal, Glenns Ferry, September 7, 1989; "Air Force Flies into Flak at Local Hearing" and "Air Force Presses On with Saylor Creek," *Idaho Statesman,* May 8, 1990; "Land Withdrawal Key to Bomb Range Expansion," *Twin Falls Times-News,* August 24, 1989; also, "Saylor Creek Foes Call Premise Faulty," *Idaho Statesman,* April 2, 1990.
26. "Field Wide Open for Proposed Bombing Range," *Twin Falls Times-News,* January 4, 1990.
27. "Air Force Flies into Flak at Local Hearing," *Twin Falls Times-News,* September 7, 1989; "Bombing Range Plan Catches Flak" and "Boos Greet Air Force at Bomb-range Meeting," *Idaho Statesman,* September 6 and 7, 1989; "Air Force Admits to Flak over Bomb Range," *Idaho Statesman,* October 8, 1989.
28. "Expansion Still Bombs with Public" and "Supersonic Flap Grounds Andrus' Support for Plan," *Idaho Statesman,* October 10, 1989; "Bombing Range Plans Generate Skepticism," *Twin Falls Times-News,* August 28, 1989.
29. "Bombing Range Expansion Threatens Desert," *Twin Falls Times-News,* August

20, 1989; "Officer Says Bomb Range May Shrink," *Idaho Statesman,* January 28, 1990.

30. "Air Force, Blaine Set to Public Hearings on Plan to Expand Bombing Range," *Idaho Statesman,* March 17, 1990; "Saylor Creek Hearing Tells of No F-4s," *Idaho Statesman,* April 3, 1990; "Critics Demand Air Force Scrap Range Expansion," *Idaho Statesman,* May 12, 1990.
31. Title unavailable, *Mountain Home News,* April 25, 1990; also, "Sonic Booms Jolt Some during Air Force Tour of Saylor Creek Range," *Idaho Statesman,* March 30, 1990.
32. Atkinson, "Range War in Idaho," *Washington Post,* May 9, 1990; title unavailable, *Washington Post,* May 12, 1990.
33. "Timetable for Range Set Back" and "Saylor Plans Put on Hold," *Idaho Statesman,* May 19, 1990; title unavailable, *Twin Falls Times-News,* May 5 and 24, 1990; "Saylor Creek Plans Delayed by Cheney," *Idaho Press Tribune,* May 20, 1990.
34. "Saylor Creek Expansion Is up in the Air," *Idaho Statesman,* May 5, 1990; "Air Force Presses on with Saylor Creek," *Idaho Statesman,* May 8, 1990; "Defense Grounds Saylor Creek Plan," *Idaho Statesman,* September 19, 1990; Nokkentved, *Desert Wings,* 33; "Range War in Idaho," *Washington Post,* May 9, 1990; title unavailable, *Washington Post,* May 12, 1990.
35. "Saylor Creek Foes Call Premise Faulty," *Idaho Statesman,* April 2, 1990; "Will Air Base at Mtn. Home Stay Open?" *Idaho Statesman,* May 24, 1990; "Andrus Says Saylor Creek Fate Hangs in Balance," *Idaho Statesman,* June 26, 1990; titles unavailable, *Idaho Statesman,* February 6 and 8, 1991.
36. Nokkentved, *Desert Wings,* 37–38.
37. "Andrus Gets Flak for Proposing Training Range," *Idaho Statesman,* May 27, 1991; "Controversy Bombards New Range Proposal," *Idaho Statesman,* June 17, 1991; title unavailable, *Idaho Statesman,* November 24, 1911; Nokkentved, *Desert Wings,* 38–40.
38. Ibid.
39. Cecil D. Andrus news release, February 8, 1991; "Andrus, State Revive, Revise Saylor Creek Bombing Plan," *Idaho Statesman,* February 6, 1991; "New Bomb Range," *Idaho Statesman,* February 8, 1991; Nokkentved, *Desert Wings,* 40–41.
40. "BLM Pushes Andrus to Find New Home for Range," *Idaho Statesman,* September 17, 1991.
41. Nokkentved, *Desert Wings,* 42–43; Gary D. Vest, deputy assistant secretary of the air force for Environment, Safety, and Health, letter to Cy Jamison, director, Bureau of Land Management, May 2, 1991; "Description of the Proposed Action and Alternatives," US Air Force planning document, May 24, 1991; "Air

Force Says Training Range Would Be Useful, Not Essential," *Idaho Statesman,* December 29, 1991.

42. Nokkentved, *Desert Wings,* 42–43; Vest, letter to Jamison; "Description of the Proposed Action and Alternatives."
43. Report and Recommendation and Order of US Magistrate Judge Mikel H. Williams, US District Court, District of Idaho, Boise, Idaho, Civ. 92–185-S-HLR, October 7, 1994.
44. Nokkentved, *Desert Wings,* 44–46; Report and Recommendation and Order of US Magistrate Judge Mikel H. Williams, US District Court, District of Idaho, Boise, Idaho, Civ. 92-185-S-HLR, October 7, 1994; Delmar D. Vail, Idaho State Director, Bureau of Land Management, Boise, Idaho, letter to Lieutenant Colonel Thomas J. Bartol, August 20, 1991.
45. "Lawyer Charges Cover-up in Desert-Impact Statements," *Idaho Statesman,* November 30, 1991.
46. "Duck Valley Reservation Residents Cast Wary Eye at Air Base Expansion," *Twin Falls Times-News,* November 10, 1991.
47. Nokkentved, *Desert Wings,* 49–51; Gov. Cecil D. Andrus, letter to Norman Guth, chairman, Idaho Fish and Game Commission, December 19, 1991; Rick Bass, *The Lost Grizzlies: A Search for Survivors in the Wilderness of Colorado* (Boston: Houghton Mifflin, 1995), 59; also, Nokkentved, *Desert Wings,* 51–52; Stockmen's Training Range Review Committee, the Owyhee Cattlemen's Association, and the "71" Association, written statement, May 5, 1992.
48. Nokkentved, *Desert Wings,* 51–52; Stockmen's Training Range Review Committee, the Owyhee Cattlemen's Association, and the "71" Association, written statement, May 5, 1992.
49. "Lawyer Charges Cover-up in Desert-Impact Statements." "Environmentalists File Suit to Stop Project," *Idaho Statesman,* May 9, 1992.
50. "Decision Made, Official Says," *Idaho Statesman,* June 24, 1992; also, "Home for a Bomb Range?" *Lewiston Tribune,* January 2, 1992.
51. Nokkentved, *Desert Wings,* 54–58; Deputy Assistant Secretary of the Air Force Gary Vest, air force memo, November 6, 1992.
52. Nokkentved, *Desert Wings,* 62–64.
53. "Baca Says Training Range Was His Undoing," *Idaho Statesman,* May 26, 1994.
54. Senator Harry Reid, *Congressional Register,* September 13, 1993, S11553.
55. "Oregon's Representatives Push Death of Owyhee Training Range," *Idaho Statesman,* October 15, 1993.
56. Nokkentved, *Desert Wings,* 65–67; letter to Secretary of the Interior Bruce Babbitt, signed by the leaders of fifteen groups opposing the proposed bombing range, October 1, 1993.

57. Nokkentved, *Desert Wings*, 72–73; Douglas N. Gladwin, declaration to US District Court, Boise, Idaho, Civ. 92-0189 S-BLW, March 15, 1996; V. Geist, letter to the Foundation for North American Wild Sheep, January 6, 1994.
58. Nokkentved, *Desert Wings*, 78–79.
59. "Economist Blasts Bombing Range Plan," *Twin Falls Times-News*, December 20, 1993.
60. Nokkentved, *Desert Wings*, 81–83.
61. David Loomis, *Combat Zoning: Military Land-Use Planning in Nevada* (Reno: University of Nevada Press, 1993), 33.
62. "Range Land Swap Skirts Law, House Chairman Says," *Idaho Statesman*, July 2, 1992.
63. Nokkentved, *Desert Wings*, 86.
64. Bruce E. Johansen, "Doctrine of Trust," in *Encyclopedia of Native American History*, ed. Bruce E. Johansen and Barry Pritzker, vol. 1 (Santa Barbara: ABC-CLIO, 2008), 614; Nokkentved, *Desert Wings*, 91–95; Bureau of Land Management, Idaho State Office, Background Paper, "Proposed Idaho Training Range National Historic Preservation Act Compliance," Boise, Idaho, May 26, 1994; "War Meetings"; also, news brief, *Owyhee Avalanche*, February 17, 1866.
65. "Military Tours Indian 'Temple,'" *Idaho Statesman*, February 18, 1994.
66. "Indian Sites on Training Range Span 5,000 Years," *Twin Falls Times-News*, January 4, 1994; "Range Foes Hear Indians' View," *Idaho Statesman*, January 9, 1994.
67. "Brad Knickerbocker Idahoans Balk at Air Force Proposal for Bomb Practice over Canyonlands," *Christian Science Monitor*, January 25, 1994; "Inouye Could Put Crimp in Range Plans," *Idaho Statesman*, April 30, 1994.
68. "'It's Crucial . . . It's Necessary,'" *Idaho Statesman*, December 9, 1993.
69. "Andrus: Range Basically Dead," "News Casts Cloud over Mtn. Home," and "Range Supporters, Opponents Comments," *Idaho Statesman*, October 5, 1994.
70. Report and Recommendation and Order of US Magistrate Judge Mikel H. Williams, US District Court, District of Idaho, Boise, Idaho, Civ. 92-185-S-HLR, October 7, 1994.
71. "Judge: Range Statement Wasn't Comprehensive," *Idaho Statesman*, October 8, 1994; "Aide: Clinton Wanted New Range Plan," *Idaho Statesman*, November 12, 1994; "Victory in Idaho: Canyon Lovers Defeat the Military," *High Country News*, November 28, 1994.
72. "Conservationists Fear Copter Carrying Chenoweth, Crapo May Disturb Bighorns," *Idaho Statesman*, April 21, 1995.
73. "Judge Rules Air Force Erred with Split EIS," *Mountain Home News*, May 17, 1995; "Ruling Could Ground Training Range," *Idaho Statesman*, May 10, 1995.

74. Idaho delegation news release and Governor Batt, May 10, 1995, local news release.
75. Title unavailable, *New York Times,* August 17, 1997.
76. Nokkentved, *Desert Wings,* 113–15.
77. Title unavailable, *New York Times,* August 17, 1997.
78. Nokkentved, *Desert Wings,* 115–16.
79. Nokkentved, *Desert Wings,* 116–19; Martha Hahn, Idaho director, Bureau of Land Management, letter to US Air Force Colonel Fred Pease, January 2, 1998; title unavailable, *Mountain Home News,* April 22, 1998; Kent Laverty, director of Idaho Wildlife Federation, news release, May 14, 1998.
80. Title unavailable, *Los Angeles Times,* June 25, 1989; *Mountain Home News,* April 22, 1998.
81. "Senate May Vote on Land Transfer to Air Force for Training," *Idaho Statesman,* May 14, 1998; also Nokkentved, *Desert Wings,* 119–22; Senator Ron Wyden, Oregon, letter to Kathleen A. McGinty, chair, Council on Environmental Quality, Washington, DC, June 9, 1998; Senator Henry Reid, comments on Senate floor, *Congressional Record,* June 25, 1998, S7068.
82. Senator Kempthorne, comments on Senate floor, *Congressional Record,* June 25, 1998, S7070; Senator Strom Thurmond, comments on Senate floor, *Congressional Record,* June 25, 1998, S7071; Senator Henry Reid, comments on Senate floor, *Congressional Record,* June 25, 1998, S7068.
83. Nokkentved, *Desert Wings,* 119–22.
84. "Training Range Pact Reached," *Idaho Statesman,* July 10, 1999.
85. "Judge OKs Agreement Allowing Air Force Base to Expand Range," *Idaho Statesman,* December 7, 1999.
86. Limerick, *Legacy of Conquest,* preface to 2011 edition.
87. Wallace Stegner, *The American West as Living Space* (Ann Arbor: University of Michigan Press, 1987), 78.
88. Nokkentved, *Desert Wings,* 54–57; Deputy Assistant Secretary of the Air Force Gary Vest, air force memo, November 6, 1992.
89. Roger Singer, interview by author, May 15, 2001.
90. Nokkentved, *Desert Wings,* 128–29; also, phone interview of Craig Gehrke by author, April 27, 2011.

Chapter 8

1. Jeff Phillips, "Great Parks, No Crowds: As Pressures on the Remnants of the West's Wilderness Increase, We Propose Six Parks for the 21st Century," *Sunset,* May 1998, 120–23.
2. Woodward, "Cowboys vs. City Slickers," *Idaho Statesman,* December 24, 2000,

1A, 6A. No book about this episode exists. All of the core quotations in the following story were taken from this feature article.

3. Phillips, "Great Parks, No Crowds," 120–23.
4. Woodward, "Cowboys vs. City Slickers."
5. Ibid.; news brief, *Owyhee Avalanche,* November 8, 2000.
6. Woodward, "Cowboys vs. City Slickers."
7. Ibid.
8. Ibid.
9. Ibid.
10. Ibid.
11. Pam Marcum, interview by author, May 17, 2000.
12. Ibid.
13. Woodward, "Cowboys vs. City Slickers."
14. Nokkentved, *Desert Wings,* 5; Sierra Club, "Wild America: Protecting the Lands of Lewis and Clark" ([San Francisco:] Sierra Club, 2000). For a discussion of the differences between a national park, a national monument, and a wilderness area, see "A National Monument, Memorial, Park . . . What's the Difference?" NationalAtlas.gov, adapted from *The National Parks: Index 1991,* National Parks Service, accessed April 27, 2011, http://www.nationalatlas.gov/articles/government/a_nationalparks.html.
15. Nokkentved, *Desert Wings,* 68; Committee for Idaho's High Desert, "Owyhee Canyonlands Briefing Sheet, Conservationist's Wilderness Proposal," February 24, 1984 (Boise, ID: CIHD).
16. Gerald Meyer, US Department of the Interior, Bureau of Land Management, Vale District–Oregon, Boise District–Idaho, Elko District–Nevada, *Recreation Area Management Plan for the Owyhee River: Oregon, Idaho, Nevada* (Vale, OR: US Department of the Interior, Bureau of Land Management, [1983]).
17. Ibid.
18. Committee for Idaho's High Desert, "Desert Notes," vol. 2, no. 1 (Pamphlets given to author); "The Owyhee-Bruneau Canyonlands Proposed National Monument," Conservationist Coalition publisher (Pamphlets given to author).
19. Roger Singer, interview by author, June 3, 2013.
20. Committee for Idaho's High Desert, "Owyhee Canyonlands Briefing Sheet, Conservationist's Wilderness Proposal," February 24, 1984.
21. Wilderness Society, "Fact Sheet on the Antiquities Act," http://wilderness.org/article/antiquities-act.
22. "Idaho's Next Monument," *Idaho Falls Post Register,* November 23, 2000; "Groups Tout Survey Results," *Twin Falls Times-News,* November 15, 2000; Owyhee Canyonlands Coalition, *Owyhee Canyonlands: A Heritage of the American West* (Boise, ID: Wilderness Society, 1997).

23. "Environmentalists to Clinton: Protect Owyhee Canyonlands," *Idaho Statesman,* November 13, 2000.
24. "Protest over Owyhee Proposal Draws Crowd" and "Q&A Helps Explain Canyonlands," *Idaho Statesman,* December 7, 2000.
25. "Chris Salove Runs away with Owyhee District 1 Vote," *Idaho Press Tribune,* May 24, 2000.
26. News brief, *Owyhee Avalanche,* November 8, 2000.
27. Barker, "The Owyhee Canyonlands," *Idaho Statesman,* December 1, 2002; Rocky Barker, interview by author, December 17, 2002.
28. Paul Rogers and Jennifer LaFleur, "Cash Cows: Tax Dollars Still Support a Wild West Holdover That Enriches Big Ranchers and Degrades the Land," *San Jose Mercury News,* November 7, 1999.
29. Ibid.
30. Ibid.
31. Ibid.
32. Ibid.
33. Ibid.
34. Ibid.
35. Ibid.
36. "Beefed-up Concerns,' *Idaho Statesman,* August 24, 1995.
37. Rogers and LaFleur, "Cash Cows."
38. Ibid.
39. Ibid.
40. Ibid.
41. Ibid.
42. Press release on the Remarks by President Clinton on Designation of National Monuments, January 17, 2001, www.whitehouse.gov/library/hot_releases/January_%2017_2001_5.html (link no longer active).
43. "Monument Maker," *Washington Post,* January 13, 2001; "Conservation Groups Go for Final Push," *USA Today,* December 14, 2000; "Babbitt: Owyhees Won't Be Set Aside," *Idaho Statesman,* January 14, 2001.
44. "Cattle Association Sets Priorities," *Idaho Statesman,* December 27, 2001; also, Barker, "The Owyhee Canyonlands," *Idaho Statesman,* December 1, 2002.
45. "Cattle Association Sets Priorities," *Idaho Statesman,* December 27, 2001; also, Barker, "The Owyhee Canyonlands," *Idaho Statesman,* December 1, 2002.
46. "Cattle Association Sets Priorities," *Idaho Statesman,* December 27, 2001; also, Barker, "The Owyhee Canyonlands," *Idaho Statesman,* December 1, 2002.
47. "Cattle Association Sets Priorities," *Idaho Statesman,* December 27, 2001; also, Barker, "The Owyhee Canyonlands," *Idaho Statesman,* December 1, 2002.
48. Barker, "The Owyhee Canyonlands," *Idaho Statesman,* December 1, 2002.

49. Ibid.; also, "Cattle Association Sets Priorities," *Idaho Statesman,* December 27, 2001.
50. "Cattle Association Sets Priorities."
51. Deanna Darr, "Unlikely Allies: Owyhee Initiative Unites Warring Factions," *Boise Weekly,* January 28, 2009.
52. Ibid.
53. Ibid.; Barker, "The Owyhee Canyonlands," *Idaho Statesman,* December 1, 2002.
54. Darr, "Unlikely Allies"; also, "Worth the Risk to Compromise" *Idaho Statesman,* December 1, 2002.
55. Ibid.
56. Ibid.; Chad Gibson, interview by author, April 26, 2011; also, Craig Gehrke, interview by author, April 27, 2011.
57. Erika Bolstad, "Land Bill Will Affect All Corners of America—Especially Idaho," *Idaho Statesman,* March 31, 2009.
58. Compiled by Brenda Bielke, "Statements on Passage of Owyhees Land Management Bill," http://www.owyheeinitiative.org/press/03-25-09_release3.htm; also, http://crapo.senate.gov/media/newsreleases/release_full.cfm?id=296546.
59. Darr, "Unlikely Allies"; also, Bruce Reichert, "An Interview with Sandra Mitchell," Outdoor Idaho, Wilderness in the 21st Century, Boise Public Television, http://idahoptv.org/outdoors/shows/wildernessinthe21stcentury/Mitchell.cfm.
60. Darr, "Unlikely Allies."
61. Ibid., also, "Implementing the Owyhee Public Lands Management Act Legislation and the Owyhee Initiative Agreement," Owyhee Initiative.org, http://www.owyheeinitiative.org/resources.htm.
62. Gibson, interview by author, April 26, 2011.
63. Gehrke, interview by author, April 27, 2011.
64. Darr, "Unlikely Allies."
65. Ibid.

Conclusion

1. Bruce Reichert, "An Interview with Mike Crapo," Outdoor Idaho, Wilderness in the 21st Century, http://idahoptv.org/outdoors/shows/wildernessinthe21stcentury/Crapo.cfm. All of the quotations in this section come from this interview.
2. Ibid.
3. Ibid.
4. Ibid.

5. Gehrke, interview by author, December 19, 2012. All of the quotations in this section come from this interview.
6. Ibid.
7. Ibid.
8. Ibid.
9. Ibid.
10. Ibid.
11. Turner, "Significance of the Frontier."
12. Patricia Limerick, prologue to *Remedies for a New West: Healing Landscapes, Histories, and Cultures,* ed. Patricia Limerick, Andrew Cowell, and Sharon K. Collinge (Tucson: University of Arizona Press, 2009).
13. Ibid., 2, 7.
14. Ibid., 8–9.
15. Joseph Campbell, with Bill Moyers, *The Power of Myth* (New York: Doubleday, 1988), 10.
16. "Ranchers Gaining in Popularity with Public," *Idaho Statesman,* February 28, 2011.

Bibliography

Abbott, Carl. *How Cities Won the West: Four Centuries of Urban Change in Western North America*. Albuquerque: University of New Mexico Press, 2008.

———. "The Federal Presence." In *The Oxford Dictionary of the American West,* edited by Clyde A. Milner II, Carol A. O'Connor, and Martha A. Sandweiss, 469–500. Oxford: Oxford University Press, 1994.

Adams, Mildretta. *Historic Silver City: The Story of the Owyhees.* Homedale, ID: Printed by the Owyhee Chronicle, 1960.

———. *Owyhee Cattlemen, 1878–1978: 100 Years in the Saddle.* Rev. ed. Homedale, ID: Owyhee Publishing Co., 1979.

Alt, David D., and Donald W. Hyndman. *The Roadside Geology of Idaho.* Missoula, MT: Mountain Press, 1989.

Applegate, Rex. *Kill or Get Killed: Riot Control Techniques, Manhandling, and Close Combat, for Police and Military.* Harrisburg, PA: Military Service Pub. Co., 1943.

Arrington, Leonard J. *History of Idaho.* Moscow: University of Idaho Press, 1994.

Arrizabalaga, Marie Pierre. "A Statistical Study of Basque Immigration into California, Nevada, Idaho, and Wyoming, 1900–1910." Master's thesis, University of Nevada, Reno, 1986.

Artiach, Jose Mari. Interview by author, June 10, 1993. Recording. Basque Museum and Cultural Center Archives, Boise, Idaho.

Barker, Rocky. Interview by author, December 17, 2002.

Barnes, Will C. *Apaches and Longhorns: The Reminiscences of Will C. Barnes*, edited by Frank C. Lockwood. Los Angeles: Ward Ritchie Press, 1941.

———. *Western Grazing Grounds and Forest Ranges*. Chicago: Breeder's Gazette, 1913.

Barthes, Roland. *Mythologies*. New York: Hill and Wang, 1972.

Bass, Rick. *The Lost Grizzlies: A Search for Survivors in the Wilderness of Colorado*. Boston: Houghton Mifflin, 1995.

Battien, Pauline. *The Gold Seekers: A 200 Year History of Mining in Washington, Idaho, Montana, and Lower British Columbia*. Colville, WA: Printed by Statesman-Examiner, 1989.

Baynton, Douglas C. "Defectives in the Land: Disability and American Immigration Policy, 1882–1924." *Journal of American Ethnic History* 24 (2005): 31–69.

Bergon, Frank. *Shoshone Mike*. New York: Viking Press, 1987.

Beristain, Nick. Interview by author, March 20, 1992. Recording. Basque Museum and Cultural Center Archives, Boise, Idaho.

Bielke, Brenda, compiler. "Statements on Passage of Owyhees Land Management Bill." http://www.owyheeinitiative.org/press/03-25-09_release3.htm.

Brown, Richard Maxwell. *No Duty to Retreat: Violence and Values in American History and Society*. Oxford: Oxford University Press, 1992.

———. "Violence." In *The Oxford Dictionary of the American West*, edited by Clyde A. Milner II, Carol A. O'Connor, and Martha A. Sandweiss, 707–11. Oxford: Oxford University Press, 1994.

———. "Western Violence: Structure, Values, Myth." *Western Historical Quarterly* 24, no. 1 (February 1993): 4–20.

"The California Gold Rush." Social Studies for Kids. Accessed June 25, 2013. http://www.socialstudiesforkids.com/articles/ushistory/californiagoldrush.htm.

Calder, Jenni. *There Must Be a Lone Ranger: The American West in Film and Reality*. London: Hamilton Press, 1974.

"Call of the Wild: A Mountain Killer Breaks Loose." *Time*, April 14, 1986.

Campbell, Joseph, with Bill Moyers. *The Power of Myth*. New York: Doubleday, 1988.

Carlson, Paul H. "Cowboys and Sheepherders." In *The Cowboy Way: An Exploration of History and Culture*, edited by Paul H. Carlson, 109–18. Lubbock: Texas Tech University Press, 2006.

"Carson River Mercury Site—Overview." Nevada Division of Environmental Protection. Accessed September 29, 2011. http://ndep.nv.gov/BCA/carsonriver/criver_2.htm.

Cawelti, John G. *The Six-Gun Mystique*. Bowling Green, OH: Bowling Green University Popular Press, 1984.

Clawson, Marion. *The Western Range Livestock Industry*. New York: Arno Press, 1979.

Committee for Idaho's High Desert. "Owyhee Canyonlands Briefing Sheet, Conservationist's Wilderness Proposal," February 24, 1984. Boise, ID: Committee for Idaho's High Desert.

Conley, Cort. *Idaho for the Curious: A Guide.* Cambridge, ID: Backeddy Books, 2003.

Cook, Stephen P. *Realizing Westward: American Character and Cowboy Mythology.* Boston: Pearson Custom Pub., 2007.

"Delamar Professorship in Biological Chemistry." Accessed June 24, 2013. http://webapps.jhu.edu/namedprofessorships/professorshipdetail.cfm?professorshipID=128.

"Delamar History!" Accessed June 24, 2013. http://www.robertwynn.com/DelamarH.htm.

"Don Shannon, Historian, Author of 'The Utter Disaster,' 'Massacre Rocks and City of Rocks,' and 'The Boise Massacre on the Oregon Trail.'" Pathways of Pioneers. Outdoor Idaho. Accessed March 28, 2013. http://idahoptv.org/outdoors/shows/pathwaysofpioneers/DonShannon.cfm.

Douglass, William A., and Jon Bilbao. *Amerikanuak: Basques in the New World.* Reno: University of Nevada Press, 1975.

———. "The Basques of the American West: Preliminary Historical Perspectives." *Nevada Historical Quarterly* 13, no. 4 (Winter 1970): 131–62.

Eiguren, Joe. Interviews by author, December 4, 1991; February 18, 1992; and March 24, 1993. Recordings. Basque Museum and Cultural Center Archives, Boise, Idaho.

Etulain, Richard W. "Basque Beginnings in the Pacific Northwest." *Idaho Yesterdays* 18, no. 1 (Spring 1974): 26–32.

———, ed. *Writing Western History: Essays on Major Western Historians.* Albuquerque: University of New Mexico Press, 1991.

Faragher, John Mack. *Rereading Frederick Jackson Turner: The Significance of the Frontier in American History and Other Essays.* New York: H. Holt, 1994.

Fiege, Mark. *Irrigated Eden: The Making of an Agricultural Landscape in the American West.* Seattle: University of Washington Press, 1999.

Fourth Biennial Report of the Fish and Game Warden of the State of Idaho, 1911–1912. Frank M. Kendall, State Game Warden, Predatory Animal Control.

Francaviglia, Richard. "Walt Disney's Frontierland as an Allegorical Map of the American West." *Western Historical Quarterly* 30, no. 2 (1999): 155–82.

"Frederic Remington." *American Masters,* PBS.org, 1991.

Garmendia Letters Collection. Basque Museum and Cultural Center Archives, Boise, Idaho.

Gates, Paul W., ed. *History of the Public Land Law Development.* Washington, DC: Zenger Publishing, 1968.

Gehrke, Craig. Interviews by author, April 27, 2011, and December 19, 2012.

Gibson, Chad. Interview by author, April 26, 2011.

Gilfillan, Archer B. *Sheep.* Boston: Little, Brown, 1930.

Gillard, Fred. "Early Theater in the Owyhees." *Idaho Yesterdays* 17 (Summer 1973): 9–15.

Goble, Dale D., and Paul W. Hirt, eds. *Northwest Lands, Northwest Peoples: Readings in Environmental History.* Seattle: University of Washington, 1999.

Gray, Dale M. "War on the Mountain." *Owyhee Outpost,* no. 22 (1991): 40–62.

Hanley, Mike, and Ellis Lucia. *Owyhee Trails: The West's Forgotten Corner.* Caldwell, ID: Caxton Printers, 1973.

Herndon, Paul. *Taylor Grazing Act 1934–1984.* Published by the State Director of Public Lands of Idaho, 1990.

Herman, Daniel Justin. *Hell on the Range: Honor, Conscience, and the American West.* New Haven, CT: Yale University Press, 2010.

Hoover, Herbert. "Message on the Dedication of Owyhee Dam." The American Presidency Project. Accessed March 28, 2013. http://www.presidency.ucsb.edu/ws/index.php?pid=23169.

"Hearing Results in Agreement to Proceed with Owyhee Initiative Legislation." News release. Office of Senator Mike Crapo, Idaho. http://crapo.senate.gov/media/newsreleases/release_full.cfm?id=296546.

A Historical, Descriptive and Commercial Directory of Owyhee County, Idaho, January 1898. Silver City, ID: Owyhee Avalanche, 1898.

Hyde, Dayton O. *The Last Free Man: The True Story Behind the Massacre of Shoshone Mike and His Band of Indians in 1911.* New York: New Dial Press, 1973.

Hyland, Andy. "16 Things: KU History Professor, Environmental Historian Recounts Personal History." Accessed January 12, 2013. http://www2.ljworld.com/news/2011/sep/12/16-things-ku-history-professor-environmental-histo/.

Idaho Wool Growers Association Letter, February 3, 1904.

"The Immigration Act of 1924 (The Johnson-Reed Act)." US Department of State, Office of the Historian. Accessed March 28, 2012. http://history.state.gov/milestones/1921-1936/ImmigrationAct.

"Implementing the Owyhee Public Lands Management Act Legislation and the Owyhee Initiative Agreement." OwyheeInitiative.org. http://www.owyheeinitiative.org/resources.htm.

Johansen, Bruce E. "Doctrine of Trust." In *Encyclopedia of Native American History,* edited by Bruce E. Johansen and Barry Pritzker. Vol. 1. Santa Barbara: ABC-CLIO, 2008.

Jordan, Bill, and William Henry Jordan. *No Second Place Winner.* Concord, NH: Police Bookshelf, 1965.

Just, Rick. "The Underground War." In *Idaho Snapshots: Stories from the Popular Radio Series,* 13–16. Meridian: Radio Idaho Press, 1990.

Keelan, Tom. "With the Miners Came the Sheep." *Boise Idaho Statesman Centennial Supplement* (1990): 2.

Landa, Sabino. Interview by author, March 18, 1992. Recording. Basque Museum and Cultural Center Archives, Boise, Idaho.

Lane, Richard H. "The Cultural Ecology of Sheep Nomadism: Northeastern Nevada, 1870–1872." PhD diss., Yale University, 1974.

Limerick, Patricia Nelson. *Legacy of Conquest: The Unbroken Past of the American West.* New York: W. W. Norton, 1987.

———. *Something in the Soil: Legacies and Reckonings in the New West.* New York: W. W. Norton, 2000.

Limerick, Patricia, Andy Cowell, and Sharon Collinge, eds. *Remedies for a New West: Healing Landscapes, Histories, and Cultures.* Tucson: University of Arizona Press, 2009.

Lingenfelter, Richard E. *The Hardrock Miners: A History of the Mining Labor Movement in the American West, 1863–1893.* Berkeley and Los Angeles: University of California Press, 1974.

Long, Jeff. *Outlaw: The True Story of Claude Dallas.* New York: Morrow, 1985.

Loomis, David. *Combat Zoning: Military Land-Use Planning in Nevada.* Reno: University of Nevada Press, 1993.

Mack, Effie Mona. *The Indian Massacre of 1911 at Little High Rock Canyon, Nevada.* Sparks, NV: Western Print. and Pub. Co., 1963.

Madsen, Brigham D. *The Shoshone Frontier and the Bear River Massacre.* Salt Lake City: University of Utah Press, 1985.

Marcum, Pan. Interview by author, May 17, 2002, Boise, Idaho.

Martin, Jonathan D. "'The Grandest and Most Cosmopolitan Object Teacher': Buffalo Bill's Wild West and the Politics of American Identity, 1883–1899." *Radical Review* 66 (1996): 92–123.

Mauk, Bill. "Cases of the Century: Claude Dallas." *The Advocate,* August 2000, 22–27.

McCall, Grant E. "Basque-Americans and a Sequential Theory of Migration and Adaptation." Master's thesis, San Francisco State College, 1968.

McDowell, Bart. *The American Cowboy in Life and Legend.* Washington, DC: National Geographic Society, 1972.

McKinney, Whitney. *A History of the Shoshone-Paiutes of the Duck Valley Indian Reservation.* Salt Lake City: Institute of the American West and Howe Bros., 1983.

Meyer, Gerald, US Department of the Interior, Bureau of Land Management; Vale District–Oregon, Boise District–Idaho; Elko District–Nevada. *Recreation Area Management Plan for the Owyhee River: Oregon, Idaho, Nevada.* Vale, OR: US Department of the Interior, Bureau of Land Management, [1983].

Milner, Clyde A. "Introduction: America Only More So." In *The Oxford Dictionary of the American West,* edited by Clyde A. Milner II, Carol A. O'Connor, and Martha A. Sandweiss, 1–7. Oxford: Oxford University Press, 1994.

Mora, Anthony. *Border Dilemmas: Racial and National Uncertainties in New Mexico, 1848–1912.* Durham, NC: Duke University Press, 2011.

Murdoch, David Hamilton. *The American West: Invention of a Myth*. Reno: University of Nevada Press, 2001.

Nokkentved, Niels Sparre. *Desert Wings: Controversy in the Idaho Desert*. Pullman: Washington State University Press, 2001.

Office of Public Affairs and the Division of Publications. "A National Monument, Memorial, Park . . . What's the Difference?" National Atlas.gov. Adapted from *The National Parks: Index 1991*. April 27, 2011. http://www.nationalatlas.gov/articles/government/a_nationalparks.html.

Olsen, Jack. *Give a Boy a Gun: A True Story of Law and Disorder in the American West*. New York: Delacorte Press, 1985.

Onderdonk, James Lawrence. *Idaho: Facts and Statistics Concerning Its Mining, Farming, Stock Raising, Lumbering, and Other Resources and Industries*. San Francisco: A. L. Bancroft, 1885.

Owyhee Canyonlands Coalition. *Owyhee Canyonlands: A Heritage of the American West*. Boise, ID: Wilderness Society, 1997.

"The Owyhee Country." Idaho State Historical Society, Reference Series, no. 200, 1964.

"Owyhee County." Idaho State Historical Society, Reference Series, no. 336, 1975.

"Owyhee County Bannock War Sites." Idaho State Historical Society, Reference Series, no. 1090, 1995.

"Owyhee County, Idaho." State & County QuickFacts, US Census Bureau. Accessed March 27, 2012. http://quickfacts.census.gov/qfd/states/16/16073.html.

"Owyhee County Idaho Gold Production." Western Mining History: Reliving the Industrial Revolution of the West. Accessed December 28, 2012. http://www.westernmininghistory.com/articles/114/page1.

"Owyhee County Profile & A Bit of History." Owyhee County, Idaho. Accessed March 29, 2013. http://www.owyheecounty.net/index1.php?countyprofile.

"Owyhee Horse and Cattle Ranches (Nineteenth Century)." Idaho State Historical Society, Reference Series, no. 1050, rev. July 1995.

Peck, Gunther. *Reinventing Free Labor: Padrones and Immigrant Workers in the North American West, 1880–1930*. Cambridge: Cambridge University Press, 2000.

Phillips, Jeff. "Great Parks, No Crowds: As Pressures on the Remnants of the West's Wilderness Increase, We Propose Six Parks for the 21st Century." *Sunset*, May 1998, 120–123.

Plew, Mark. *BSU Archaeology Reports*. Boise, ID: Boise State University, 1986.

Prendergast, Alan. "The Law and Claude Dallas." *Rolling Stone*, December 9, 1982, 30–34, 71.

Raine, William MacLeod, and Will C. Barnes, *Cattle, Cowboys, and Rangers*. Garden City, NY: Doubleday, Doran, & Co., 1930.

Reichert, Bruce. "An Interview with Sandra Mitchell." Outdoor Idaho, Wilderness in the 21st Century, Boise Public Television. http://idahoptv.org/outdoors/shows/wildernessinthe21stcentury/Mitchell.cfm.

———. "An Interview with Mike Crapo." Outdoor Idaho, Wilderness in the 21st Century, Boise Public Television. http://idahoptv.org/outdoors/shows/wildernessinthe21stcentury/Crapo.cfm.

Report of the Commissioner of Agriculture, 1891. Washington, DC, 1892.

Robbins, Roy M. *Our Landed Heritage: The Public Domain, 1776–1936*. Lincoln: University of Nebraska Press, 1962.

Roesch, Ethel A. "Basques of the Sawtooth Range." *Frontier Times,* April–May 1964: 28–36.

Rogers, Paul, and Jennifer LaFleur. "Cash Cows: Tax Dollars Still Support a Wild West Holdover that Enriches." *San Jose Mercury News,* November 7, 1999.

Ross, Clyde P. "Mining History of South-Central Idaho." Moscow: Idaho Bureau of Mines and Geology, July 1963.

Sawyer, Byrd Wall. *Nevada Nomads: A Story of the Sheep Industry*. San Jose, CA: Harlan-Young Press, 1971.

Schwantes, Carlos A. *In Mountain Shadows: A History of Idaho*. Lincoln: University of Nebraska Press, 1991.

Shaddock, Louise. *Andy Little: Idaho Sheep King*. Caldwell, ID: Caxton Printers, 1990.

"A Short History of Silver City, Idaho." Historic Silver City, Idaho. Accessed December 28, 2012. http://www.historicsilvercityidaho.com/.

Sierra Club. "Wild America: Protecting the Lands of Lewis and Clark." [San Francisco:] Sierra Club, 2000.

Silen, Sol. *La Historia de los Vascongados en el Oeste de los Estados Unidos*. New York: Las Novedades, 1917.

Sims, Robert C., and Hope Benedict, eds. *Idaho's Governors: Historical Essays on Their Administrations*. Boise, ID: Center for Research Grants and Contracts, Boise State University, 1978.

Singer, Roger. Interview by author, May 15, 2002. Recording. Basque Museum and Cultural Center Archives, Boise, Idaho.

"Site of Utter Party Massacre." Idaho State Historical Society, Reference Series, no. 233, June 1993.

Slotkin, Richard. *The Fatal Environment: The Myth of the Frontier in the Age of Industrialization, 1800–1890*. New York: Atheneum, 1985.

———. *Gunfighter Nation: The Myth of the Frontier in Twentieth-Century America*. Norman: University of Oklahoma Press, 1998. First published 1992 by Atheneum.

———. *Regeneration through Violence: The Mythology of the American Frontier, 1600–1860*. Middletown, CT: Wesleyan University Press, 1973.

Speer, Robert. "Protecting Idaho's Desert Lands." ***Boise Weekly,*** December 16–22, 1999, 15–16.

Stapilus, Randy, and Marty Peterson. ***Idaho 100: The People Who Most Influenced the Gem State.*** Carlton, OR: Ridenbaugh Press, 2012.

Starrs, Paul F. ***Let the Cowboy Ride: Cattle Ranching in the American West.*** Baltimore: Johns Hopkins University Press, 1998.

Stegner, Wallace. ***The American West as Living Space.*** Ann Arbor: University of Michigan Press, 1987.

Supreme Court of the United States. October Term, 1916. No. 379. Secundino Omaechevarria, Plaintiff in Error, vs. State of Idaho. In Error to the Supreme Court of the State of Idaho. Washington, DC: Judd & Detweiler, Printers, November 4, 1916.

Templeton, Earl. "Annual Grazing G Report, District 6." Humboldt National Forest. Winnemucca, Nevada.

"Territorial Government in Idaho, 1863–1869." Idaho State Historical Society, Reference Series, no. 48, 1963.

Thomas, John L. ***A Country in the Mind: Wallace Stegner, Bernard DeVoto, History, and the American Land.*** New York: Routledge, 2000.

Tullidge, Edward. ***History of Salt Lake City.*** Salt Lake City, 1886.

Turner, Frederick Jackson. "The Significance of the Frontier in American History." Paper presented to the American Historical Association at the World's Columbian Exposition, Chicago, Illinois, July 12, 1893.

Ugalde, Marcelino. Interview by author, July 9, 2002.

Warren, Kim Cary. ***Quest for Citizenship: African American and Native American Education in Kansas, 1880–1935.*** Chapel Hill: University of North Carolina Press, 2010.

Welch, Julia Conway. "Two Legends." ***Owyhee Outpost,*** no. 26 (June 1995): 1–8.

Welke, Barbara Young. ***Law and the Borders of Belonging in the Long Nineteenth Century United States.*** New York: Cambridge University Press, 2010.

Wells, Merle. "The Context of Gubernatorial Politics in Idaho." In ***Idaho's Governors: Historical Essays on Their Administrations,*** edited by Robert C. Sims and Hope Benedict. Boise, ID: Center for Research Grants and Contracts, Boise State University, 1978.

———. ***Gold Camps and Silver Cities: Nineteenth Century Mining in Central and Southern Idaho.*** Moscow: Idaho Department of Lands, 1983.

Wentworth, Edward. ***America's Sheep Trails: History, Personalities.*** Ames: Iowa State College Press, 1948.

West, Elliott. "Five Idaho Mining Towns: A Computer Profile." ***Pacific Northwest Quarterly*** 73 (July 1982): 108–20.

White, Richard. "Frederick Jackson Turner and Buffalo Bill." Accessed August 1, 2013. http://www.studythepast.com/his378/turnerandbuffalobill.pdf.

———. *"It's Your Misfortune and None of My Own": A History of the American West.* Norman: University of Oklahoma Press, 1991.

Wilderness Society. "Fact Sheet on the Antiquities Act." Internal publishing.

"William F. Cody 'Buffalo Bill' (1846–1917)." New Perspectives on the West. PBS.org. Accessed August 1, 2013. http://www.pbs.org/weta/thewest/people/a_c/buffalobill.htm.

Worster, Donald. *An Unsettled Country: Changing Landscapes of the American West.* Albuquerque: University of New Mexico Press, 1994.

Young, Brigham. Brigham Young Papers, 1857–1877. Utah Historical Society. Salt Lake City.

Zhu, Liping. *A Chinaman's Chance: The Chinese on the Rocky Mountain Mining Frontier.* Niwot: University Press of Colorado, 1997.

Zumbo, Jim. "Last Day of the Wardens." *Outdoor Life,* July 1981, 5–7.

Index

Note: page numbers in *italics* refer to illustrations.

Achabal, Juan, 107
Ada County Limit Club, 110–11
Adam, Andy, 133
agriculture: effect on landscape, 86; irrigation and, 22, 26, 27, 124; modern, 27; on reservations, 26
Ainsworth Mining Co., 52
Air Force: land controlled by, 176; and Owyhee Initiative, 221–22, 226. *See also* Saylor Creek Bombing Range expansion
Aldecoa, Domingo, 103
Alexander, Jan, 28
American exceptionalism, 122
Andrews, Victor C., 172, 176, 177, 183
Andrus, Cecil, 181, *181*, 184–87, 189–90, 194–95
Antiquities Act of 1906, 202, 203, 211, 219–20
Apollo Minstrels, 44
Archabal, John, 111
Archabal Sheep Co., 24
Arrington, Leonard, 127
Arrowrock Dam, 124

Babbitt, Bruce, 189, 190, 210, 218, 220
Baca, Jim, 189–90, 193
Ballard, D. W., 49, 50, 51, 52
Banks, Don, 205
Bannock Indians, 16, *17*, *18*, 18–19, *20*, 60, 61, 63–65
Bannock War of 1878, 63, 64
Basabe, Tom, 182, 217–18
Basque immigrants, *95*; assimilated, acceptance of, 107, 108, 110–11, 114; demographics of, 94, 96; immigration quotas and, 113; migrations, 93–94; nativism and, 114; number of, 95, 108–9; plans to return home, 94, 95, 107, 108; prejudice against, 88–89, 108; successful, 107; and World War

I, 109–11. *See also* Omaechevarria, Secundino
Basques, in sheep ranching, 22, 24, ***93***, 95–97, ***97***; and closing of open range, 113; and disregard for the land, 104, 107; and economic opportunity, 88, 93; limited experience of, 96; local resentment of, 99, 106–7, 108; murder of, in Denio ranch party, 72, ***73***, 74; number of, 95–96; positive contributions of, 96–97; "tramp bands" and, 105–6; violence against, 101–3
Beachy, William "Hill," 23, 51
Bear River Massacre, 63–64
Bennett, James Gordon, 119
Bicknell, R. F., 88, 91, 100, 101
Big Quiet, Owyhee county as, 15, 29
Billy the Kid, 129, 130–31
Black, William, 36, 61
Blue Bucket, 38
Blue Ribbon Coalition, 203
Border Dilemmas (Mora), 114
Brackett, Bert, 172, 176, 198
Brandeis, Louis, 112, ***112***
Brown, Richard, 6–7, 45
Brubacher, Esther, 54–55
Bryan, D. C., 32
Buffalo Bill's Wild West Show, 120, ***120***; American exceptionalism as message of, 121–22; at Columbian Exhibition (Chicago, 1893), 4, 121–22, 235; imitators of, 122; touring of, 120; and Western myth, 4, 119–21, 235–36
Buffalo Horn, 19, 64
Bukowsky, Grace, 181
Buntline, Ned, 120
Bureau of Land Management (BLM): environmentists' pressure on, 210, 213–14; grazing rights and, 89, 141, 216; land controlled by, 203; Owyhee Canyonlands preservation and, 203, 205, 210, 211, 227; progressive tightening of range laws by, 138; recreational use statistics, 209; resentment of, 138, 213–14; and Saylor Creek Bombing Range expansion, 183, 186–87, 189–90, 195, 198, 200; Shoshone-Paiute Tribes and, 222
Bush, George H. W., 211
Bush, George W., 5

Calder, Jenni, 118
California gold rush, 35
Cambron, Ben, 79, 80, 81
Cambron, Harry, 72, 74, 79, 80–81
Campbell, Joseph, 235–36
Canary, Martha "Calamity Jane," 118
Carlin, Don and Eddy, 141–42, 144, 157
Carson, Kit, 119, 120, 130
Carter, James E. "Jimmy," 211
cattle grazing rights: amount of land involved in, 215; ranchers' legal victories in, 104; compensation for loss of, 198–99; corporations and, 215–16; and environmental damage, 215–16, 219; environmentalists and, 206, 207, 210, 214–15, 216, 217, 222, 224, 228; as essential for cattle industry, 218–19; federal restrictions on, 89, 105, 128, 213–14; federal "subsidies" and, 215–19; legal basis of, 89, 98–100; number of ranchers holding, 215; Owyhee Canyonlands preservation and, 204–5, 224; permit system for, 217, 218; taxpayer groups and, 216. ***See also Omaechevarria v. State of Idaho*** (1918)

cattle ranchers: appeal of myths about, 117; economic pressure on, 216, 217, 218–19; environmental laws and, 204, 213–15, 217–18, 220; and federal intrusion, 213–14; as "more American" than shepherds, 88–89; Owyhee Canyonlands preservation and, 204–6; Owyhee Initiative and, 222, 223, 224, 228; and Saylor Creek Bombing Range expansion, 172, 175–76, 182, 184, 188, 197, 201; shepherd "tramp bands" and, 97; trail drive by, ***205***; turn to government for support, 103, 114
cattle ranching, 19–22; alternatives to, 206–7, 207–8, 218; brands, 24; conflicts with sheep ranchers, 20–22; environmentalists' opposition to, 206, 207, 214–15, 217, 222; history of, 90–91; and Indian food supply, 66; productivity of, 216; small ranches, decline in, 217; women ranchers, 25
Cheney, Richard "Dick," 183
Chenoweth, Helen, 196
Christensen, Eric, 189
Citizen Alert, 181
City Slickers (film), 131
Civilian Conservation Corp, 127–28
Civil War, and Idaho politics, 19, 50
Clinton, William J. "Bill," 189, 193-195, 200-202, 204, 211–12, 216, 218–20
Cody, William F. "Buffalo Bill," 4, 119–21, ***121***, 122, 129–30. *See also* Buffalo Bill's Wild West Show
Coeur d'Alene Indians, ***17***, 60
Columbian Exhibition (Chicago, 1893), 3, 121–22, 235
Complete Life of George A. Custer (Whittaker), 119
Connor, Patrick Edward, 37, 61
conquest: as American legacy, 6, 235; collaborative model and, 235–36; Western myth and, 129–30
Cooper, James, 174, 175, 179–80
Cooper, John, 181, 182, 183–84
corporations: grazing subsidies and, 215–16; miners' funding and, 32, 33–34, 35, 41–42, 54; and mining boom, 34, 41–42, 54; and mining law, 54; and Western myth, 41–42, 54
Craig, Larry, 173–74, 195, 196, 198, 211
Crapo, Mike, 189, 195, 196, 220, 221, ***221***, 226–27, 231–32
Curtis, E. J., 49
Custer, George A., 129
Custer's Last Stand, 119, 120

Daggett, Mike. *See* Shoshone Mike
Dallas, Claude: as anachronistic, 156, 160, 161, 170–71; appeals, 169; capture of, 153–55, ***155***; character of, 133–34, 134–36, 137, 138–39, 140; contempt for authority, 135, 137, 144, 158, 170, 171; early life and family of, 133–34, 135, 151–52, 160; escape and recapture, 161–66, ***162***; Fish and Game's pursuit of, 142–45; illegal hunting by, 136–37, 139–40; killing of Fish and Game wardens, 145–46; life while in flight, 155–56; local critics of, 153, 170; as loner, 136; myth surrounding, 149, 150–51, 152, 155–56, 160–61, ***161***, 163, 165, 169, 170, 171; in Paradise Valley, Nevada, 135, 138–40; parole hearing for, 169–70, 171; and polarized positions on government, 149, 152, 153, 156, 158, 160; in prison, 160, 168–69, 169–70,

171; release from prison, 171; search for, 147–53; self-defense claim of, 157–58, 170; supporters of, 148–49, 152–53, 156, 158, 161–62, 164, 165, 167–68, 170; trial and sentencing, 157–60; trial on escape charges, 168–69; warden's bodies, disposal of, 146–47; work as cowboy, 134–37
Defense Authorization Bill of 1999, 198, 201
Defense Base Closure and Realignment Commission, 185–86
DeLamar Mine, 30
democracy, federal power and, 201
Denio, Mattie and Will, 72
Department of the Interior, 219
Dewey, William, 23
DiFazio, Peter, 190
Disney, Walt, 130
Donnelly, J. P., 75, ***75***, 78–79, 85
Douglass, William, 96–97, 113
Duck Valley Reservation, 18, ***21***, 26, 57, 77, 179, 190, 193–94, 196–97
dude ranches, 127, 131

Echohawk, Larry, 195
Elms, Conley, 142–47, ***143***
Elms, Michael, 147, 159
Engle Act of 1958, 192
Enlarged Homestead Act (1909), 124
entertainers, in boom towns, 44
environment: new emphasis on, 130, 131; role in history, 6; settlers' effects on, and Indian food supplies, 66–67, 86; settlers' imposition of homogeneity on, 86
environmentalists: and cattle grazing rights, 206, 207, 210, 214–15, 216, 217, 222, 224, 228; and sensitivity to people, 233; in modern Idaho, 29; and Owyhee Initiative, 221–24; Saylor Creek Bombing Range expansion and, 172, 175–76, 180, 182, 183, 184, 187–88, 190–91; support for federal involvement, 131. ***See also*** Owyhee Canyonlands national park/monument designation
Erramouspe, Peter, 72, 73

Faragher, John Mack, 5
The Fatal Environment (Slotkin), 85
federal government: conflicts with local government, 219; control of Western lands, 105, 106, 123–24, ***123***, 128–29, 176; as employer, 128–29; and grazing rights, 89, 105, 213–14; infrastructure and, 128; and Native Americans, conquest of, 18–19, 26; Native American treaty violations, 4, 18–19; and Owyhee River Dam, 22; public's views on, in Dallas case, 149, 152, 153, 156, 158, 160. ***See also*** Bureau of Land Management
federal involvement in West: conflict with Native Americans and, 37, 59, 62–63, 64; early weakness of, 46; expansion of after 1890s, 124; frontier forts and, 37–38, 63; Great Depression and, 127–28; increase in, 30; local collaborative decision making and, 227–28, 232; as modern concern, 29, 131; and origin of big government, 201; pervasiveness of, 123–24, ***123***; and resource exploitation, 124–25; transition from facilitator to regulator, 8; World War II and, 129. ***See also*** Owyhee Canyonlands national park/monument designation; Saylor Creek Bombing Range expansion

Federal Land Policy and Management Act of 1976, 209
federal troops: as defense against Native Americans, 37, 62–63; lawless behavior by, 62–63, 63–64; mining conflicts and, 49, 50, 52
Fish and Game Department: Dallas's killing of wardens from, 145–46; as overzealous, 158, 168; and Saylor Creek Bombing Range expansion, 185, 187, 191, 192–93, 195, 198. *See also* Dallas, Claude
Fite, Katie, 206, 208, 227, 228
Fogus, David, 36–37, 38, 40, 48, 49, 54
Fort Hall Reservation, *18*, 26, 57, *61*, 63, 64, 83
Fremont, John Charles, 130
French, Permeal, 24
frontier: and American values, 6; Jackson on closing of, 3–4; as place of ethnic mingling, 6. *See also* Western myth

Garaitandia, Domingo, 103
Gehrke, Craig, 195, 201, 221, 224, 228, 232–34
General Revision Act of 1891, 104–5
Gibson, Chad, 224, 228
Give a Boy a Gun (Olsen), 160, *161*
Golden Chariot Mining, 23, 46–52
gold rush (1860s): amounts of ore removed, 30, 33, 36, 39, 40, 46, 52, 53; fame of, 16–18, 40; influx of population in, 23, 36, 38, 39, 40–41; and rush to invest, 41–42; start of, 35–36; stories of disappointment, 38–39; success stories, 23, 30, 36–37, 39. *See also* mining; prospectors and miners
gold rush claims, struggle to stake and defend, 32–34, 46–51, 52–53; and government intervention, 34–35, 49–51, 51–52, 54; losses of life and property from, 34, 48, 51–52, 53; poor claim records and, 46; slowness of legal system and, 47; and Western myth, 54
government: friction between levels of, 76, 86; increasing presence of, grazing rights disputes and, 103, 114; increasing presence of, mining rights disputes and, 34–35, 49–51, 51–52, 54; polarized positions on, Dallas case and, 149, 152, 153, 156, 158, 160; and public order, 34–35, 49–51; role in Shoshone Mike's Band incident, 85–86; and Western expansion, facilitation of, 114; and Western violence, 6–7. *See also* federal government
Grand Staircase Escalante National Monument, 204–5
Grant, Fred, 212, 220
Grayson, Beachy & Co., 46, 51, 90
Grayson, George W., 46, 51
grazing rights disputes: environment concerns in, 107; and federal government, increased role of, 103, 114; history of, 89; increased crowding and, 104; and itinerant shepherds ("tramp bands"), local resentment of, 96–98, 99, 105, 106–7, 108–9; legal battles, 103; national forest system and, 105–6, 107; Owyhee Initiative and, 223; racial and ethnic tensions underlying, 103; Taylor Grazing Act of 1934 and, 113; violent confrontations, 101–3; World War I and, 109. *See also* cattle grazing rights; *Omaechevarria v. State of Idaho* (1918); sheep grazing rights
Great Depression, and federal role, 127–28
Greater Owyhee Legal Defense (GOLD), 187, 188, 189, 195, 200

Great Train Robbery (1903 film), 129
Grey, Zane, 127, 133
Grimes, George, 35–36
Guffey, James M., 23

Hanley, Mike, 205–6, 208
Hansen, John, 68–69
Hardiman Brothers, 90
Harrison, William Henry, 105, 106
Hays and Ray mine, 32–34
Helfrich, Prince, 209
Herman, Daniel, 54, 114
Hickok, "Wild Bill," 118
Hoagland, Jerry, 223, 224
Hoffman, Ted, 212, 223
Hogle, Ed, 79, 80
Holgate, John C., 36, 48
Homestead Act of 1862, 90
Honey, Art, 28
Hoover, Herbert, 22
Hornback, J. M., 42
Howard, Ted, 179, 222

Ida Elmore mining Co., 46–51, 52
Idaho: establishment of, 19; statehood, 56; state seal, 31
Idaho Farm Bureau, 203
immigrants: as mine workers, 40–41; quota system for, 89, 113–14. *See also* Basques, in sheep ranching
Immigration Act of 1924, 89, 113–14
Indiano, Bert, 72
Indian Reorganization Act of 1934, 26
Inouye, Daniel, 194, 199
Irving, Washington, 138

James, Jesse, 130
Johnson, Lyndon B., 129–30
Jordan, Michael, 36, 38

Kelly, John, 44–45
Kelly, Milton, 34
Kempthorne, Dirk, 189, 190, 195, 196, 198, 200
Kennedy, John F., 129–30
Kootenai Indians, *17*

Lamb, Graham, 70, 76, 77, 78, 80
L'Amour, Louis, 127, 133, 136
land: federal ownership of, 105, 106, 123–24, ***123***, 128–29, 176; federal sale of, 124–25; as "public trust," 206, 207, 208
land use, struggle over: as chronic issue, 30; collaborative local decision making in, 227, 228–29, 231–34; ecological impact of, 30. *See also* grazing rights; Owyhee Canyonlands national park/monument designation; Saylor Creek Bombing Range expansion; *other specific topics*
Laxague, John, 72
The Legacy of Conquest (Limerick), 201, 235
Leslie, H. E., 43–44
Limerick, Patricia, 6, 59, 201, 235
Lincoln, Abraham, 19, 38
Little, Andy, 96–97
local collaborative decision making on land use, 227, 228–29, 231–34
Lockhart, Sam, 51–52
Lodge, Edward, 159–60, 169, 196
London, Jack, 133
Long, Jeff, 134, 160, ***161***, 165
Lowry, Tim, 213–14, ***215***
Lucky Twenty Miners, 36
Lyon, Caleb, 38, 62

Mackenzie, Donald, 15
Manning, Lindsay, 179, 193, 194
Marlboro Man, 4, 130, 206
Martinez, Dan, 166, 170
Mauk, Bill, 168, 170
McBride, John R., 49, 51–52
McCarthy, John, 221, 223
McKay, Richard and Anna, 166
media: Dallas case and, 150–51, 152, 157, 160, 163–64, 165, 169–70; and Shoshone Mike, 84–85; Owyhee Canyonlands preservation effort and, 211
Meiers, Richard, 185
Meiners, Bill, 212
Meyr, Herb, 177, 181, 184, 192
Minear, A. P., 40
mining: appeal of myths about, 117; boom towns, 18, 43–45; and corporate power, 34; and Native Americans, 37, 54–55, 60–61, 66; environmental impact of, 54; immigrants and, 40–41; infrastructure and, 42; law governing, 54; and social cohesion, 42, 43; technology for, 40, 41–42. ***See also*** gold rush (1860s)
Mining and Scientific Press, 41–42
Minoletti, Nancy, 166
minorities, as early settlers, 24, 30
Mitchell, Sandra, 222, 227
Monohan, Joseph, 25
Moore, Christoper Wilkinson, 23
Mora, Anthony, 114
More, J. Marion, 36–37, 40, 51–52, ***53***
Morning Star mine, 39, 40, 41–42, 52
Morris, Randy, 178–79, 181–82
Mountain Home Air Force Base, ***175***; composite wing planned for, 185, 186, 187, 188, 191–92, 195; local support for, 176, 183; Owyhee Initiative and, 226; Pentagon threats to close, 177, 181, 184, 185, 186, 197; relocation of F-4 fighters to, 176–77; training needs at, 29, 174–75
Murdoch, David, 122, 125–26
Murphy Outpost Days, ***27***, 28
mythology, Slotkin on, 85

national forests: grazing rights in, 105–6, 107; visitors to, 131
national monuments, power to designate, 211
national parks: cattlemen's interest in expanding, 105; growth of, 105, 106
National Wild and Scenic River System, 210, 211
Nationwide Rivers Inventory, 210
Native Americans: assimilation of, 114; definition of as Other, 86; displacement by mining, 37, 54–55, 60–61, 66; federal jurisdiction over, 63; food supply of, 66–67, 86; forced turn to farming, 18–19; forcing of onto reservations, 18, 26; friendly settler relations, 67–69; inaccurate portrayals of in American myth, 4; modern reservation life, 26; and New Deal, 127–28; and Owyhee Canyonlands conservation, 220, ***221***, 221–22, 226, 228; and Saylor Creek Bombing Range expansion, 172, 175–76, 179, 188, 189, 191, 193–94, 195, 196–97, 198; settlers' hatred of, 62; and livestock theft, 58; treaties, U.S. violation of, 4, 18–19; U.S. conquest of, as origin of federal government aggressiveness, 201; U.S. trust responsibility and, 193; and Western myth, 59, 86, 122, 130–31. ***See also specific tribes***

Native Americans' conflict with settlers, 18–19, 37, 57–59, 61–64; as avoidable, 59, 69; deprivations leading to, 60; extermination as goal of, 58, 62; increase in over time, 59–61; intensity of, 60; and intervention of federal government, 59, 62–63; miners and, 37–38; and settlers' desire for protection, 62, 64; settlers' desire to punish, 76; vigilante justice and, 59; and Western myth, 59
Native American tribes of Owyhee County, 16, *17*
Nettleton, Tim, 147, 149, 150, 151, 155, 156, 159, 164, 167, 169
Newlands Reclamation Act (1902), 124
Newman, Paul, 194
new western historians, 4, 6–7
Nez Perce Indians, *17*, 60
Nielsen, Cortland, 152
Nielsen, George, 138, 139, 140–41, 144, 147, 153, 158
Nixon, Richard M., 211
No Duty to Retreat (Brown), 7
Northern Paiute Indians, 16, *17*, *20*, 26, 60, 61
North West Co., 15
Northwest Vigilantes, 45–46

Oakley, P. A. "Annie," 118, 122
Obama, Barack, 225, *226*
off-road vehicles, as issue, 202, 203, 207, 213, 223, 227
Olsen, Jack, 160–61, *161*, 165, 167
Omaechevarria, Secundino, 88, 91, 95–96, 113
Omaechevarria v. State of Idaho (1918): appeals of, 106; defense in, 100–101, 106, 112–13; facts of case, 88; prosecution witnesses, 98–100; Supreme Court ruling, 111–13; xenophobic context of, 89
Omnibus Public Lands Management Act of 2009, 225–27, *226*
open range, closing of, 113
Oregon Steam Navigation Co., 33
Oro Fino Mine, 39, *39*, 40, 52
Other, in U.S. history, 86–87
Otter Massacre, 61
Our Country (Strong), 122
Outlaw (Long), 160, *161*, 165
Owyhee Canyonlands, *11*, *203*, *229*; public attention to, 202, 207; as recreational area, 209, *209*; size of, 208; wildlife and geology of, 208–9
Owyhee Canyonlands Coalition, 187, 190, 191, 200, 210–11
Owyhee Canyonlands national park/monument designation, 220; claims of low impact of, 202–3, 207, 210–11, 212; Congress and, 203, 211–12, 220; environmentalists' efforts toward, 202, 210–12, 220; environmentalists' views on, 206–8, 207, 214–15, 217, 222; and fear of federal intrusiveness, 203, 204–6, 212–13; and grazing rights, 204–5; Obama and, 225–27; opposition to, 203, 212–13; Owyhee Initiative compromise on, 220–28; and private control, supporters of, 213; public opinion on, 207, 211; ranchers' concerns about, 204–6, 223; scientific research unit created by, 225; wilderness designation for, 224–25. *See also* Owyhee Initiative
Owyhee County: boundaries of, 19; county seat, 30; demographics, 28–29; economy, early, 19–20, 19–22, 23, 56–57; economy, modern, 27–28; establishment of, 19; map of, *21*; modern, profile of, 25–31; naming of,

15; Owyhee Canyonlands preservation and, 203; and Owyhee Initiative, 220–29; prehistory of, 16; topography and geology, *11*, *13*, 15–16, 19. ***See also*** settlement of Owyhee County

Owyhee Initiative, 220–28, *221*; collaborative approach of as model, 227–29, 231–34; criticisms of, 227; groups excluded from, 222; groups supporting, 226; implementation of recommendations by, 225–27; logic behind, 220; negotiation and compromise by, 222–25, 228–29; stewardship council, 223, 224, 227–28

Owyhee Mill Co., 33–34

Owyhee Mountains, *12*; mining in, 16–18, 32–34, 37, *39*, 40, 46–51, 52–53; and Western myth, 7–8

Owyhee River, *209*, 209–10

Owyhee River Dam, 22, *24*, 124

Owyhee Soil Conservation District, 221–22

Owyhee Wild and Scenic River Study, 209–10

Paiute Indians. ***See*** Northern Paiute Indians; Shoshone-Paiute Tribes

Peck, Charles, 32, 33

Pend d'Oreille Indians, 60

Pentagon efforts to increase land holdings, 173–74. ***See also*** Saylor Creek Bombing Range expansion

Pinchot, Gifford, 105

Pittman, Key, 108

Pogue, Bill, *141*; body, Dallas's hiding of, 146–47; body, search for, 147–48, 150, 158; killing of, 145–46; as overzealous, 156, 157, 158, 168; pursuit of Dallas, 141–45

Pogue family, 150, 159, 160, 164, 171

politics, and Western myth, 5, 125, 129–30

politics in Owyhee County: modern, 27; post-Civil War, 19, 50

Polk, James K., 35

Poorman Co., 32–34, 52

Poorman Mine, 18, 32–34, *33*

presidents, and Western myth, 5

Presley, Lee, 181

prospectors and miners: miners unions, 53–54; need for corporate funding, 32, 33–34, 35, 41–42, 54; willingness to face danger, 35, 53–54

public order on frontier: and government intervention, 34–35, 49–51; range of organizations to preserve, 38, 45–46

railroads, 19–20, 23, 56, 90

Railroad Stage Lines, 23

Reagan, Ronald W., 5, 130, 211

Reclamation Service, U.S., 22, 124

Reid, Harry, 190, 194, 199

Remedies for a New West (Limerick), 235

Remington, Frederic, *125*, 125–26

Richardson, Albert D., 40

Robbins, Orlando, 49–50, 52

Robison, John, 223, 224, 227

rodeos, 127

Roosevelt, Theodore "Teddy," 5, 106, 125–26, 129, 211

Russell, Charles, 137, 142

Sagebrush Rebellion, 131

Salinger, Matt, 165

Salove, Chris, 212, 221, *221*

Saylor Creek Bombing Range, 173, 174–75, *180*, *199*

Saylor Creek Bombing Range expansion:

Air Force alienation of public, 201; Air Force concessions on, 197, 200; Air Force strategy in, 195–96, 196–97; apparent demises of proposal, 183, 184, 194–95; behind-the-scenes deals in, 184, 197, 201; coalition against, 172, 175–76, 187, 188, 190–91, 195–96, 196–97; Congress and, 183, 186, 189, 190, 192, 194, 196, 198, 199–201; and democracy, lost faith in, 201; environmental impact statement for, 177, 180–81, 183, 186–87, 190, 193, 194, 195, 196, 197, 198; government agencies opposed to, 186–87, 188, 189–90, 192–93, 195, 198; government's relentlessness in, 180, 189, 195–96; growth of opposition to, 177–78; Idaho "working group" on, 182, 183; intended uses of, 174, 181, 183, 187; local supporters of, 176, 183; and moratorium on military land withdrawals, 184; need for, as issue, 172, 173, 175, 176–77, 179–80, 182, 183–84, 185–86, 191–92, 193, 196; Owyhee Initiative and, 232–33; projected impact of, 191; public hearings on, 178, 180–84, 186, 188, 198; residents' concerns about, 178–79, 181–82; size of, 172, 173, 177; small victories of opposition, 200, 201; state support of, 181, 184–89, 192, 193, 196; threats to close base and, 177, 181, 184, 185, 186, 197; vision of West as issue in, 180

Scouts of the Plains (Buntline), 120

Seidlitz, Aden, 227

settlement of Owyhee County, 15, 16; and conflict with Native Americans, 18–19; economic development, 19–22; minorities and, 24, 30; notable figures in, 23–25, 30–31

Shea, Con, 24, 90

Shea, Patrick, 198

sheep grazing rights: destructiveness of, as issue, 98, 100–101, 105, 107; laws restricting, 99–100; lawsuits on, 105–6; in national forests, 105; "tramp bands" and, 98

sheep ranching, 20–22; history of, 91–92; and Indian food supply, 66; introduction to America, 91; newcomers, local resentment of, 100; as opportunity for Basque immigrants, 88, 93; settlers' low opinion of, 91–92; World War I and, 109. ***See also*** Basques, in sheep ranching

shepherds: difficult life of, 92–93; foreign, resentment of, 100, 101–2; itinerant ("tramp bands"), 97–98, 99, 104, 105, 106–7, 108, 110; work routine of, 92. ***See also*** Basques, in sheep ranching

Shoshone Indians, 16, ***17***, 18–19, ***18***, 26, 57–59, 60, 61, 63

Shoshone Mike: death of, 78–79; family of, 65, 67–68, 69; names of, 64–65; tribal affiliation of, 65

Shoshone Mike's Band: charges against, 58–59, 70, 76–77; conflict with Tranmer brothers, 57–58, 69–70; flight and pursuit, 58, 59, 70–78, ***73***, ***75***; friendly relations with settlers, 67–69; Indians' losses and, 59–60; migratory lifestyle of, 66–67; and murder of Denio ranch party, 72–74, ***73***; overtaking and defeat of, 78–82, ***83***; public perception of posse as heroes, 80, 84–85; reported confession by, 84; reward offered for, 75, 76, 80–81; role of government in capture of, 85–86;

straddling of Indian and white worlds, 65; surviving members, fate of, 80, 83–84, 85; and Western myth, 84–85; and Western values, 86
Shoshone-Paiute Tribes: and Owyhee Initiative, ***221***, 221–22, 225, 226, 228; and Saylor Creek Bombing Range expansion, 179, 188, 190, 191, 193–94, 195, 196–97, 198
"The Significance of the Frontier in American History" (Turner), 3–4
Silver City, *26*, 27, 30, 40, *43*, *44*; services available in, 43–45; violence in, 51–52
Silver Tunnel Co. of Idaho, 41–42
Simonds, Grant, 227, 228–29
Simplot, J. R., 217
Simplot Livestock Co., ***205***, 217
Singer, Roger, 201, 210
Sitting Bull, 4, 120, ***121***
Slotkin, Richard, 7, 85, 137
Snake River: agriculture and, 22; dams on, 22, 23, 57, 66
Sonnichsen, Carl, 118
Springer (Sheriff), 49, 52
State of Idaho v. Luis Yturaspe (1911), 102
Stauffer, E. A., 100
Stegner, Wallace, 201, 202
Stevens, Jim, 140–41, 144–47
Stock-Raising Homestead Act of 1916, 124–25
Strong, Josiah, 122
Sutter, John, 35
Swisher, George, 88, 98–99, 104
Symms, Steve, 174, 189

Taylor, Dean, 148–49
Taylor Grazing Act of 1934, 89, 113, 128
Thorson, Ralph "Papa," 163
Tindall, Bill and Margaret, 204–6
Tolmie, Harold, 212, 221, ***221***
tourism: New West amenity tourism, 130; as replacement for cattle ranching, 206–7, 207–8, 212
Trade Dollar Consolidated Mining and Milling Co., 22, 23
Tranmer, Frank, 57–59
Tranmer, Guy, 57–59
Tranmer, J. F., 70, 77
Trueblood, Ted, 15
Turner, Frederick Jackson, 3–4, 5, 28–29, 121, 234
Turner, Ted, 131
Tuttle, Daniel S., 44
Twain, Mark, 4, 138

Umatilla Indians, 64
Urie, Nimrod, 57, 70, 77
Ute Indians, 65
Utter Party Massacre, 18

values, American: closing of frontier and, 6; film Westerns and, 129–30; violence and, 6–7, 45; Western myth and, 4–7, 118
values, Western, honor and conscience in, 86
Vest, Gary, 173–74, 178, 182, 184, 186
vigilantism: and campaigns against Native Americans, 59; and frontier, order on, 38, 45–46; and U.S. culture, 7, 45
violence, source of in U.S. culture, 6–7, 45
The Virginian (Wister), ***126***, 127, 133

Ward Massacre, 61
Washoe process, 40
water: agriculture and, 22, 26, 27, 124;

competition for, 22; government water projects, 124; as issue in Owyhee Canyonlands conservation, 206, 207, 213, 223, 224
Wayne, John, 129, 155
Welke, Barbara Young, 114
Weller, Gene, 155, 158
West: shifting conception of, 5; as site of early federal expansion, 201
West, Elliot, 41
West, Mort, 78, 84
Western myth: and American values, 4–7, 118; appeal of, 4, 7, 28, 30–31, 117, 233–34, 236; in art, 125–27; commercialization of, 4, 130, 236; corporations and, 41–42, 54; "Custer's Last Stand" and, 119; development of, 7; Easterner's lost hopes and, 118; environmentalists and, 219, 233; ethnic diversity and, 41, 65–66; exploitation of by cattle ranchers, 215; in films, ***126***, ***128***, 129, 130–31; international appeal of, 116–18, 129; interplay of real and mythic in, 119; in literature, 127, 133; mining violence and, 54; modern inversions of, 130–31; as national heroic past, 118; and national identity, 118; Native Americans and, 59, 86, 122, 130–31; ongoing viability of ranching and, 216, 219; Owyhee Canyonlands conservation and, 206, 207, 208; parallels to religious faith, 131–32; politics and, 5, 125, 129–30; power of to affect positive change, 234, 235; sanitizing of figures in, 118; Shoshone Mike's Band and, 84–85
Westerns (films): international influence of, 116–18, 129; Western myth and, ***126***, ***128***, 129, 130–31
Western Shoshone Reservation, 57. ***See also*** Duck Valley Reservation
White, Richard, 6
Whittaker, Frederick, 119
Widnall, Sheila, 194, 196
Wiebe, Robert, 124
Wilderness Society, 201, 203, 220, 221–22, 226, 228
Wilkins, Kitty, 25
Williams, Mikel H., 195, 196
Wilson, Hoyt and Coco, 134, 156–57
Wilson and Co., 50–51
Wister, Owen, 125, ***126***, 127, 133
women, as early settlers, 24–25
World's Congress of Historians and Historical Students (1893), 3–4
World War I: and Basque immigrants, 109–11; and Western resources, 124–25
World War II, and federal involvement in West, 129
Worster, Donald, 6, 30
Wyden, Rob, 199

Yellow Hair, 120